turquoise

A chef's travels in Turkey

turquoise

Greg and Lucy Malouf

PHOTOGRAPHY BY LISA COHEN
AND WILLIAM MEPPEM

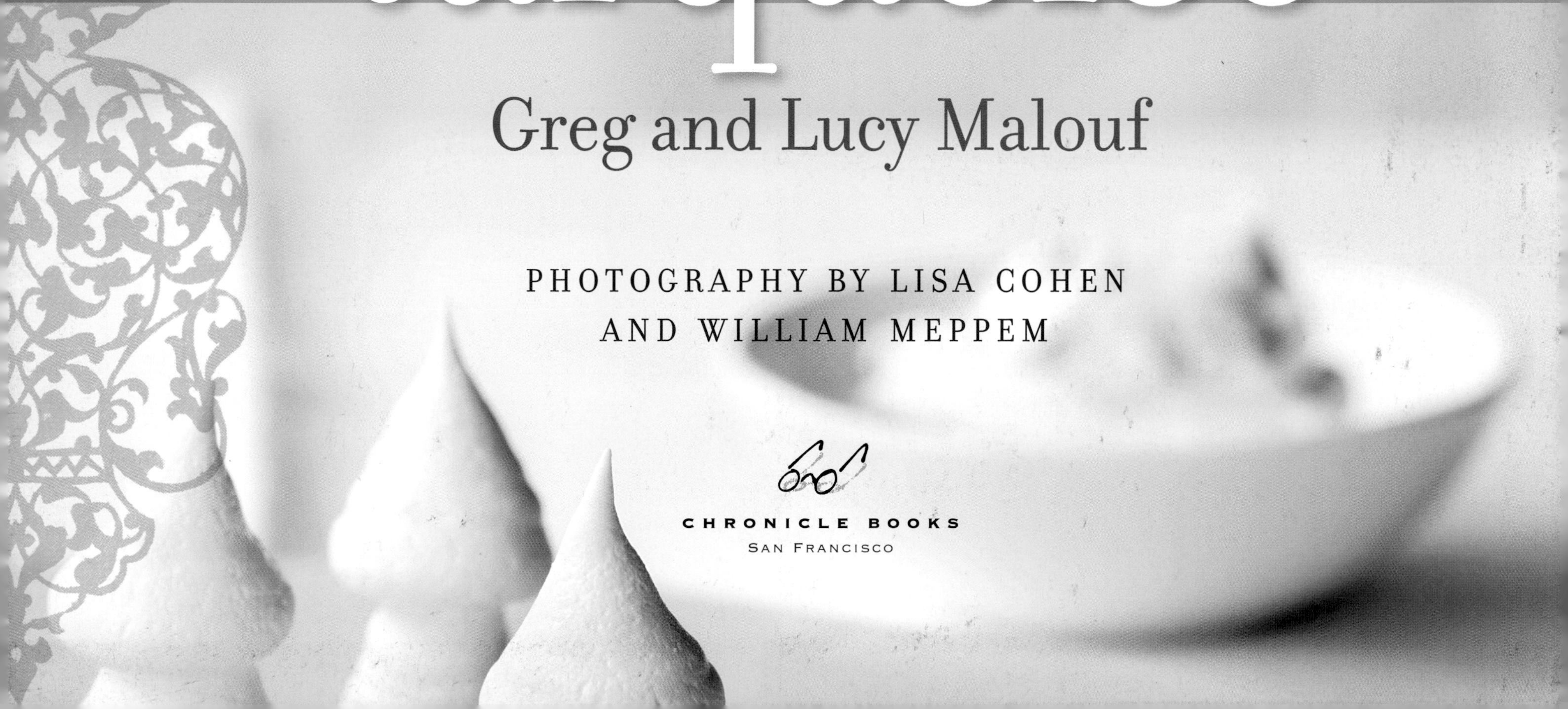

CHRONICLE BOOKS
SAN FRANCISCO

First published in the United States
in 2008 by Chronicle Books LLC.

First published in 2007 by
Hardie Grant Books
85 High Street
Prahran, Victoria 3181, Australia
www.hardiegrant.com.au

Text © Greg Malouf and Lucy Malouf
Photography © Lisa Cohen
Food photography © William Meppem
Additional photography by Lucy Malouf on pages 53, 240
and 242

ISBN: 978-08118-6603-3

Cataloguing-in-Publication data is available from the
National Library of Australia (ISBN 978 1 74066 513 1)

Edited by Patricia Cortese and Caroline Pizzey
Jacket and text design by Trisha Garner
Photography by Lisa Cohen and William Meppem
Typesetting by Trisha Garner and Megan Ellis
Food styling by Caroline Velik
Maps on pages xii and 13 by pfisterer + freeman
Typeset in Corporate A BQ, Mrs Eaves and The Sans
Printed and bound in China by C&C Offset Printing

10 9 8 7 6 5 4 3 2

Chronicle Books LLC
680 Second Street
San Francisco, California 94107

Contents

Preface

"What on earth do you want to write a book about Turkish cooking for?" asked my sister-in-law, when I told her that Greg and I were planning a trip to Turkey. "What's it going to be called? 'One-hundred-and-one ways with eggplant'?"

A quick poll of our friends revealed that most did indeed think of Turkish food as being limited to endless versions of oily braised eggplant, with a few sticky pastries and limp döner kebabs thrown in for good measure. Yet we had read plenty of books that described Turkish food as one of the greatest cuisines in the world, and numerous magazines and newspapers were busily printing stories about a revitalized Istanbul—the new "cool" travel destination. It seemed that a trip to explore the country's culture and cuisine was not to be missed.

Greg has vivid memories of holidaying in Istanbul while working as a young apprentice chef in Austria. Over the course of the many weeks we spent planning our culinary adventure, his eyes would light up as he described a city of crumbling ruins, glittering mosques and smoky teahouses. He spoke, too, of the mass of humanity that thronged the streets and alleyways of the Grand Bazaar; of the fishermen beneath the old Galata Bridge frying the day's catch on portable grills in their old wooden boats; and of the *simit* sellers wandering among the crowds, pushing their little carts stacked with golden rings of bread. He had tales of pudding shops and pastries, a ferry ride up the Bosphorus to the Black Sea and long nights drinking rakı as the whirling gypsy music grew ever wilder.

It all seemed impossibly romantic, this dream of the Orient, and I couldn't wait to see it for myself.

And it was all still there—well, nearly all. The rickety old Galata Bridge that Greg remembered so clearly has gone, replaced by a sturdier modern version, and 21st-century safety regulations mean that fish sandwiches are no longer cooked on those little old wooden boats, but instead are sold from a series of food stands along the Eminönü waterfront. But these were minor disappointments. During the five weeks we spent travelling across Turkey, we found it to be a magical place beyond our wildest expectations; a country that famously straddles continents—and even time itself.

This mingling of the past, present and future is perhaps most evident in Istanbul, where old neighborhoods are steeped in memories of violence and glamour, decay and opulence. Yet it takes only a short stroll through crowded streets to newer suburbs like Beyoğlu and Nişantaşı—with their Modern Art Museum, cutting-edge design studios, glitzy nightclubs and vibrant café culture—to witness signs of the capital's recent cultural revival and determination to reclaim its heritage as one of the world's great cities.

While there's a tendency to focus on Istanbul as being the beating heart of Turkey, the reality is that it forms only a tiny fragment of the country's landmass and plays but one part in the country's long and varied history. Outside Istanbul we discovered an ancient land layered with history and of extraordinary natural beauty–craggy mountain ranges, wide empty steppe lands and a vast coastline that touches three different seas. It's a land washed in brilliant white sunshine, where a deep blue sky merges with a green sea to create a distinctive and memorable turquoise.

And what of the food? Well, ironically, there was very little eggplant to be found on restaurant menus during our visit, as Turkish cooking is by and large dictated by the seasons. So, instead of eggplant, we enjoyed the tail-end of winter's finest produce: roasted chestnuts and hot, sweet, milky drinks of *sahlep* from street vendors, firm white turbot, plump mussels and salty anchovies from the sea and, best of all, gorgeously perfumed amber quinces. Toward the end of our visit spring was beginning to make its presence felt: the markets were filling up with tender green almonds and spiky artichokes, while myriad varieties of wild greens were arriving from the gardens of the Mediterranean and Aegean, along with crisp cucumbers and a few tiny, sweet strawberries.

Food is, of course, both the product and expression of a culture, and in Turkey we found this to be profoundly different from and more exciting than anything we had been expecting. It has been said that one of the greatest qualities of the Turks has been their willingness to adapt, and through the centuries successive Turkish rulers–culminating perhaps with the Ottomans–have shown their ability to embrace diverse lands and ethnic groups, varying religions and different cultural mores. This quality is joyously expressed in Turkey's architecture and art, and in its food. The food that we enjoyed on our travels–whether in the smallest Anatolian village or cosmopolitan Istanbul–all helps to tell Turkey's rich and varied history.

And it's a story that's still being told. While visitors to Turkey may bemoan the limited menus on offer in restaurants that cater predominantly to tourists, we implore you to search just a little further afield to discover the authentic regional food on offer all across Turkey. You'll find it in humble village restaurants, in city soup kitchens, crowded *meyhanes* and, most accessibly, on the streets. You just have to be bold enough to move off the well-trodden tourist path. There are definite signs of a slow-burning renaissance in the country's food scene. Growing numbers of chefs around the country–although perhaps most obviously in Istanbul–seem to have a renewed pride in their country's broader food traditions and are drawing on the past to create a brilliant culinary vision for Turkey's future.

Now is perhaps the time to point out that this is definitely not a traditional Turkish cookery book–after all, there are plenty of these around, many of them written by people far better qualified than we are. In *Turquoise* we wish to share the story of our journey with you, to inspire you to learn more about this country and about the aromas, flavors and textures of its wonderful cuisine.

While some of the recipes generously shared with us by the new friends we met are definitely authentic, for the most part, they are Greg's recipes–inspired by the people, the ingredients and the dishes we discovered on our travels. As such, the tale we tell in *Turquoise* of the country and its food is highly subjective, reflecting our own particular passions and interests, but we hope that in some small way it captures the essence of Turkish food.

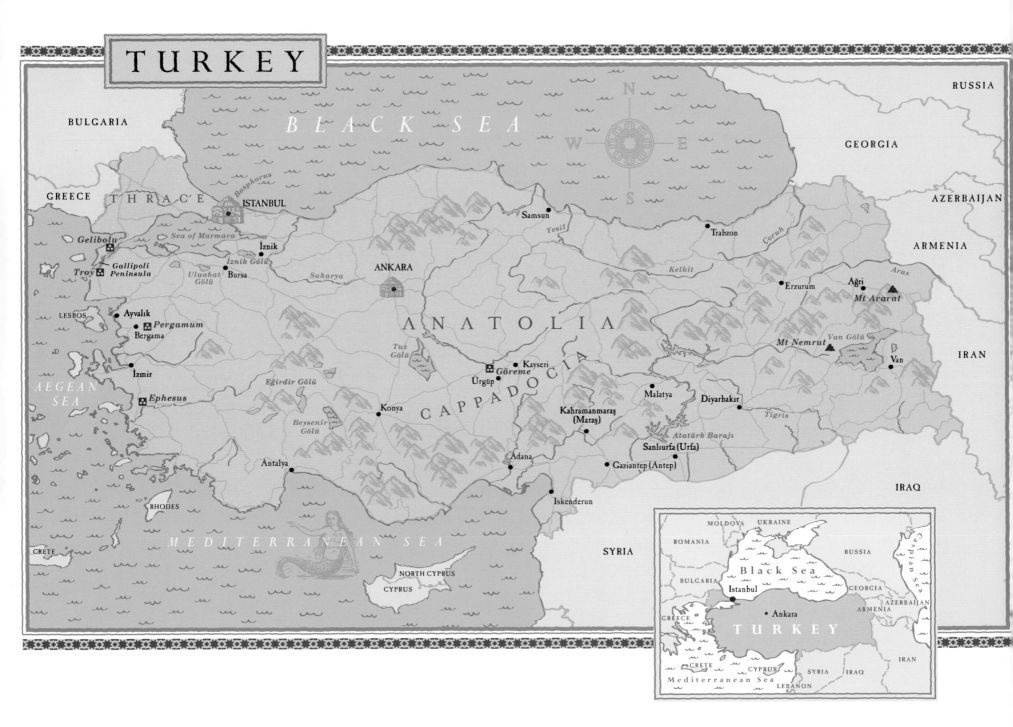

Introduction

A COUNTRY OF MANY PASTS AND PEOPLES

Modern Turkey is surely one of the most intriguingly positioned countries in the world, linking, as it does, the two continents of Europe and Asia. Only around 3 percent of the landmass is in Europe, however—the region of Thrace, which spreads from the northern shores of the Bosphorus Strait up into the southeastern tip of the Balkan Peninsula.

The remaining geographically diverse landmass is in Asian Turkey, also known as Anatolia or, in ancient times, as Asia Minor. A glance at the map shows that Anatolia is a large peninsula, jutting westward out of Asia to nudge up close to European soil at the Gallipoli Peninsula and Istanbul. In fact, Anatolia and Thrace are separated by three bodies of water, the Bosphorus, the inland Sea of Marmara and the Dardanelles. At the closest point, in the city of Istanbul, the two continents are a mere half mile apart, and are linked by two long suspension bridges.

To those of us who are used to thinking of Turkey as a beach-holiday paradise, it comes as a surprise to learn that mountain ranges are Turkey's most distinctive geographic feature—rising from all four points of the compass to embrace the vast central steppes of Anatolia like a chunky necklace. On our recent visit, we rose early one morning to fly southeast from Istanbul deep into the Anatolian heartland. It was a clear sunny morning and the plane flew for what seemed like thousands of miles over wildly dramatic, snow-drenched mountain ranges. Neither Greg nor I had made this trip before and we were stunned by the extraordinary magnificence of the country's landscape. There's a sense of danger lurking beneath these brooding peaks, too; around 80 percent of the country sits in an active tectonic zone and earthquakes are a frequent and unpredictable menace.

As a peninsula, Turkey is surrounded on three sides by water and boasts more than 4,000 miles of thickly forested and spectacularly beautiful coastline. To the north, Turkish fishermen catch turbot, tuna, mackerel and salty anchovies (*hamsi*) from the free-flowing waters of the Black Sea; to the west, the Aegean Sea is dotted with islands, big and small, while the sunny Mediterranean shores to the south lure thousands of vacationers every year.

As well as being spectacularly beautiful, Turkey has a long and fascinating history. It is a country that has won and lost greatness, where successive empires have trampled each other underfoot in their determination to seize this jewel of the Mediterranean. There can be little doubt that its geographic location, straddling seas and continents, goes a long way to explaining Turkey's rich and varied history.

The Anatolian peninsula is crisscrossed by ancient trading routes from East to West, while control of the straits, which divide modern-day Istanbul, allowed successive empires to regulate the movement of ships between the Black Sea and the Mediterranean. It is little wonder that wave upon wave of invaders from all directions have washed through the country from the earliest days of civilization.

Archaeological remains suggest that indigenous nomadic tribes roamed the mountains and central plains of Anatolia more than 8,000 years ago, and the fertile plain around Konya is thought by many to be the original "cradle of civilization," the home of Çatalhöyük, one of the world's oldest cities.

For many centuries before Turkic tribes from the Asian steppes began their incursions into Anatolia, nomadic herders wandered the high mountain plateaus and valleys with their flocks of sheep and goats. The first recorded inhabitants of the area were the Hittites, a highly successful Indo-European race who had migrated to Anatolia, Mesopotamia and Syria around 2000 BC. Then, from around 1200 to 500 BC, Anatolia was colonized by various races of peoples, including Phrygians from the north, Lydians from the east and Cimmerians from the west, while Greeks began establishing city-states along Anatolia's Aegean coast.

The Persians swept into Anatolia around 550 BC and remained in control until around 334 BC, when the young Alexander the Great stormed across the Dardanelles in a burst of Hellenistic fervor. But Alexander's expansion was too swift and too ambitious and his empire was doomed to fail. When he died, the empire fragmented and Anatolia became a battleground of civil wars between his squabbling generals.

During the second century BC, the Roman Republic embarked upon its own eastward expansion. After crushing their ancient enemies, the Carthaginians and the Greeks, they gradually moved in on Anatolia, establishing the Roman province of Asia in 129 BC, with its capital at Ephesus. Even though they had defeated the Greeks, the Romans were swift to absorb elements of Greek art and culture, which they spread throughout their empire, along with other benefits, such as law, medicine, hygiene and civil engineering know-how. Under Roman rule, Anatolia enjoyed the benefits of Greco-Roman culture, prosperity and relative peace for around 400 years.

The next major milestone in Turkish history occurred in 330 AD, when the Roman Emperor Constantine the Great decided to move his capital from Rome to the ancient town of Byzantium in Thrace. It was renamed Constantinople in his honor and, as the western half of the Roman Empire collapsed, began a long and glorious life as the capital of successive great empires.

The best of Roman and Greek culture and customs flourished during the Byzantine Empire and Christianity's foothold strengthened. Constantinople was for several centuries the richest city in the world and exquisite relics and monuments of the era, such as the splendid Haghia Sophia cathedral, remain to this day.

The Byzantine Empire reached its peak under Justinian I, who ruled from 526 to 565 AD; under his leadership the empire spread across Asia Minor, the Balkan Peninsula, Egypt, Syria and Palestine. He was also able to reclaim land lost in Italy, southern Spain and the north of Africa.

Because of its size and its economic and political strength, the Byzantine Empire for a long time was able to protect Europe from increasingly frequent attacks by invaders such as the barbarians from the north of Europe, Arab Muslims from the south and Turkic tribes from Central Asia. But Justinian's death opened the floodgates to a wave of attacks on all fronts against the empire, now teetering on the verge of bankruptcy.

By the eleventh century, a particularly ambitious tribe of Turks called the Seljuks had begun to invade and capture territories west of their homeland in the steppes of Central Asia. Having conquered Armenia, Palestine and most of Persia they moved in on Anatolia.

In 1071, at the Battle of Manzikert, the Seljuks defeated a Byzantine army, and that was the beginning of the end of Byzantine control of Asia Minor. The Seljuks were Muslim converts from Central Asia, east of the Caspian Sea, and they were the first Turkish people to rule in Anatolia. During their rule, the capital was moved to Konya in the southwest of Anatolia, and the Greek language and Christian religion were gradually replaced by Turkish and Islam.

Under Seljuk rule, Konya became a center of learning and culture, attracting artists, musicians and scholars from all around the Arab world. It was home to the Sufi mystic poet Jalal al-Din Rumi, founder of the Whirling Dervish order. Another great hallmark of Seljuk culture was their monumental architecture, with its sculpted and carved stonework. They built mosques, hospitals, colleges and bridges, and, perhaps most famously, established a network of grand caravanserais—hostelries—to provide accommodation for merchants travelling across their country.

From the eleventh century, the Christians in western Europe became very nervous about the Turkish invaders, and the latter's successful capture of Palestine—the Holy Land—prompted a call to arms in the form of military expeditions known as the Crusades. This was a period of great turmoil for Anatolia, where rival armies of Seljuks and Crusaders battled it out for control, especially in the south.

For the great city of Constantinople, still teetering under Byzantine control, the twelfth and thirteenth centuries were turbulent times, swinging between fabulous wealth (and a flowering of the city's art and architecture), disastrous misrule and civil war. The city itself was even sacked by Crusaders—in a fit of fury about the city's failure to follow through on promises of support.

By the thirteenth century, another force emerged. Mongol armies swept into Anatolia, crushing everything and everyone in their path.

With the Mongol defeat of Seljuk forces, Anatolia fragmented into a number of independent Turkic-ruled states. The most significant of these was overseen by a warlord called Ertuğrul, whose son, Osman, founded the dynasty known as the Ottomans, which would become one of the greatest empires the world has ever seen.

By the end of the fourteenth century, the Ottomans had conquered most of western Anatolia and Thrace, Greece and much of the Balkan Peninsula. The jewel in the crown, Constantinople, finally fell to Ottoman forces led by Mehmed II in 1453, bringing to a close forever the Byzantine era.

The fall of Constantinople and the establishment of the Ottoman Empire sent shock waves of fear around Europe. It was a fear that came to be tinged with awe and respect, though, and to this day the West is still dazzled by the very idea of the Ottomans. It was an era that came to mean opulence and excesses beyond our wildest dreams—grand mosques, luxurious palaces and lush gardens, lavish feasting, jewels, harems and massive armies.

Within fifty years the city of Constantinople had risen to even greater heights under Sultan Suleiman the Magnificent. While his achievements led him to be known as "Magnificent" in the West, within his own empire he was called Suleiman Kanunı—"the Lawgiver." But he was recognized, in both the West and the East, as one of the great rulers of the sixteenth century. An effective legislator and administrator, he was also a poet and philosopher, a patron of the arts and a great spiritual leader. His reign was seen to be a time of great cultural achievement and religious and ethnic tolerance.

Suleiman was an extremely successful military leader, under whose leadership the Ottoman Empire nudged its way right up to the city walls of Vienna. By the time of his death in 1566, the empire's extent was some 9,000 square miles, spanning three continents, including much of the Middle East and North Africa, the Arabian Peninsula and Persia, Greece and the Balkan States and reaching as far north as Slovakia and Austria.

Sadly, the Ottoman dynasty had peaked. Suleiman's successors were not of his caliber. A series of mediocre sultans, such as the infamous Selim the Sot, focussed their energies on enjoying the riches of their territories, rather than ruling them, and by the eighteenth century the empire had lost many of its European territories. It continued to slowly spiral into decline, becoming increasingly susceptible to external forces, and further weakened by nepotism, bureaucracy and the dangerously corrupt Janissaries. This powerful and elite corps of Imperial guards was ostensibly there to guard the sultan but, like a modern-day military junta, they ruled the roost with an iron fist.

During the nineteenth century, the winds of nationalism began to blow from Europe into the Ottoman Empire, threatening the country's well-established and successful "millet" system of local government—a system that allowed ethnic and religious minorities to self-govern, side by side with their Turkish neighbours. For many centuries Turkey had been a country where diversity was tolerated, and even encouraged (if largely for reasons of economy). Now, amid bitter fighting, the empire started to fracture as its minority peoples began to seek their independence. In 1832 the Kingdom of Greece was created, and soon the Serbs, Bulgarians, Albanians, Arabs and Romanians all sought their own freedom.

Then the Armenians in the east of Anatolia decided it was their turn to claim independence. In 1914 the Ottomans joined World War I on the side of the Austro-Hungarian Empire and Germany, so the Armenians decided to align themselves with neighboring Russia in the hope of securing their own republic.

These events provided the backdrop for what is still one of the most bitterly contested events in Turkey's recent history. A series of Armenian uprisings led to a massacre of the local Muslim population. Retribution came in the form of deportation and massacre of the Armenians by the Turkish government. To this day, the subject provokes heated disputes and denials: the Turks call the Armenians traitors, while the Armenians claim they were victims of an official policy of genocide. The exact number of deaths on each side remains unclear, with each offering up its own set of "proofs" to support its cause. From an outsider's perspective, the whole painful episode seems likely to remain a thorn in the country's side for many years to come.

Despite a flurry of internal reform initiatives, implemented in a vain attempt to halt the empire's slow decline and to make it more "European" and modern, the crumbling wreck of the Ottoman Empire was finally finished off in the aftermath of the Great War. Despite a few isolated successes for the Turks, such as driving back the British from the Dardanelles during the notorious Gallipoli campaign, the Allies ultimately won the war in 1918.

Having assumed control of Istanbul, the Allies planned a devastating carve-up and redistribution of the Ottoman Empire's remaining lands. For the Turks, one of the cruellest outcomes of defeat was the Allies' proposal to hand over Smyrna (İzmir) to Greece, and in 1919 the Greeks duly invaded to claim their prize.

This insult was the straw that broke the camel's back and a backlash was inevitable. Bitterly resentful of the broken government's inability to defend the country, Mustafa Kemal, a highly ambitious military hero, decided to take matters into his own hands. His dissatisfaction with Ottoman governance had been bubbling along even before the Greek invasion and this was to be his moment of glory.

In the face of Greek invasion, Kemal's nascent resistance movement garnered support from the Turkish people, leading to the Turkish War of Independence and the eventual formation of the Turkish Republic, with Kemal himself as president.

With the ousting of Greek forces, the Allies' ambitions for divvying up the Ottoman Empire faded fast and the reenergized Turks found themselves in a position to renegotiate their borders and territories. Perhaps most famously, the Treaty of Lausanne in 1923 instigated a series of population exchanges between Turkey and Greece. As a result around 1.25 million Greeks who had lived happily along the Aegean coast of Turkey for hundreds of years were forced to move to Greece, and nearly half a million Muslims were repatriated from Greece back to Turkey.

This was only one of a series of changes that swept through the country as a result of Kemal's leadership. He had a vision for rebuilding Turkey and dragging it into the twentieth century. What he considered to be "backward" Islamic traditions were outlawed—the fez was banished, as was the Arabic alphabet and the practice of polygamy. Islam lost its status as the state religion, with secular law replacing Islamic law. All Turks were ordered to choose a family name, instead of the traditional single given name. Kemal himself was given the name Atatürk—father of the Turks—as a mark of respect and honor.

Today the ghost of Atatürk still walks the land and his image is a constant presence—sometimes benign, sometimes stern, but always there. Luridly tinted photographs of the former leader peer down from every carpet shop, teahouse and posh hotel; his bronze torso dominates every village square and his face stares up at you from every Turkish lira. And yet, as visitors, our impression was that Turkish people seem to have mixed feelings for their former leader. They revere, admire and grumble about him, all in the same breath, uncertain as to whether all his moves have taken Turkey in the right direction.

At the moment, though, Turkey is experiencing something of a cultural and economic rebirth, largely fueled by current government reforms aimed at hastening the country's move toward Europe. It still remains to be seen whether Turkey will succeed in its bid to secure a European-oriented future for itself, or whether it will return to political Islam.

Regardless of how its story unfolds, these are unquestionably exciting times for Turkey. Long dreary decades of nationalism and stultifying parochialism are at last being swept away and it feels very much like a country poised on the brink of greatness. At the very least, it seems to be rediscovering a new sense of confidence in its own identity—an identity that will hopefully embrace the best of East and West instead of pitting these different forces one against the other.

THE FOOD

From the research and reading we did before our trip, and from the places we visited on our travels through Turkey, we found that there's a definite tendency to divide Turkish food into two camps: Ottoman and Anatolian. In other words, a distinction between the food of the urban rich and the food of the rural poor. The reality, of course, is far more complicated. Turkish cooking today is an interweaving of many different but complementary strands that together create a gorgeous and vibrant culinary tapestry.

Both rural Anatolian and sophisticated Ottoman cuisines are a legacy of the country's rich and varied history, the complex interchange and cross-fertilization of culinary traditions and influences that have washed through the country down the centuries. Their ingredients and recipes are drawn from such diverse parts of the world as Central and Far East Asia, Persia, Arabia, the Balkans and the Mediterranean.

Irrespective of the origin of a dish, the same principles of respect and enjoyment apply to cooking and eating. As is the custom in most countries around the Middle East and eastern Mediterranean, Turks enjoy taking time over their food. Families eat together rather than in shifts, as is so often the case in Western countries. Meal times are for togetherness and sharing, not for eating with one eye on the television. Food is on the table to be savored and lingered over, rather than rushed through. And even in big, modern cities like Istanbul this attitude is still present more often than not.

Growers, sellers and consumers all share a respect for the food they eat. Turks are fussy about the quality of their food and demand that it be the best, the freshest, the most intensely flavored. This means that produce markets are almost always limited to what is seasonally available—you won't find expensive strawberries in Turkish market stalls in the middle of winter.

And when it comes to food preparation, the same respectful approach applies. As one Turkish food writer told us: Turkish food is not about experimentation, it is about technique—about cooking a particular dish in the time-honored way, in the very best way you can.

Turks have no fear of simplicity either, and many dishes are pleasingly unfussy. Some of the best meals we ate on our travels were the simplest: a spanking fresh piece of turbot hot from the pan and topped with a wedge of lemon; a cold salad of wild greens braised in olive oil; a piece of white cheese accompanied by a little cube of honeycomb. In Turkey, eating is about enjoying the essential nature of an ingredient, rather than masking it with fancy sauces or garnishes. Which is not to say that Turks don't make good use of fresh herbs and spices—but they are used judiciously, to enhance rather than overwhelm.

This simplicity is perhaps the hallmark of what we in the West know as *cucina povera*—the cooking of the poor. It's a style of cooking and eating that makes the most of very little, and is typical of village—Anatolian—cooking. Until the last ten years or so, regional dishes

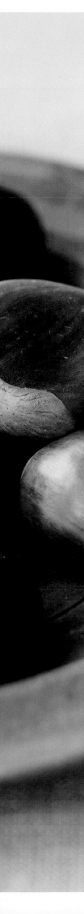

were virtually unknown outside their place of origin, but with the constant daily influx of rural Turks into the big cities (as many as a thousand people are said to move to the capital every day) regional dishes are becoming better known. And there are increasing numbers of chefs, such as Musa Dağdeverin from Istanbul's Çiya restaurant, who recognize the importance of preserving these ancient cooking traditions in the face of the inevitable Westernization of the food industry.

Part of the pleasure of eating in a country with a genuinely seasonal kitchen is the discovery of the different regional ingredients and dishes. Turks respect that food follows the natural rhythm of the seasons and the expectation is that produce will have been grown or reared within a few hundred yards (or at the most a mile or so) of their own kitchen. So it's not unusual to find dishes that vary widely from region to region: in southeastern Anatolia they make pilaf from bulgur wheat rather than rice; along the Aegean coast baklava is made using olive oil, rather than the traditional clarified butter; and near the Black Sea bread is made from corn, rather than wheat.

As well as broad-brush regional variations, there are also endless variations from village to village. On our travels we tasted dishes in central Anatolia and in Gaziantep that our Istanbul friends had never heard of, let alone tasted. Musa Dağdeverin, who travels the length and breadth of the country sourcing and recording traditional dishes, has an ever-increasing repertoire of more than a thousand recipes drawn from his research. It is said that you're unlikely to eat the same dish in his restaurant twice in one year.

While it's likely that some Turkish dishes can trace their origins back to the pastoral nomads who roamed the mountains and valleys of Anatolia thousands of years ago, many more have been brought to the country by successive waves of occupiers. The famous Turkish dumplings known as *mantı*, for instance, are believed to have been brought to Turkey by the Uyghur Turks, who ventured into Anatolia in the eighth century from their kingdom, in what is now Xingjiang, northern China. The predilection for stuffing vegetables as well as pasta is a widespread feature in both cuisines today. Another shared invention was the concave iron cooking pan that the Chinese call a wok and which is known in Turkey as a *çin tavası*.

Another group of Turks to bring their culinary habits to Anatolia were the Seljuk Turks from Central Asia. They were horse-riding nomads who enjoyed a meat-heavy diet of game animals such as hare and rabbit, deer, horse and camel, as well as sheep. It's generally believed that methods of spicing, pressing and then air-drying lumps of meat hung from saddles originated with these Turks, as did the method of spearing small morsels of meat on any kind of makeshift skewer and cooking it quickly over a fierce open fire.

Fermented dairy products, such as yogurt and cheeses, were also believed to have been brought to Anatolia by the Seljuks, as were flat breads and bulgur wheat dishes. When the ambitious Seljuks reached Persia in the eleventh century, they encountered another highly sophisticated culture and cuisine. From the Persians they learned about combining fruit with meat—a method that survives in many Turkish *yahni* (stews) to this day. The Seljuks also learned how to cultivate rice, offering the Persians bulgur wheat by way of exchange.

On their travels westward, the Seljuks took with them all the culinary lessons learned along the way. And in Anatolia they experienced yet another new range of ingredients, such as seafood, olive oil, herbs, fruits and vegetables, quickly making them their own. This was a time of great creativity in the kitchen, producing a varied and increasingly complex cuisine.

It was a few hundred years later, though, that things really began to get interesting on the Turkish food scene—when another tribe of nomadic Turks, the Ottomans, captured Constantinople and established the most powerful and successful Islamic empire the world had ever seen. From the beginning it was clear that food was important to the Ottomans. The conquering sultan, Mehmet II, had a massive four-domed kitchen installed in his new Topkapı Palace, which was gradually extended over successive centuries to form the complex that remains today.

As well as feeding the sultan and his family, the Topkapı kitchens fed the government and cabinet ministers, foreign ambassadors and the Janissary Corps, all of whom lived within the palace grounds. On average this amounted to 5,000 hungry people every day. The quantities of food prepared were staggering. Meticulously maintained kitchen records list items like "60,000 sheep," "100,000 pigeons," "2,000 pounds of cloves and nutmeg," and "206 pounds saffron"—all of which were simply gathered in from the provinces by imperial command.

It hardly seems surprising that the palace kitchens were run with ruthless efficiency. At its largest, there was a team of almost 1,400 specialist cooks and assistants, and specialist cooking guilds emerged, each highly protective of their own particular trade and craft.

The Ottoman Empire was vast, spanning at its height three continents, and the chefs in the palace kitchens were the beneficiaries of exciting foodstuffs that flooded into the capital every day from all corners of the empire. In what was surely a forerunner to today's "fusion" cooking, hundreds of new and exotic dishes were created in the palace kitchens, many with equally exotic names, such as Sultan's Delight, the Imam Fainted, Ladies' Thighs, Harem Navels and Nightingale Nests. Some were inspired by cultures that had been absorbed into the Ottoman Empire, such as Arabic and Persian; others were a legacy of the previous Seljuk reign, while others still emerged from the great melting pot of peoples that was Constantinople in the sixteenth and seventeenth centuries.

Feasts at the palace were famously lavish and extravagant. Visitors to the court would be overwhelmed by the feasting. As many as 300 dishes were presented upon exquisitely embroidered cloths and eaten from silver dishes; meals would be eaten against a background of music by the light of a thousand flickering candles. Indeed, the rituals surrounding the meal, the manner of presentation and the surroundings were almost as important as the food itself. This style of banqueting was about total surrender to sensual pleasures.

As the Roman Empire had discovered to its cost several hundred years earlier, this sort of overindulgence can only lead to trouble in the end. Throughout the eighteenth and nineteenth centuries the Ottoman Empire slowly declined, amid stories of madness, murder and mayhem within the palace and a gradual fragmentation of its territories.

From the nineteenth century onward, the increasingly corrupt and inefficient Ottoman government earned itself the title "Sick Man of Europe," and within the country pressure grew to implement Western-style economic and political reform. What this meant for the food scene, in the cities, at least, was the emergence of a new "restaurant" culture, something almost unheard of in traditional Ottoman society. With this "Westernization," neighborhoods such as Pera (now Beyoğlu) and Galata came into their own. Pera, which had always been home to the city's minority communities and European merchant classes, now began to attract even more foreign travellers, as well as the city's Ottoman elite who flocked there in droves to patronize new European-style cafés and eating houses. The Turkish word for restaurant, *lokanta*, came into use around this time, taken from the Italian word *locanda*, meaning inn.

Outside influence on the food itself, though, remained very limited, apart from a bit of "Frenchification." When Atatürk began his reforms of the new Turkish Republic in the 1920s, the emphasis shifted back toward unification and nationalization and "foreign" foods were very definitely off the menu. To this day Turks are famously conservative in their eating habits and deeply resistant to any messing around with their traditional dishes. And who can blame them when so much of it is so good? There has been some inevitable Westernizing of Turkish restaurant menus, of course; in recent times returning emigrants and new "workers" in the country have brought with them their favorite items. Italian gelati, German schnitzel and the ubiquitous French fries are all commonplace now, but, thankfully, the "Golden Arches" have yet to make a significant impact on the Turkish culinary landscape.

While Turks may well be determined to preserve and protect their food traditions, it seems that it is not entirely at the expense of innovation. The winds of change do seem to be blowing—or at least wafting gently—through the country's food scene. In recent years, for instance, a small number of passionate chefs have been introducing Istanbullus to the pleasures of rural "peasant" food, while still others have taken the first tentative steps toward experimenting with classic dishes and ingredients. There will always be purists who are horrified by this sort of "messing around" with traditional dishes, of course, but we are all for progress and evolution in the kitchen. And, in the end, perhaps the most important culinary legacy that the Ottomans left to modern-day Turkey is the importance of taking risks and a willingness to experiment. After all, has it not been demonstrated that out of such boldness and creativity, greatness has come?

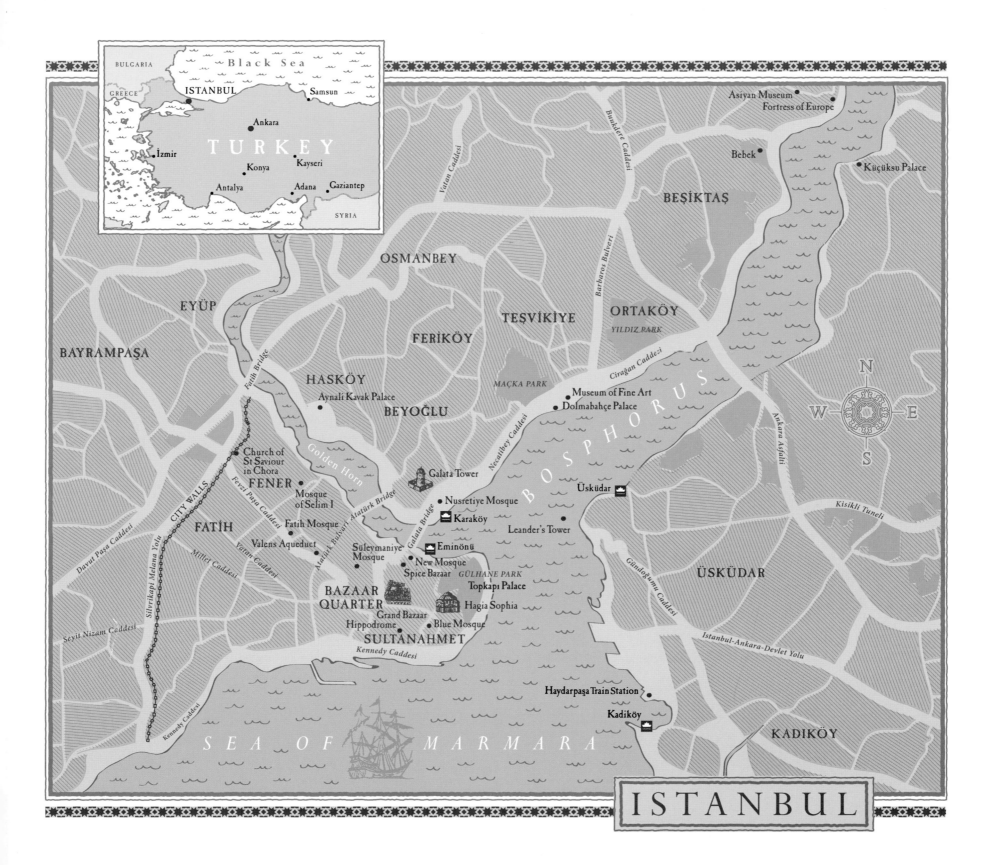

ISTANBUL

Istanbul—Turkey's delight

[SOUPS]

Greg had meticulously detailed lists of the dishes he intended to sample in the coming weeks … "The Imam swooned," "Sultan's delight," "Something for the husband," "Nightingale nests," and the irresistibly named "Harem navels."

O n the early-morning flight to Istanbul from London's Luton Airport, Greg and I compared notes. In my scruffy journal were the names of ancient mosques and museums, palaces and spice bazaars. In his own smart black travel diary, Greg had meticulously detailed lists of the dishes he intended to sample in the coming weeks. I peered over his shoulder and read at random "The Imam swooned," "Sultan's delight," "Something for the husband," "Nightingale nests," and the irresistibly named "Harem navels." Farther down the page I saw listed: Turkish tea, fried-fish sandwiches, chicken breast pudding and, naturally enough, Turkish delight. My mouth watered in anticipation, made keener by the fact that I was actually very hungry. Our predawn start had meant we'd missed breakfast, and the "no-frills" flight offered nothing at all worth spending our remaining few English pounds on. But, we agreed, it would probably be all to the good that we'd land hungry; we had a lot of eating ahead of us.

Then, Asia was beneath us: the dreary, brown plains of northwestern Turkey. Our plane landed, seemingly in the middle of nowhere, at Istanbul's new Sabiha Gökçen Airport. It was a good bone-shaking hour by minibus to the splendors of the great Ottoman city and our sense of excitement grew as we bumped along at breakneck speed through the barren landscape. Gradually the terrain changed to thickly

Although geographically in the West, it is in the old city where you most feel you are in the Orient—in Constantinople.

forested hills, then a scattering of satellite apartment complexes broke the monotony and finally we were nearing the vast sprawling suburbs of Istanbul.

All of a sudden the traffic thickened and slowed. We were hemmed in by a queue of honking trucks, crossing the Boğaziçi Bridge over the fast-running waters of the Bosphorus Strait. The traffic ground to a halt, and for a few magical moments we found ourselves suspended in limbo between Asia and Europe.

It was the perfect vantage point to appreciate fully the vast and expanding metropolis of modern Istanbul, which swept before us along the European shoreline of the Bosphorus. Gazing out to the northeast we saw massive tanker ships plowing through the choppy waters toward the Black Sea. And to the southwest, spread out in the distance like a dream, was the famous Istanbul skyline. Our hearts quickened and we wound down the windows to make out more clearly the cascading domes of the city's great mosques, with their delicate spires and minarets glinting in the weak afternoon sunshine of late winter.

This was where we were heading: to Sultanahmet, the old imperial city, with its palace and mosques, its steamy bathhouses and ancient bazaars. Although geographically in the West, it is in the old city where you most feel you are in the Orient—in Constantinople.

For more than a thousand years Constantinople was the glorious capital of Byzantine Christendom, and a glittering beacon of sophistication for western Europe, mired as it was in the Dark Ages. And then, for the next few hundred years, Constantinople rose to even dizzier heights as the capital of the Turkic Ottoman Empire, the most powerful force in Europe and Asia.

For our first few nights in Turkey we were staying in Sultanahmet, where the steep narrow streets bristle with reminders of this great and glorious past. Our hotel was in the shadow of the graceful domes and six elegant minarets of the Blue Mosque and after settling ourselves into our rooms we wandered out to explore the neighborhood.

Rain clouds were gathering overhead and the streets were deserted. A solitary *simit* seller trudged through the drizzle, weighed down by a tray of sesame-encrusted

bread rings. We made our way toward the Hippodrome—or Sultanahmet Square as it is known today—which was empty apart from a handful of elderly men in raincoats, who sat on park benches sharing a bag of hot roasted chestnuts. It was hard to imagine that this was once an ancient racetrack, where rival chariot teams raced around to the cheers of a 120,000-capacity crowd.

We were ready for lunch, but before feeding our baser appetites we felt bound to satisfy our souls. Just beyond the northern end of the Hippodrome stands the jaw-droppingly lovely Hagia Sophia, Istanbul's most famous monument. Built by the Emperor Justinian in the sixth century, it was the greatest church in Christendom for nearly a thousand years and to this day is still thought by many to be the most beautiful church ever built.

Converted to a mosque after the fall of Constantinople to the Turks in 1453, Hagia Sophia now boasts fountains and minarets, but the power of its vast soaring interior, the brilliance of its glittering mosaics and the sense of awe that it inspires have been undiminished—even by the scaffolding (courtesy of UNESCO-funded restoration work) that rose skyward into the dome.

And so on to lunch; something quick and easy, we were all agreed. The surrounding streets were lined with grungy-looking tourist restaurants and *hazır yemek*, the Turkish version of self-service, cheap-and-cheerful cafés. But Greg had other ideas. "We need to find a *pideci*," he announced. "I've got to have a *lahmacun*." No surprises there! Lahmacun—the Turkish equivalent of his favorite Lebanese lunch, *lahme bi-ajeen*, is the Eastern version of lamb-topped pizza. The best *pide* restaurants have wood-fired ovens and will usually offer a limited range of other options—kebabs and soups—as well.

By chance, we happened upon a wonderful Black Sea–style *pide* restaurant in a street tucked away between the Sultanahmet streetcar line and the Grand Bazaar. There were simple soups and salads, and in front of a large wood-fired oven two young men were working briskly in tandem, rolling and stretching out dough, forming the traditional long boat shapes, adding a variety of toppings and thrusting

the *pide* into the deep glowing recesses. The smell was intoxicating and we eagerly gave our order.

A few minutes later the food started arriving: two golden puffs of nigella-flecked bread emerged from the oven and landed in front of us with a trio of accompaniments. There was a dish of spicy red pepper paste, creamy whorls of butter and tangy white cheese. Next came deep bowls of steaming red soup—a popular Turkish "peasant" dish that was thick with lentils, enlivened with a spritz of lemon and a sprinkling of dried mint. We scooped and dunked and sipped greedily, and then the main event arrived. There was Greg's *lahmacun*, a crisp dough base smeared with spicy lamb paste and sprinkled with hot red pepper flakes. The *pide* were long and skinny, with the edges rolled in to contain the generous toppings: egg and spicy *sucuk* sausage and melting soft white cheese.

There may not have been swooning Imams, or delighted Sultans, but we all agreed, for a simple soup and sandwich lunch, and our first meal in Turkey, things just don't get much better than that!

Hot yogurt soup with chicken threads and corn

Versions of creamy hot yogurt soup can be found across Turkey, and it's thought to have originated with the nomadic herdsmen that settled in Anatolia a thousand years ago. At its simplest, it is flavored with dried mint and may be thickened with rice, chickpeas, bulgur or barley. For this recipe I add sweet corn kernels and threads of chicken to make it more substantial.

1 large chicken breast on the bone
1 small onion, cut into quarters
1 stick celery
½ lemon
1 sprig thyme
2 bay leaves
1 small stick cinnamon
½ teaspoon white peppercorns
1½ quarts Chicken Stock (page 41)
4 ounces short-grain rice
½ cup sweet corn kernels
1 pound Greek-style yogurt
2 teaspoons cornstarch
¼ cup water
1 egg, lightly beaten
sea salt
freshly ground black pepper
2 ounces unsalted butter
1 tablespoon dried mint
dried red pepper flakes to serve (optional)

Put the chicken, vegetables, lemon, herbs, cinnamon, peppercorns and stock into a large, heavy-based saucepan. Bring to the boil, skimming away any fat and impurities that rise to the surface, then lower the heat immediately. Simmer very gently, covered, for 5 minutes. Turn off the heat and leave the chicken in the stock for 20 minutes.

Pull the chicken meat off the bone and shred it as finely as you can. Reserve for later. Strain the stock into a large, heavy-based saucepan, then add the rice and slowly bring to the boil. Simmer gently, covered, for 30 minutes until the rice has broken down and begun to thicken the soup. Add the corn kernels.

To stabilize the yogurt, beat it in a large bowl until smooth. Mix the cornstarch with the water, then stir it thoroughly into the yogurt with the egg. Gently stir a spoonful of the hot soup into the yogurt mixture, then pour this back into the barely simmering soup. Cook at a bare simmer for about 10 minutes, stirring in one direction only. Be sure not to let the soup boil or the mixture will curdle.

When ready to serve, add the shredded chicken to the soup and season with salt and pepper, then ladle the soup into warmed serving bowls. Quickly sizzle the butter in a small frying pan, then add the mint and heat until foaming. Swirl the sizzling butter into each bowl of soup, sprinkle with red pepper flakes, if using, and serve.
SERVES 6–8

Chicken and vermicelli soup with egg and lemon

This is a Turkish version of everyone's favorite chicken noodle soup, but instead of being a clear broth, the soup is rich and creamy. The "body" is created by using grated onion; the soup is then finished with an egg and lemon mixture, which thickens it further, makes it velvety-smooth and adds a vibrant lemon flavor.

It's essential to use a really good homemade chicken stock for this soup, such as the one on page 41 (alternatively, use your own recipe or a top-quality stock purchased from a deli). With good stock to hand, this soup can be pulled together in a matter of minutes. (Please don't be tempted to use stock cubes, though!)

1 small red onion, peeled and coarsely grated
¼ cup olive oil
1 ounce unsalted butter
1 long green chile, seeded and finely shredded
2 ounces vermicelli noodles
3 ⅓ cup Chicken Stock (see page 41)
½ pound chicken breast, skin removed
3 egg yolks
juice of ½ lemon
½ teaspoon hot paprika
sea salt
freshly ground white pepper
⅓ cup shredded flat-leaf parsley leaves

To make the soup, place the onion in a sieve. Press lightly with the back of a spoon and leave to drain for 5 minutes or so, discarding the juice.

Heat the oil and butter in a large, heavy-based saucepan, then sauté the onion over a low heat for 3 minutes. Add the chile and sauté for another minute. Roughly break up the vermicelli noodles and add them to the pan with the chicken stock and simmer gently for 10 minutes. Cut the chicken breast into ¼-inch dice and add to the pan, stirring gently over a very low heat for a minute.

In a small mixing bowl, whisk the egg yolks with the lemon juice. Ladle a spoonful of the hot soup into the egg mixture and whisk gently. Pour this back into the barely simmering soup, whisking continuously. Cook at a bare simmer, whisking gently, until the soup starts to thicken. Be sure not to let the soup boil or the mixture will curdle.

When the soup has thickened, add the paprika and season generously with salt and pepper. Stir in the parsley, then ladle the soup into warmed bowls and serve with hot buttered toast.

SERVES 6

Spicy lamb soup with lemon peel and rice

This soup combines all my favorite flavors: the sweet pungency of cinnamon and cumin, a mild chile heat and a subtle underlying lemony tang. The addition of rice makes it feel particularly comforting, too. In my view, it's the perfect soup!

¼ cup olive oil

1 onion, diced

2 cloves garlic, finely chopped

1 teaspoon ground cumin

½ teaspoon hot paprika

½ teaspoon black peppercorns, lightly crushed

5 sprigs thyme

1 long red pepper, seeded and diced

1 long red chile, seeded and diced

⅔ pound lamb shoulder, cut into 1 cm cubes

1 stick cinnamon

1 bay leaf

long strip of peel from ½ lemon

1 quart Chicken Stock (page 41)

⅓ cup short-grain rice

Heat the oil in a large, heavy-based saucepan. Sauté the onion and garlic for a minute, then add the spices, thyme, red pepper and chile. Sauté over a low heat for another 5 minutes, until the vegetables soften.

Stir in the lamb until coated with the spiced onion mixture. Add the cinnamon stick, bay leaf, lemon peel and stock. Bring to the boil, skimming away any fat and impurities that rise to the surface, then lower the heat immediately. Simmer very gently, covered, for 45 minutes, or until the meat is tender. Skim from time to time. Add the rice to the pan and cook for another 15 minutes.

When ready to serve, ladle the soup into warmed bowls.

SERVES 6–8

Beyran soup—slow-cooked lamb soup with garlic and green chiles

This hearty soup comes from Gaziantep in the southeast of Turkey, where it's eaten as a warming breakfast dish—especially during the long cold winters. Beyran is served in soup restaurants known as *metanet lokantasi*, which translates as building strength of body as well as spirit.

It requires a fair amount of strength and spirit to eat a traditionally made *beyran* as it includes sheep's cheek and the solid tail fat from the fat-tailed sheep found all around the Middle East. (This solid white fat is the cooking medium of choice in the eastern and southern parts of the country, but it is rather terrifying to Western palates.) An authentic *beyran* is also full of garlic, and you'll probably be offered a couple of sweet and spicy cloves to munch on as a breath-freshener as you head off to join the world again. Our tamed-down version uses lamb shanks, which provide a similarly melting texture without the fat. For the truer Gaziantep experience, add the extra garlic clove at the last minute.

3 lamb shanks
1 whole head of garlic, cut crosswise
1 onion, cut into quarters
1 carrot, cut into quarters
2 bay leaves
2 quarts water
⅓ pound short-grain rice
1½ teaspoons extra-virgin olive oil
additional 1 clove garlic, roughly smashed (optional)
chile flakes to serve
lemon wedges to serve
long green chiles to serve

Put the lamb shanks, garlic, onion, carrot, bay leaves and water into a large, heavy-based saucepan. Slowly bring to the boil, skimming away any fat and impurities that rise to the surface, then immediately lower the heat. Simmer very gently, covered, for 1½ hours, skimming from time to time. Check after an hour and top up with more water if necessary.

Remove the pan from the heat, then carefully ladle the stock into a container, discarding the solids but reserving the lamb shanks. (Don't be tempted to tip everything into a sieve: the less you disturb the solids at this stage, the clearer the final broth will be. I find the best method is to use a sieve to keep the solids submerged while you ladle out the liquid.)

Rinse the rice thoroughly under cold running water. Bring to the boil with 1¼ cups reserved lamb stock in a small saucepan, then lower the heat and drizzle in ½ teaspoon of the extra-virgin olive oil. Simmer gently, covered, for 15 minutes or until the rice is tender.

While the rice is cooking, remove the meat from the lamb shanks and tear it into small shreds. Bring the remaining stock, the shredded lamb, smashed garlic clove, if using, and remaining extra-virgin olive oil to a gentle simmer.

When ready to serve, place a spoonful of rice in the center of each warmed bowl and distribute the shredded lamb evenly between them. Pour on the hot stock, then sprinkle the soup with chile flakes and serve with lemon wedges, long green chiles and plenty of soft Turkish bread alongside. Squeeze on the lemon, then crunch on the chiles and chew on the bread as you slurp up the soup!
SERVES 6–8

Red lentil "peasant" soup with sizzling mint butter

Although essentially a home-style dish, versions of this hearty soup can be found in restaurants all around Turkey. The lentils break down during cooking, so the soup becomes almost creamy in the mouth. I like to add fine bulgur wheat toward the end of the cooking time, which adds a pleasing texture and makes the soup even more of a hearty winter warmer. The flavor is further enhanced by adding a drizzle of paprika- and mint-infused butter just before serving.

The soup thickens as it cools, so if you plan to reheat it, you may need to thin it with a little extra stock. Serve with warm Turkish bread.

2 tablespoons olive oil
1 large onion, finely diced
1 carrot, finely diced
2 cloves garlic, finely chopped
1 teaspoon ground cumin
1 teaspoon hot paprika
1½ teaspoons sweet paprika
1 tablespoon tomato paste
7 ounces red lentils
1½ quarts Chicken Stock (page 41)
¼ cup fine bulgur
1 vine-ripened tomato, cut into quarters and seeded
sea salt
freshly ground black pepper
2 ounces unsalted butter
½ teaspoon dried mint
lemon wedges to serve

Heat the oil over a low heat in a large, heavy-based saucepan. Stir the onion, carrot and garlic around in the hot oil, then add the cumin, hot paprika and 1 teaspoon of the sweet paprika and sauté for 5–8 minutes, until the vegetables soften.

Stir in the tomato paste and cook for a minute. Add the lentils and chicken stock and bring to the boil. Cover the pan and cook over a medium heat for 20 minutes, stirring from time to time.

When the lentils have broken down and become creamy, add the bulgur. Dice the tomato finely, then add to the pan, season with salt and pepper and simmer for 10 minutes.

When ready to serve, ladle the soup into warmed serving bowls. Quickly heat the butter in a small frying pan until it foams, then add the remaining sweet paprika and the dried mint. Swirl the sizzling butter into each bowl of soup and serve with wedges of lemon.

SERVES 6–8

Swiss chard soup with chickpeas and barley

This soup was inspired by a dish we ate at the Müzedechanga restaurant at Istanbul's Sabanci Museum. We'd just visited a fascinating exhibition about Ghengis Khan and ate lunch in the sunshine looking out over the beautiful museum gardens, with the Bosphorus in the distance.

The soup was full of Swiss chard and chickpeas—just the sort of earthy flavors I love—and the pearl barley gave it a lovely chewiness. Even though it's not really Turkish, I can't resist serving this soup with a dollop of yogurt.

6 ounces dried chickpeas
2 tablespoons olive oil
1 small onion, finely diced
3 sticks celery, finely diced
2 cloves garlic, finely chopped
½ teaspoon ground allspice
½ teaspoon ground cinnamon
5 sprigs thyme
½ pound Swiss chard leaves (stems removed), shredded
4 ounces pearl barley
1½ quarts Chicken Stock (page 41)
2 bay leaves
1 long red chile, seeded and shredded
½ vine-ripened tomato, seeded and diced
sea salt
freshly ground black pepper
lemon juice to serve
Greek-style yogurt to serve

Soak the chickpeas overnight in plenty of cold water.

Heat the oil in a large, heavy-based saucepan. Sauté the onion, celery and garlic over a low heat for 5–8 minutes, until the vegetables soften. Add the spices, thyme and Swiss chard, then toss everything around in the pan for a few moments.

Drain and rinse the chickpeas and add them to the pan with the pearl barley, stock and bay leaves. Bring to the boil, then lower the heat and simmer, covered, for around an hour or until the chickpeas and barley are tender.

Add the chile and tomato and season generously with salt and pepper. When ready to serve, remove the bay leaves and the thyme stalks. Ladle the hot soup into warmed bowls, then add a squeeze of lemon juice and a generous spoonful of yogurt to each.
SERVES 6–8

Soups

In Turkey soups are eaten all day long—from early-morning breakfasts through to late-night snacks. They are a key part of any festive banquet, and are generally the first food to soothe a hungry stomach at the end of Ramadan fasting days. In winter, soups are the comfort food par excellence, and the cure for all ills—even hangovers! Soups are not considered as just the opening act to Turkish meals; more often than not they will be the star turn.

In fact, there are entire restaurants, known as *çorbacı* (from *çorba*, the Turkish word for soup) that serve nothing but soup—some even specialize in a particular kind of soup. The most famous of these are probably *işkembeci* (tripe soup restaurants), which often stay open until the early hours of the morning serving up their potent hangover cure to those who've overdone the rakı. It's hard to know whether it's the tripe that works the sobering-up magic, or whether it's the traditional, fierce accompaniments of garlic, vinegar and chiles.

One of the most enjoyable meals we had on our Turkish journey was in the southeastern city of Gaziantep, where we ate a fortifying soup called *beyran* (see page 30). Although delicious, *beyran* is a fairly challenging dish that many might want to eat only a few times a year. Made from the sheep's cheek and enriched with a big blob of solid white fat from a special Middle Eastern breed of sheep, you can almost feel your arteries hardening as you slurp it down.

The range of soups on offer is vast. There are simple vegetable soups thickened with a handful of rice, pasta or legumes; others are made from any part of the animal—from the head to the tail. A whole subsection of soups are yogurt based; some contain green vegetables, like spinach, and others serve as the liquid vehicle for tiny rolled dumplings or stuffed *mantı*. One of the best-loved soups is *tarhana*, which is a soup base made from a sun-dried, fermented mixture of bulgur wheat and yogurt. A sort of precursor to Cup-a-Soup!

The one thing that all Turkish soups have in common, from the humblest Black Sea milk soup to the most elegant banquet soup, is the way they make so much out of very little. Above all, they are nourishing and economical and the mainstay of most home cooking.

Red pepper soup with bulgur, chickpeas, mint and chile

A hearty soup chock-full of grains and legumes, this makes a lovely winter's lunch with some crusty bread and a light salad.

Pekmez, or grape molasses, is available from Turkish food stores.

7 ounces dried chickpeas

¼ cup olive oil

1 onion, finely diced

1 long red pepper, seeded and finely chopped

1 long red chile, seeded and finely chopped

1 teaspoon dried mint

1 tablespoon *pekmez*

14-ounce can chopped tomatoes

1½ quarts water or vegetable stock

3 ounces coarse bulgur

⅓ cup shredded mint leaves

¼ teaspoon hot paprika

juice of ½ lemon

Soak the chickpeas overnight in plenty of cold water.

Heat the oil in a large, heavy-based saucepan. Sauté the onion, pepper, chile and mint over a low heat for 5–8 minutes, until the vegetables soften. Add the *pekmez* and sauté for a further minute.

Drain and rinse the chickpeas and add them to the pan with the tomatoes and 1 quart of the water or stock. Bring to the boil, then lower the heat and simmer, covered, for around 30 minutes. Add the bulgur to the pan with the remaining liquid and simmer, covered, for a further 10 minutes, stirring from time to time.

When ready to serve, stir in the shredded mint, paprika and lemon juice. Ladle the soup into warmed bowls and serve piping hot.

SERVES 6–8

Pumpkin soup with a yogurt swirl

A touch of cardamom and chile lifts this soup into a rather exotic realm and the spices are beautifully counterbalanced by the creamy, sweet yogurt swirl. *Pekmez*, or grape molasses, is available from Turkish food stores.

2 tablespoons olive oil
1 ounce unsalted butter
2 leeks, white part only, roughly chopped
3 cloves garlic, roughly chopped
½ teaspoon ground cinnamon
¼ teaspoon ground cardamom
½ teaspoon freshly ground black pepper
3 teaspoons *pekmez*
1 small butternut pumpkin (about 1¾ pounds), peeled and diced
1 long red chile, seeded and roughly chopped
1 bay leaf
1¼ quarts Chicken Stock (page 41)

YOGURT SWIRL
7 ounces Greek-style yogurt
1 teaspoon *pekmez*
pinch of sea salt

Heat the oil and butter in a large, heavy-based saucepan. Sauté the leeks and garlic for a few minutes, then add the spices and sauté over a low heat for 5–8 minutes, until the leeks soften.

Stir in the pumpkin, chile and bay leaf, then add the stock. Bring to the boil, skimming away any fat and impurities that rise to the surface, then lower the heat immediately. Simmer, covered, for 30 minutes.

Remove the pan from the heat and fish out the bay leaf. Puree the soup in batches in a blender or with an immersion blender until very smooth and creamy. If you want it to be supremely silky-smooth, pass the soup through a fine sieve.

Beat the yogurt with the *pekmez* and salt in a small bowl until smooth. When ready to serve, ladle the soup into warmed bowls and swirl in a generous dollop of yogurt.
SERVES 4–6

Fresh tomato and orzo soup with Gruyère croutons

We were fascinated to discover a type of Gruyère from Kas in the far east of Turkey.
Its sweet nutty flavor complements the sweetness of the soup beautifully.

2 tablespoons olive oil
1 teaspoon unsalted butter
1 shallot, finely diced
½ teaspoon honey
1 heaping teaspoon tomato paste
8 large vine-ripened tomatoes, skinned, seeded and roughly chopped
1 bay leaf
⅓ cup orzo pasta, cooked
1 quart Chicken Stock (page 41)
1 tablespoon lemon juice
2 tablespoons shredded flat-leaf parsley leaves

GRUYÈRE CROUTONS
6 slices day-old baguette, cut on the diagonal
½ clove garlic
4 ounces Gruyère, grated
sweet paprika for dusting

Heat the oil and butter in a large, heavy-based saucepan. Sauté the shallot for a few minutes until soft and translucent, then add the honey and tomato paste and cook for a few more minutes. Add the tomatoes, bay leaf, orzo pasta and stock. Bring to the boil slowly, skimming away any fat and impurities that rise to the surface, then lower the heat immediately. Simmer very gently, covered, for 20 minutes, skimming from time to time.

To make the Gruyère croutons, preheat your grill to its highest setting. Toast the baguette on one side, then rub the untoasted side with garlic and top with Gruyère. Grill until golden and bubbling, then dust lightly with paprika.

When ready to serve, stir the lemon juice and parsley into the soup. Ladle the soup into warmed bowls over the cooked orzo pasta and float the hot Gruyère croutons on top.
SERVES 6–8

Fish soup with young fennel and rakı

Rakı is the national drink of Turkey and its anise flavor brings out the fennel in this seafood soup brilliantly. Serve with plenty of hot crusty bread.
If you are unable to find rakı, substitute arak, ouzo or Pernod.

2 tablespoons olive oil
1 onion, finely chopped
1 leek, white part only, finely chopped
1 clove garlic, finely chopped
2 small bulbs fennel, cored and sliced lengthwise
2 long red chiles, split lengthwise and seeded
2½ tablespoons Seafood Spice Mix (page 319)
1½ quarts Crab Stock (page 41)
1 teaspoon sea salt
16 mussels, scrubbed and bearded
4 red mullet, filleted
2 small calamari, cleaned
7 ounces cooked chickpeas
2 ripe tomatoes, seeded and diced
1 generous tablespoon rakı
2 ounces raw shrimp meat
extra-virgin olive oil to serve
flat-leaf parsley leaves, finely shredded, to serve

Heat the oil in a large, heavy-based saucepan or an enameled pot and add the onion, leek, garlic, fennel and chiles. Add the spice mix, reserving a teaspoon. Sauté over a medium heat for a couple of minutes, stirring to coat the vegetables with the spices. Add the stock and season with salt. Simmer gently, uncovered, for about 20 minutes, or until the vegetables are very tender. Skim from time to time.

Meanwhile, discard any mussels that refuse to open after a sharp tap. Check the fish fillets for any lingering pin bones. Cut the calamari tentacles into short lengths. Split the tubes lengthwise and score the inside of each in a criss-cross pattern, then cut into quarters.

Lightly dust the fish and calamari with the remaining spice mix. Add the chickpeas and tomatoes to the pan and splash in the rakı. Add the mussels, prawns, fish fillets and calamari, then increase the heat and cook, covered, for 3–4 minutes until the mussels begin to open.

Serve immediately from the pan at the table, distributing the seafood, vegetables and broth between warmed bowls. Add a drizzle of extra-virgin olive oil and a little parsley to each bowl.

SERVES 8

Golden avgolemono with shrimp, chicory and rice

Egg and lemon sauces and soups are a distinctive component of both Turkish and Greek cookery. Using eggs to add richness was a common feature of medieval cookery, and the egg–lemon combination is believed to have been a Byzantine idea, taken up by the sophisticated kitchens of the Ottoman sultans.

The appeal of avgolemono (as they are known in Greek) or *terbiye* (Turkish) sauces and soups is that they are rich and velvety-smooth, with a refreshing lemony flavor.

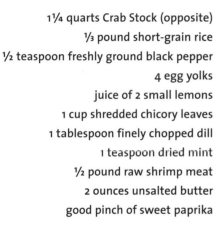

1¼ quarts Crab Stock (opposite)
⅓ pound short-grain rice
½ teaspoon freshly ground black pepper
4 egg yolks
juice of 2 small lemons
1 cup shredded chicory leaves
1 tablespoon finely chopped dill
1 teaspoon dried mint
½ pound raw shrimp meat
2 ounces unsalted butter
good pinch of sweet paprika

Heat the stock in a large, heavy-based saucepan, then add the rice and pepper and bring to the boil. Lower the heat and simmer, uncovered, for 20 minutes.

In a small mixing bowl, whisk the egg yolks with the lemon juice. Ladle a spoonful of the hot stock into the egg mixture and whisk gently. Pour this back into the barely simmering soup, whisking continuously. Cook at a bare simmer, whisking gently, until the soup starts to thicken. Be sure not to let the soup boil or the mixture will curdle.

Add the chicory, dill, dried mint and shrimp meat to the pan and simmer gently for 3 minutes, or until the shrimp are barely cooked. Meanwhile, quickly heat the butter in a small frying pan until it foams, then add the paprika. When ready to serve, ladle the soup into warmed serving bowls and swirl on the sizzling butter.
SERVES 8

Crab stock

A wonderful, fragrant stock I like to use for all sorts of seafood soups, stews and braises, instead of the more prosaic fish stock. It should be used within 24 hours of being made, or it can be frozen for up to 3 months.

4½ pounds crabs
5 ounces olive oil
4 sticks celery, roughly chopped
2 onions, roughly chopped
4 cloves garlic, roughly chopped
½ teaspoon fennel seeds, roughly crushed
14-ounce can diced tomatoes
½ cup sherry
long piece of peel from 1 orange
20 strands saffron, roasted and crushed
2 bay leaves
12 sprigs thyme
4¼ quarts water

Remove the underbody from the crabs and pull away the spongy gills ("dead man's fingers"). Cut each body in half and bash the shells and claws into large pieces.

Heat the oil in a large, heavy-based saucepan to smoking point. Sauté the crab pieces briefly over a high heat, then add the celery, onion, garlic and fennel seeds and sauté for 2 minutes. Stir in the tomatoes, sherry, peel, saffron, bay leaves and thyme, then add the water. Bring to the boil, skimming away any fat and impurities that rise to the surface, then lower the heat immediately. Simmer, uncovered, for an hour, skimming from time to time.

Carefully ladle the stock into a container, discarding the solids. (Don't be tempted to dump everything into a sieve: the less you disturb the solids at this stage, the clearer the final broth will be. I find the best method is to use a sieve to keep the solids submerged while you ladle out the liquid.) Refrigerate or freeze for later use.
MAKES 2½ quarts

Chicken stock

You can use this stock as a base for any recipe that calls for chicken stock. The quantities given here are enough to make around 2½ quarts, and the stock can be frozen quite happily for up to 3 months.

6½ pounds chicken carcasses
1 onion, cut into quarters
2 sticks celery, roughly chopped
1 leek, white part only, roughly chopped
2 cloves garlic, halved
½ teaspoon black peppercorns
1 bay leaf
3 sprigs thyme

Rinse the chicken carcasses and then put them into a 5-quart stockpot. Pour on enough water to cover the bones generously and add the remaining ingredients. Bring to the boil, skimming away any fat and impurities that rise to the surface, then lower the heat immediately. Cover the pot and simmer very gently for 2 hours, skimming from time to time.

Carefully ladle the stock into a container, discarding the solids. (Don't be tempted to dump everything into a sieve: the less you disturb the solids at this stage, the clearer the final broth will be. I find the best method is to use a sieve to keep the solids submerged while you ladle out the liquid.)

Refrigerate for up to three days or freeze for later use.
MAKES 2½ quarts

A day on the Bosphorus

[DIPS]

Istanbul is a city dominated by the sea, whose lifeblood has always been the saltwater that flows through and around it.

The second night in Istanbul I was awakened in the small hours by squabbling seagulls on the rooftops outside my window. As I peered out into the chilly night, past the looming bulk of the Blue Mosque, I could sense the distant presence of the rain-swept Bosphorus, grey and sullen in the predawn light.

It was a reminder that Istanbul is a city dominated by the sea, whose lifeblood has always been the saltwater that flows through and around it. Not only is the city itself split in two by the deep and dark waters of the Bosphorus, but the European side is also rift by a smaller inlet, the Golden Horn. And then there are those two seas: the vast and mysterious Black Sea to the north, and the smaller Sea of Marmara abutting the Aegean, to the south. Few other cities are so advantageously positioned between land and water, or have been fought over so continuously or determinedly through the centuries as a result.

Then, through the squally rain, the mosque's speaker crackled into life and the first prayer call of the day rose up and out into the lightening sky. There was little chance of getting back to sleep so I stayed in my spot at the window, watching the sky gradually lighten and the wind and rain die down; a good thing, too, as we had plans that day for a boat trip on the Bosphorus.

The Galata Bridge was bristling with fishing rods and down on the waterfront the morning's catch was being hauled ashore to be cooked over wood-fire grills and made into the famous Istanbul fish sandwiches.

This nineteen-mile strait is famous for being one of the busiest and most difficult-to-navigate waterways in the world. An estimated 50,000 vessels plow back and forth between the two shores and the two seas every year. Tiny one-man rowboats do daily battle with massive freight trawlers and oil tankers, while lumbering old-fashioned commuter ferries, private pleasure boats and fancy cruise ships weave their way around each other.

Later that morning we made our way down to the Eminönü quay to watch the action. The Galata Bridge was bristling with fishing rods and down on the waterfront the morning's catch was being hauled ashore to be cooked over wood-fire grills and made into the famous Istanbul fish sandwiches. As we pushed our way through the crowds that were bustling around the ferry stations, the aroma of frying fish became too much for us. At a small kiosk, we watched eagerly as a couple of piping hot fish fillets were deftly flipped into bread rolls. We scoffed them down greedily. Now we were ready for our excursion.

Our ferryboat was starting to fill with tourist passengers all set for a day on the water. Its bulky prow rose and fell on the lazy swell of the tide, and hungry seagulls circled, on the hunt for the odd piece of discarded fish sandwich. We clambered aboard and found a well-positioned spot in the front of the boat. The horn blew low and loud; the boat drew away from the quay and the seagulls moved into place, dipping and swooping into the boat's choppy wake.

For many centuries, before the city began its expansion in earnest, the Bosphorus was a lovely broad waterway, its banks fringed with rolling green hills and thick forests and dotted with pretty little fishing villages. Today, the densely populated suburbs of Istanbul sprawl along its entire length, almost as far as the Black Sea. As the boat began its zig-zag journey, with the smell of brine in our noses, we were filled with a sense of excitement—heading toward the open sea, leaving the chaos of the city behind. And there was an even greater pleasure to be had from seeing that city revealed from a distance, allowing, as it did, an entirely different, more peaceful perspective.

Scenes from everyday Istanbul life, past and present, were unfolding on either side of the strait. We saw modern museums and ornate nineteenth-century palaces,

As the boat began its zig-zag journey, with the smell of brine in our noses, we were filled with a sense of excitement—heading toward the open sea, leaving the chaos of the city behind.

grand hotels, pretty mosques and decrepit apartment buildings that seemed to be collapsing into the water. And on both sides, here and there we passed lovely wooden villas known as *yalı*, with their carved wooden balconies, high shuttered windows and gently sloping roofs. The *yalı* were built by wealthy Ottoman families during the eighteenth and nineteenth centuries as waterside summer residences, where they would go to escape the sweltering heat of the city. Sadly, many have disappeared completely; others have rotted into ruin. They stand dark and derelict, their once smartly painted woodwork now bleached a dirty gray-brown.

Farther on, at the narrowest part of the Bosphorus, we passed the crenellated towers and walls of Rumeli Hisarı. This mighty fortress was built by Mehmet II in 1452 as part of his highly organized siege of Constantinople. His intention was to cut the city off from any assistance that might arrive by sea, and the plan worked a treat. Within a year the capital was wrenched from Christian Byzantium forever. But while Constantinople flourished under its new Ottoman rulers, the fortress itself had served its purpose and quickly fell out of use.

We disembarked at Kanlıca, a sleepy little village on the Asian side of the Bosphorus famous for its yogurt. The pretty harbor was encircled by tall timber houses and the water was crowded with brightly painted fishing boats. We wandered around the village square enjoying the sunshine for a while before ducking into a café overlooking the water for some refreshment. We learned that, traditionally, Kanlıca yogurt was made from a mixture of cow's milk and ewe's milk and was thick enough to cut with a knife. Today, most of the local product is sold pre-set in tubs and one of the main reasons for its popularity is that it comes ready-sweetened with powdered sugar—something of a novelty in a country where mass-produced,

gloopy Western-style yogurt, thick with artificial fruit flavors and colors, was unheard of until quite recently.

On the menu there was a range of yogurts we could choose from, either plain or topped with jam, molasses, confectioners' sugar or honey. At the table next to ours, a young couple were scooping up tiny spoonfuls of the stuff and slipping it into each other's mouths. We smiled at them. They smiled at us. "There's a lot of yogurt to choose from here," we said. "Ah yes," replied the young man. "Turkish people take their yogurt seriously!" On their advice we chose the unsweetened variety, which was indeed delicious: brilliantly white, thick and creamy, with a pure, mild flavor. We enjoyed it drizzled with local honey, accompanied by a cup of strong black tea poured from a gently bubbling samovar.

Reenergized, we decided it was time to head back to the city. The Istanbul ferry didn't call back at Kanlıca until much later that afternoon, so, undaunted, we decided to brave one of the busy local buses. More by luck than good planning, we got onto a bus for Istanbul, and were delighted to spot the young yogurt-lovers from the Kanlıca café sitting in front of us. We smiled at each other in recognition and gratefully accepted their help in changing buses at the busy Mecidiyeköy bus station. An hour or so later we passed the massive İnönü soccer stadium, famous for being the only sporting venue in the world where fans can view two continents simultaneously. There was a match on that evening and it was apparent from the crowd that the supporters had other things on their mind than the view. The police were out in force, clearly anticipating trouble. They took up their places in serried ranks; they all wore visors, with riot shields held high and truncheons at the ready. The young couple in front of us on the bus were amused by the look on our faces. "Turkish people take their soccer seriously!" they told us.

Haydari

Thicker than *cacık*, this is made from strained yogurt—*süzme*—which is very like the Middle Eastern *labne*. *Haydari* is often mixed with mild red or green chiles and spread on little toasts or toasted flat bread. It's also delicious with all sorts of grills—meats, seafood, poultry, *köfte* and kebabs.

Strained yogurt is worth making to try in a variety of dips. Try it also with hot and spicy soups or serve as an accompaniment to grilled meats and poultry, rice dishes and even with desserts. This quantity will make about 3/4 pound, enough to make *haydari* or for you to try both Whipped Feta Dip (page 58) and Soft White Cheese and Walnut Dip (page 62).

STRAINED YOGURT
1 pound Greek-style yogurt

1 clove garlic
1 teaspoon sea salt
½ cup finely chopped dill
1 long green chile, seeded and shredded
sweet paprika to serve
extra-virgin olive oil to serve

To strain the yogurt, spoon it into a clean muslin or cheesecloth square or tea towel. Tie the four corners together and suspend the bundle from a wooden spoon over a deep bowl. Refrigerate overnight to drain. (You can use the strained yogurt in other savory or sweet recipes, and flavor accordingly.)

To make *haydari*, tip the strained yogurt into a large bowl. Crush the garlic with the salt, then beat into the yogurt with the dill and chile. Taste and adjust seasoning if necessary. Chill, covered, until ready to eat. Transfer to a serving bowl or plate and garnish with a sprinkle of paprika and a drizzle of oil.
SERVES 4–6

Cacık

Although *cacık* is a popular meze dish in Turkey, it's also served as an accompaniment to pastries, meat and rice dishes and can be diluted with ice-cold water to make a refreshing summer soup.

You'll find *cacık* flavored with all sorts of green herbs, but mint or dill are the most commonly used.

Cacık varies in consistency and can be very runny. It is usually made from ordinary natural yogurt, so if you prefer it thicker, as we do, then use a thick Greek-style or tub-set variety.

1 clove garlic
sea salt
1 pound Greek-style yogurt
2 Lebanese or Persian cucumbers, seeded and grated (skin on)
⅓ cup finely chopped dill
1 teaspoon dried mint
squeeze of lemon juice

Crush the garlic with 1 teaspoon salt, then beat with the yogurt, cucumber and herbs in a large bowl. Season with salt and lemon juice to taste. Chill, covered, until ready to eat.
SERVES 4–6

[Clockwise from left] Hot Red
Pepper Paste (page 59), *Cacık*
(opposite), Soft White Cheese and
Walnut Dip (page 62)

Yogurt

A stroll through the dairy section of any Turkish market reveals the Turks as a nation of yogurt lovers. In fact, most of the country's milk production goes toward making yogurt—whether it is from cow, goat, sheep or even water buffalo milk. Turks tend not to use low-fat cow's milk, and yogurt devotees will know that the higher fat content of the latter three animals makes even more delectably creamy yogurt (these are increasingly available in the West). A delicious type of Turkish yogurt that we discovered on our travels is *kaymaklı* yogurt, which has a thick layer of clotted 'cream' on the surface.

Unflavored yogurt appears on the table at every mealtime and is served with just about anything, including soups, stews, kebabs, pilafs, stuffed vegetables and salads. It is often flavored with garlic and herbs, such as fresh dill and mint, to be made into side dishes like *cacık* and *haydari*; or strained to make soft fresh cheese and eaten with jam, honey or confectioners' sugar as a delicious breakfast or snack. And if it's not being eaten, it's being drunk as the cooling, slightly salty drink *ayran*.

Yogurt is one of the most ancient foods known to man. Evidence exists of fermented milk products being produced almost 4,500 years ago, and the Turks are just one of many peoples who like to claim responsibility for its creation. There is no clear proof as to where or how it was first made, but the earliest yogurts can be traced back to nomadic horse-riding peoples of Central Asia, who made both yogurt and cheese from milk produced by their small goat and sheep flocks and from their horses. The evidence suggests that milk was often transported in goat-skin bags strapped to the saddles, and the earliest yogurts were probably fermented spontaneously by wild bacteria.

In Turkish markets and dairy shops you'll generally find two kinds of yogurt: *sıvı tas* and *süzme*. Sıvı tas is the standard yogurt and can vary in consistency from fairly runny to thick and creamy; it's used to make most yogurt-based sauces and is diluted with iced water to make *ayran*. *Süzme* is a very firm, strained yogurt that's made by hanging *sıvı tas* in a muslin bag overnight to drain away the whey. The longer the hanging time, the thicker the result. If allowed to drain for a couple of days, it becomes a creamy soft cheese with a light tangy flavor; delicious spread on bread with a drizzle of extra-virgin olive oil. Sadly, strained yogurt is not widely available in Western countries, but it is incredibly easy to make your own at home (see page 54).

Whipped feta dip

This dip was one of my first-ever creations as a young chef and I still love it. It's utterly simple, but the balance of salty cheese, hot mustard and tangy yogurt is just brilliant. Although the mustard is not strictly Turkish, variations of little cheese dips are very popular as part of meze selections. If you want to add another dimension of flavor, add a teaspoon of mild honey to the processor along with the mustard and strained yogurt.

Serve this dip with raw vegetables or warm or toasted flat bread. You could even thin it down with olive oil to dress a robust romaine lettuce salad.

8 ounces sheep's feta
⅓ pound Strained Yogurt (page 54)
1 generous teaspoon Dijon mustard

Soak the feta in cold water for around 10 minutes to remove excess salt, changing the water twice. Crumble the feta roughly into a food processor and puree for a minute, pushing the mixture down from the sides once or twice. Add the strained yogurt and mustard and puree again until very smooth and creamy. Chill, covered, until ready to eat. This dip will keep for up to a week.
SERVES 4–6

Silky celery root dip with lime

I was inspired to make this dip after a wonderful meal at Istanbul's famous Doğa Balık. Although best known for its seafood, the restaurant also has a mind-bogglingly large number of meze dishes on display, and diners are encouraged to make their own selection. This unusual dip has a refreshing, mild celery flavor and a delectable silky-smooth texture. The lime juice is not very Turkish, but it adds a lovely citrus zing. Serve as a dip with warm or toasted bread, or as an accompaniment to grills and roasts.

2 celery roots (about 1½ lbs)
2 cloves garlic, peeled and smashed
1 quart milk
juice of up to 1 lime
⅓ cup olive oil
sea salt
freshly ground white pepper

Peel the celery roots and cut into even-sized pieces. Place in a saucepan with the garlic and milk and bring to the boil. Lower the heat and press a piece of baking paper, cut to the size of the pan, down over the celery root. Simmer gently, covered, for around 30 minutes, or until the celery root is very soft.

While the celery root is still hot, put it into a blender or food processor with half the cooking liquor and half the lime juice and blend to a velvety-smooth puree. With the motor running, slowly drizzle in the olive oil to form an emulsion. Season with salt and pepper, then add more lime juice to taste. Chill, covered, until ready to eat.
SERVES 4–6

Hot red pepper paste

On our very first day in Istanbul we ate in a tiny *pide* restaurant. The first thing to arrive on the table was a small pot of spicy red pepper paste, a dish of butter and a plate of crumbled white *lor* cheese. We ate these with big puffed-up rounds of flat bread, straight from the wood-fired oven, and thought we'd arrived in heaven. This is our version of the pepper paste—it is quite chile-hot, so a little goes a long way. Serve it on warm flat bread with chilled unsalted butter and *lor*. If you can't get ahold of *lor*, then another crumbly white cheese, such as feta or a mature goat cheese, will do nicely.

3 long red peppers

3 long red chiles, seeded

1 teaspoon pomegranate molasses

½ teaspoon dried mint

2 tablespoons shredded mint leaves

2 tablespoons extra-virgin olive oil

2 green onions, finely diced

1 small Lebanese or Persian cucumber, peeled, seeded and diced

juice of 1 lemon

1 teaspoon sea salt

½ teaspoon freshly ground black pepper

Preheat the oven to 400°F. Roast the peppers and seeded chiles for 20 minutes on a foil-lined jelly-roll pan, turning once, until the skins blister and char. Remove from the oven and leave to cool.

When cool enough to handle, peel the skins away from the peppers and pull away the seeds and membranes. Roughly chop the peppers and put into a blender. Use a sharp knife to scrape the flesh of the chiles away from the skins—this is easier than trying to peel them. Add the chile flesh to the blender with the remaining ingredients. Whiz to a fine purée, then taste and adjust the balance of salt and lemon if necessary. Chill, covered, until ready to eat. This dip will keep for up to 3 days.

SERVES 4–6

Creamy fava bean pâté with grated-egg dressing

When we first saw a slab of this pale green pâté on a tray of meze dishes in Istanbul's Refik restaurant, we had no idea what it was. It's made by pouring a thick bean purée into a mold and chilling it until it sets firm. The resulting pâté has a smooth, creamy texture and its mild flavor is quite addictive. Although the grated egg is not really Turkish, I find it adds color and texture and an extra flavor dimension.

Serve drizzled with olive oil, chopped dill, paprika and lemon, or, if you want to be a bit fancy, Dill and Lemon Dressing (page 115). Cut off little slices and eat with warm or toasted flat bread.

Fava beans are simply dried broad beans, and are available whole (skins on) or split (skinless). Try to find the split skinless kind if you can.

7 ounces split fava beans
¼ cup olive oil
2 onions, chopped
drizzle of honey
1 small clove garlic, sliced
3⅓ cups water
juice of 1 lemon
sea salt
freshly ground white pepper
1 hard-boiled egg, finely grated
extra-virgin olive oil to serve
chopped dill to serve
sweet paprika to serve
pinch of chile flakes to serve
lemon wedges to serve

Soak the dried beans overnight in plenty of cold water, and remove the skins if necessary.

Heat the oil in a large heavy-based saucepan, then add the onions and sauté for a few minutes over a medium heat. Stir in the honey and sauté for 5 minutes. Drain and rinse the beans and add them to the pan with the garlic, water and lemon juice. Bring to the boil, then lower the heat and simmer, uncovered, for around an hour, or until the beans are tender. If there is still liquid in the pan, increase the heat and bubble vigorously until it has evaporated, taking care that the mixture doesn't stick and burn.

Blend the beans to a smooth purée in a blender. The mixture will be very thick and creamy. Season with salt and pepper. Pour into well-oiled molds or a greased shallow plastic tray. Chill, covered, overnight.

When ready to eat, turn the pâté out onto a serving plate or cut into little squares or diamond shapes. Scatter on the grated egg, then drizzle with the extra-virgin olive oil and sprinkle on the dill, paprika and chile flakes. Serve with lemon wedges.
SERVES 4–6

Soft white cheese and walnut dip

Simple to make, this dip is nice and peppery, and the walnuts give it a pleasing crunch. Serve as a spread for fresh crusty bread or smeared on croutons as an appetizer with predinner drinks.

⅔ cup walnuts

6 ounces feta

2 tablespoons Strained Yogurt (page 54)

2 tablespoons chopped flat-leaf parsley leaves

½ teaspoon freshly ground black pepper

1 tablespoon extra-virgin olive oil

Preheat the oven to 350°F. Scatter the walnuts onto a jelly-roll pan and roast for 5–10 minutes until a deep golden brown. Pour the nuts into a tea towel and rub well to remove as much skin as possible. Chop the walnuts finely and toss in a sieve to remove any remaining skin and dust.

Put all the ingredients into a large bowl and mash everything together thoroughly with a fork. Taste and adjust the seasoning.

SERVES 4–6

Smoky eggplant purée

A perennial favourite on the meze table. Serve with crusty bread, or with thin flat bread, opened out, brushed with a little olive oil and baked in the oven until crisp and golden.

1–2 eggplants (about 1½ pounds)

1 small clove garlic

sea salt

1 teaspoon extra-virgin olive oil

6 ounces Greek-style yogurt

juice of ½ lemon

2 tablespoons finely chopped flat-leaf parsley or mint leaves

Prick the eggplants all over with a fork and set them directly on the naked flame of your stove top. Set the flame to low–medium and cook for at least 10 minutes, turning constantly until the whole eggplant is charred. Remove from the flame and place on a cake rack in a plastic bag so the juices can drain off. Allow the eggplants to cool for about 10 minutes. (If you don't have a gas stove, stand the eggplants under the broiler, set to high, turning them regularly until charred. You won't get quite the same smoky flavor, but the effect is reasonable.)

When the eggplants are cool, gently peel away the skin from the flesh, taking care to remove every little bit or the dip will have a bitter burnt flavor. Put the flesh into a colander, then press gently and leave to drain for 5–10 minutes.

Put the drained eggplant into a bowl, then crush the garlic with 1 teaspoon salt and beat into the eggplant with the oil, yogurt and lemon juice. Chill, covered, until ready to eat. Transfer to a serving dish, add extra salt to taste, sprinkle on the herbs and serve.

SERVES 4–6

Taramasalata

The spice bazaar in Istanbul has a section crammed full of little shops selling Russian and Iranian caviar and *bottarga*—the salted pressed roe from gray mullet. Upmarket Turkish restaurants sometimes sell *bottarga*, sliced wafer-thin and chilled. Few of us can afford this luxury, but *taramasalata* is almost as delicious. These days gray mullet roe is scarce and you're more likely to be able to find smoked cod roe.

Serve with warm or toasted bread.

4 ounces gray mullet or smoked cod roe
2 thick slices good-quality white bread, crusts removed
1 clove garlic, roughly chopped
juice of 1–1½ lemons
1 cup olive oil
1 cup vegetable oil
3 ounces water

Lightly rinse the roe under cold running water.

Chop the bread roughly, then put it into a bowl and pour on enough water just to cover. Leave for a few moments, then squeeze it firmly. Whiz the bread, roe, garlic and the juice of 1 lemon to a paste in a food processor.

Combine the oils and start to drizzle into the processor with the motor running as if making a mayonnaise. Begin with 3 ounces, then loosen the mixture with 2 tablespoons water. Continue to add oil and water in similar amounts, and finish with the remaining lemon juice. The purée should be light, fluffy and a delicate, pale-golden pink. Taste and adjust the seasoning. Chill, covered, until ready to eat. The *taramasalata* will keep for 4–5 days.
SERVES 4–6

Almond *tarator*

This recipe was developed by my good friend Mick "Johnstone" Van Warmelo, chef at Olive restaurant in Hong Kong, where I consult. It is wonderful served as a dip with raw vegetables or to accompany seafood or lamb dishes, and the garlicky tang is particularly good with Crumbed Lambs' Tongues (page 169).

9 ounces blanched almonds
3 cloves garlic
sea salt
juice of 1 lemon
3 tablespoons champagne vinegar
1 tablespoon honey
4 egg yolks
2¼ cups olive oil
3–5 ounces lukewarm water
freshly ground black pepper

Pulse the almonds in a food processor until roughly crushed. Crush the garlic with 1 teaspoon salt and add to the almonds with the lemon juice, vinegar, honey and egg yolks and pulse until smooth and creamy. With the motor running, slowly drizzle in about half the oil, followed by half the water to loosen and stabilize the mixture. Slowly drizzle in the rest of the oil to form a thick, creamy mayonnaise—add a little more water if it is too thick. Season with pepper and check for salt—you may need to add a little more.

To give the *tarator* a smoother, finer texture, you can blend the mayonnaise in a blender on high for a few minutes.
MAKES 3 cups

Leaning toward Europe

[VEGETABLES]

We had spent the first few days in
Istanbul exploring the city's past;
now it was time to leap into its present.

We had spent the first few days in Istanbul exploring the city's past; now it was time to leap into its present. This meant a stroll across the Galata Bridge to Beyoğlu, where the city leans most determinedly toward Europe.

The suburb of Beyoğlu encompasses a steep hill on the northern side of the Golden Horn and has always been home to the city's minority of foreign residents. In the thirteenth century the area was given by the emperor to the Genoese as a gift for their support of Constantinople in its ongoing battles with the Crusaders. Under the Genoese, Pera, as they called it, became a flourishing trading colony, and the Galata Tower, one of Istanbul's most distinctive landmarks, was built. Over successive centuries, Greeks, Armenians, Arabs and Jews all established communities here. At the height of the Ottoman era, Pera was home to wealthy European merchants, and signs of nineteenth-century grandeur can still be spotted in the neighborhood's Beaux Arts, Romanesque and Ottoman architecture.

Today, as then, İstiklal Caddesi is the main thoroughfare. Although it's no longer the Grande Rue lined with fancy boutiques, fashionable coffee houses and embassies, it still retains some of its former charm. There's a cute little streetcar that trundles its way through the thousands of pedestrians; you spy once-glamorous Art Deco facades wedged in between graffitied concrete boxes, while old-fashioned pudding and confectionary shops seem to coexist quite happily with the predictable chain stores and fast-food restaurants.

We met up with our friend Sedat Arpalik outside Hacı Bekir, Istanbul's most famous Turkish delight shop, and queued behind a smartly dressed businessman

At the height of the Ottoman era, Pera was home to wealthy European merchants, and signs of nineteenth-century grandeur can still be spotted in the neighborhood's Beaux Arts, Romanesque and Ottoman architecture.

with a neatly waxed mustache who was taking his time making a selection from the vast array of exquisitely pretty *lokum*. But our eyes were drawn to a large pot of warm halvah. This was something new, which we couldn't resist trying. The shop assistant ladled some beige sludge into a small paper cup. It was a little like eating hot, semisweet, sesame-flavored sand—but curiously addictive—and it fortified us against the chilly wind outside.

Sedat was keen to show us something of Istanbul's "cool" side. An Australian-born Turk, he'd moved back to the city only a few months before to project-manage a building development.

"There's definitely a new energy about the place," he told us, cutting a path through the crowds and turning down a narrow side street. "The neighborhoods around İstiklal are really funky these days; you've got artists, musicians, filmmakers and designers all moving in. And if you think it's busy now, you should come here at nighttime. The place is heaving!" We were making our way down Nevizade Sokak, Istanbul's most vibrant eating precinct. "I come here most nights for a beer," Sedat confessed. "In the summer you can barely move for the crowds of people, the wandering gypsy-musicians and street peddlers trying to flog you a rose or two. It's just wild."

For now, though, we were headed for lunch at Refik, which proved to be far from new and trendy but rather a much-loved fixture on the Istanbul food scene. To get there, we had to pass though Balık Pazarı, the district's famous fish market. All around us were stalls overflowing with spanking fresh sea bass, pimple-backed turbot and huge pans of gleaming blue-black mussels. There were also pickle shops and variety meat butchers; cheese stalls and kebab stands; hardware stores selling samovars and tea glasses, mops and electric toasters—all the usual stuff of a busy Oriental bazaar.

Refik was an unassuming, homey place, tucked away down a narrow cobbled lane. We were grateful to step out of the chilly spring air into its cozy, dimly lit interior. Sedat explained that it was one of the city's oldest eateries, called a *meyhane*. *Meyhanes* are traditional inns, serving alcohol alongside small meze dishes.

"This place was started more than fifty years ago," he said. And as we took our seats under a tatty display of faded black-and-white photographs he pointed out a

ruddy-faced man standing by the glassed-in display cabinet. "That's the original Refik," he whispered. "I believe he's well into his seventies now but he still comes in every day." Mr Refik, looking as if he'd been enjoying a few glasses of rakı, the traditional accompaniment to meze, smiled cheerily and plonked a bottle down in front of us.

A few minutes later a waiter arrived bearing a large tray of tiny meze plates from which we made our selection: new-season's artichokes braised in olive oil, a salad of creamy poached brains doused in lemon juice, two slabs of tangy feta, grilled mushrooms and a bowl of thick mint-spiked yogurt. These were followed in quick succession by spicy chunks of grilled liver and crisp-fried red mullet. It was all wonderfully fresh, flavorsome and unpretentious.

Warmed by a few glasses of rakı, we felt ready to head back out into the cold afternoon. Sedat had plans for us, beginning with dessert in a traditional pudding shop. We were easily seduced by the vast trays of sticky, amber quinces served with rich *kaymak*—clotted cream made from buffalo milk—and a bowl of delicate *muhallebi*, a milk pudding perfumed with rose water.

Our tour of Beyoğlu continued as we cut back across İstiklal Caddesi to head for Fransız Sokağı, a chichi and newly spruced up "French" street, complete with gas streetlights, wrought-iron balconies and pretty pink and yellow pastel paintwork. No matter that it all felt just a bit too prettified; at this time of the late afternoon it was busy with young folk out on the terraces enjoying tea, a beer or a quick game of backgammon in the weak sunshine. After dark, Sed told us, diners spill out into the street to enjoy their moules marinières and pommes frites, while the roof terraces are packed with revelers into the wee small hours.

For now, we forged on to Çukurcuma, which is perhaps the artiest of Istanbul's trendy neighborhoods. Its narrow cobbled streets are home to funky little art galleries, pricey antique shops and grungy little dives selling all sorts of bric-a-brac. We clambered over a mound of excavated tarmac where the road was being dug up to lay new electricity cables—par for the course in this city—and almost fell over a film crew filming an episode of a Turkish "soap." It's that kind of neighborhood.

We cut back to head for Fransız Sokağı, a chichi and newly spruced up "French" street, complete with gas streetlights, wrought-iron balconies and pretty pink and yellow pastel paintwork.

Later that night Sed took us to Changa restaurant, where Turkey's embrace of Europe is most smartly on display. It's situated just off busy Taksim Square in an area pulsing with neon, nightclubs and greasy döner kebab stands. The traffic was at a standstill as we squeezed our way across the narrow street toward a discreet entrance.

Changa has led the way for modern dining in Istanbul and its sleek minimalist interior within a narrow Art Nouveau townhouse was undeniably alluring. The decor was as cutting edge as anything you'd find in London, Sydney or New York—all chrome, glass and Eames chairs beneath original painted plaster ceilings. It even had a glass porthole cut into the ground floor so the foodie customers could spy on the kitchen action beneath their feet. The clientele were clearly a modern kind of Turk, too, with plenty of turtlenecks and black-rimmed spectacles on display.

Pleasingly, the food lived up to the stylish standard of the restaurant's design. After studying the menu, it came as no surprise to learn that the famed New Zealand–born fusion-king Peter Gordon had a hand in the menu. As with his other restaurants in London and Auckland, the menu was brimming with original ideas—many with a clear Turkish bent. We shared a soup of Swiss chard and *sucuk* sausage, slices of tongue with a crust of spicy *çökelek* cheese, a superb confit of duck with a pistachio- and raisin-studded pilaf and tender little lamb chops served with a smoked-bulgur pilaf.

Changa isn't the kind of place that your average Turk would rush to. It's expensive for a start—even for those of us spending a tourist dollar. And Turkish people have a rather protective approach to their cuisine; at heart they don't really approve of it being messed around with. But Changa's customers were the sort of well-heeled, Western-oriented set that would happily rush to try something a bit new and different. And they seemed to be enjoying the food immensely, confident that its Turkishness was not being overly compromised.

As we went to hail a taxi, a group of giggling young Turkish women spilled out from a nearby doorway in a cloud of cigarette smoke and "doof-doof" music. We were intrigued to see another example of the way East and West blend so harmoniously in Istanbul, for although several girls were displaying bare midriffs, a couple of others were wearing headscarfs.

Crunchy zucchini flowers stuffed with *haloumi*, mint and ginger

12 baby zucchini with flowers attached

vegetable oil

olive oil

all-purpose flour for dusting

2 eggs, lightly beaten with a little water

sea salt

freshly ground black pepper

SUMAC CRUMBS

finely grated zest of 2 limes

½ teaspoon chili powder

1 teaspoon fennel seeds, lightly roasted and crushed

2 teaspoons ground sumac

7 ounces dried bread crumbs

HALOUMI STUFFING

4 ounces *haloumi*, washed

2 ounces mozzarella

1 small clove garlic

½ teaspoon salt

generous pinch of ground cardamom

generous grind of black pepper

¼ teaspoon freshly grated ginger

2 tablespoons finely shredded flat-leaf parsley leaves

1 heaped teaspoon finely chopped mint leaves

½ teaspoon dried mint

To make the crumbs, leave the lime zest out on a plate to dry overnight or put it into a very low oven for 30 minutes. This will intensify the lime flavor. Mix the zest with the remaining ingredients and set aside.

To make the stuffing, grate the *haloumi* and mozzarella into a bowl. Crush the garlic with the salt and stir into the bowl with the remaining ingredients.

Carefully open each zucchini flower and pinch out the stamen. Roll a lump of the cheese stuffing into a thumb-sized sausage shape and gently stuff it into the flower. Twist the top of the flower to seal.

Heat equal quantities of the oils in a deep-fryer or saucepan to 400°F. Set up a little production line of flour, egg wash and the crumb mixture. Dust each zucchini flower lightly with flour, then dip it into the egg and, finally, gently roll it in the crumbs.

Carefully fry the flowers in the hot oil, no more than four at a time, until the crumbs turn crisp and golden. Remove and drain on paper towels, and repeat with the remaining flowers. Season lightly and serve straight away.

SERVES 4

İmam bayıldı

Purists will have to forgive me for messing around with Turkey's most famous dish. I love using tiny eggplants, which are the perfect size to serve as an accompaniment to roast or grilled lamb dishes. You could also serve them at room temperature as part of a meze selection. And as for the goat's cheese—well, I think it adds an incomparable creamy tang to this luscious dish.

Pekmez, or grape molasses, is available from Turkish food stores. You'll find the red pepper paste used here in Middle Eastern food stores.

6 small eggplants (3–4 inches long)
sea salt
olive oil
4 ounces soft goat cheese

GARLIC PASTE
1 tablespoon olive oil
5 cloves garlic, sliced
2 teaspoons ground coriander
1 teaspoon sea salt

SPICY TOMATO SAUCE
¼ cup olive oil
1 large onion, finely diced
1 teaspoon sweet paprika
1 teaspoon mild Turkish red pepper paste
6 vine-ripened tomatoes, skinned, seeded and chopped
¼ cup finely chopped flat-leaf parsley leaves
1 tablespoon finely chopped French tarragon
zest of ½ lemon
1 tablespoon pekmez
3 ounces water
sea salt
freshly ground black pepper

Slit the eggplants in half lengthwise from the base to ½ inch below the stalk. Ease each one open—keeping it joined at the stalk—and use the tip of a small sharp knife to score the flesh inside. Sprinkle one side generously with salt and squeeze the eggplant together, then leave to drain in a colander for 30 minutes. Meanwhile, preheat the oven to 350°F.

Rinse the eggplants thoroughly, then sprinkle them inside and out with oil. Arrange in a jelly-roll pan and roast for 10 minutes. Transfer the eggplants to a container with a lid, then seal and leave to steam and cool down.

To prepare the garlic paste, heat the oil in a heavy-based frying pan. Add the garlic and sauté for a few minutes, taking care not to let it color. Put into a mortar with the coriander and salt and grind to a thick paste.

To make the sauce, heat the oil in a heavy-based frying pan and sauté the onion until soft and translucent. Stir in the paprika and pepper paste and sauté for another 2 minutes, then add the tomatoes, herbs, lemon zest, pekmez and water and season with salt and pepper. Bring to the boil, then lower the heat and simmer, uncovered, for an hour, stirring occasionally. It should reduce to a very thick, sticky sauce. Refrigerate until needed.

When ready to cook the İmam bayıldı, preheat the oven to 350°F. Arrange the eggplants in a large baking dish. Carefully lift up the top half of each eggplant and smear a little garlic paste inside, pushing it down into the soft flesh. Smear a heaping spoonful of sauce inside each eggplant as well and dab in a little goat's cheese. Press the top down again to form a kind of sandwich. Drizzle with oil and bake for 10–12 minutes until the sauce is bubbling and the cheese oozing. Allow to cool and serve cold or at room temperature.

SERVES 6

Braised broad beans with artichokes and *pastırma*

Fresh broad beans cooked in olive oil are a popular meze dish in Turkey. Sometimes they are cooked and eaten in the furry outer pod, especially in the Aegean region, but podded or whole they are usually flavored with fresh dill. In this recipe I have taken inspiration from a Spanish dish and substituted *pastırma*—the spiced, cured beef popular across Turkey—for the more traditional *jamon iberico*.

Serve these beans cold or warm as part of a meze selection, with crusty bread to mop up the juices.

²⁄₃ pound fresh broad beans in the pod, shelled

1 clove garlic

½ teaspoon sea salt

⅓ cup extra-virgin olive oil

6 fresh artichoke hearts, cut into quarters and kept in a bowl of acidulated water with 2-3 tablespoons lemon juice

12 pearl onions, peeled and halved

1 teaspoon dried mint

¼ teaspoon freshly ground black pepper

1 sprig thyme

5 ounces Chicken Stock (page 41)

juice of ½ lemon

2 tablespoons chopped dill

4 ounces *pastırma*, shredded

Blanch the broad beans in a saucepan of boiling water and refresh briefly under cold water. When cool, peel off the skins.

Crush the garlic with the salt. Heat ¼ cup of the oil in a heavy-based frying pan and add the drained artichokes, pearl onions and garlic and salt. Sauté over a low heat for a few minutes, then add the mint, pepper, thyme, stock and lemon juice. Bring to the boil, then lower the heat and simmer, uncovered, for 8–10 minutes, until the artichokes and onions are tender. Add the beans and dill and cook for a further minute, then put into a warmed serving bowl.

Heat the remaining oil in a separate frying pan. Fry the shredded *pastırma* until golden brown, then remove from the heat and drain off any excess oil. Scatter over the beans and serve straight away.

SERVES 6

Bitter greens, artichokes and shallots with poppy seeds

This dish was inspired by one we ate at Çiya restaurant in Istanbul. There were many meze dishes of wild greens we enjoyed that day but we fell in love with the combination of strong, bitter greens and the barely discernible nutty crunch of poppy seeds. In this version a squeeze of lemon juice and a pat of butter at the end soften the bitterness. Serve this dish warm or at room temperature as part of a meze selection. It also makes a great lunch dish with a poached or fried egg and some warm flat bread.

¼ cup extra-virgin olive oil

6 fresh artichoke hearts, cut into quarters and kept in acidulated water

12 small shallots, peeled and halved

1 leek, white part only, cut lengthwise into thin strips and washed

1 teaspoon poppy seeds, lightly crushed

¼ teaspoon hot paprika

¼ teaspoon freshly ground black pepper

ground sumac

1⅓ pounds chicory, roots trimmed

5 ounces Swiss chard, shredded lengthwise

5 ounces Chicken Stock (page 41)

squeeze of lemon juice

2 ounces unsalted butter

Heat the oil in a heavy-based saucepan and add the drained artichokes, shallots and leek. Sauté over a low heat for a few minutes, then add the poppy seeds, paprika, pepper and 1 teaspoon sumac and cook for a further couple of minutes. Add the chicory, Swiss chard and stock. Bring to the boil, then lower the heat and simmer, uncovered, for 8–10 minutes until the artichokes and onions are tender.

Remove the pan from the heat, then stir in the lemon juice and butter well and put into a warmed serving bowl. Sprinkle with a little more sumac and serve.

SERVES 6

Turlu vegetable pot

Turlu is the Turkish word for mix, and this vegetable dish is the Turkish equivalent of ratatouille. It is wonderful made when summer vegetables are at their peak. Serve warm, as a vegetarian main course, and accompany with plenty of yogurt on the side and crusty bread to soak up all the juices.

The pickled green chiles mentioned can be made following the recipe on page 316, or they can be bought from a deli.

1 zucchini, cut into ½-inch dice

1 eggplant, peeled and cut into ½-inch dice

sea salt

1 carrot, cut into ½-inch dice

2 kipfler potatoes, peeled and cut into ½-inch dice

2 artichoke hearts, cut into quarters and kept in acidulated water

1 small red onion, cut into ½-inch dice

2 cloves garlic, finely sliced

2 long red peppers, roasted, peeled and cut into ¾-inch dice

2 pickled green chiles, shredded

2 vine-ripened tomatoes, skinned and chopped

1 tablespoon coriander seeds, lightly toasted and crushed

good pinch of ground allspice

good pinch of ground cinnamon

freshly ground black pepper

¼ cup olive oil

5 ounces water

2 tablespoons apple or champagne vinegar

1 teaspoon sugar

1 cup cooked chickpeas

zest and juice of ½ lemon

½ cup chopped flat-leaf parsley leaves

Toss the zucchini and eggplant with 2 teaspoons salt and transfer to a colander. Leave to drain for 30 minutes, then rinse thoroughly and pat dry.

Using your hands, toss all the vegetables in a large bowl with the spices and oil. Heat a heavy-based frying pan and sauté the coated vegetables in batches over medium heat until lightly golden.

Transfer the vegetables as they are done to a large casserole dish, then lastly add the water, vinegar and sugar. Stir gently and bring to the boil. Lower the heat, then cover and cook gently for 30–40 minutes or until tender. Toward the end of the cooking time, stir in the chickpeas.

Remove the pan from the heat, then taste and adjust the seasonings. Add the lemon zest and juice and the parsley and serve.

SERVES 4

Large mushrooms baked with smoky chile

Turkish recipes make good use of the various types of paprika available, which range from sweet and delicate to deeply smoky to bitingly hot. I particularly like the combination here, of sweet and smoky paprikas, which bring out the earthy meatiness of mushrooms.

This makes a wonderful, hearty winter lunch dish that you could serve on its own with a big blob of yogurt and perhaps a simple green leaf salad. It also makes a great accompaniment to a grilled steak or roast—slice the meat and serve it on top of the baked vegetables so the juices intermingle.

3 tabelspoons olive oil

1 large red onion, cut into large dice

2 cloves garlic, roughly smashed

½ teaspoon smoky paprika

1 teaspoon sweet paprika

1 teaspoon ground cumin

1 tablespoon sherry vinegar

6 large mushrooms, stems removed

2 vine-ripened tomatoes, cut into quarters

2 long red chiles, split and seeded

2 long green chiles, split and seeded

few sprigs thyme

sea salt

½ teaspoon freshly ground black pepper

2 ounces butter

3 ounces water

Preheat the oven to 350°F. Heat the oil in an ovenproof frying pan. Add the onion, garlic and spices and sauté for around 5 minutes until soft. Stir in the vinegar.

Place the mushrooms on top of the onions, stem-sides up, and tuck the tomatoes, chiles and thyme in and around them. Season with salt and pepper and scatter bits of butter over the mushrooms. Pour in the water and transfer to the oven. Bake for 20 minutes, or until the vegetables are tender.

Set the pan over a high heat on the stove. Spoon the juices over all the vegetables so they are moist, and cook vigorously until you are left with a concentrated sauce. Taste and adjust the seasoning and serve straight away.
SERVES 6

Vegetables

While the eggplant is unquestionably king in Turkish cooking, the Turks, in fact, use a veritable cornucopia of vegetables. Which is not surprising really, when you consider that Turkey's vast landmass covers a diverse range of geographical terrains and climates—from the sun-kissed Mediterranean to lush valleys and mountain pastures and the fertile plains of central Anatolia.

Turkish cooking is mainly based upon the seasons, and this is especially true when it comes to fruit and vegetables (although some, like onions, garlic, potatoes and fresh herbs are grown all year round). Artichokes and broad beans signal the arrival of spring; in the summer, eggplant, okra, tomatoes, peppers and zucchini are at their plump, tasty best; while in the autumn and early winter people make good use of cabbages and celery root, pumpkins, leeks, carrots and spinach.

A very popular way to cook vegetables is in olive oil—a distinct category of dishes known as *zeytinyağlı*—and usually served at room temperature as part of a meze selection, or on their own, with plenty of crusty bread to mop up the lusciously oily cooking juices. This method of cooking is generally agreed to have been encountered by the Turks after settling in Anatolia. Olive trees had long been cultivated along the Mediterranean and Aegean coastlines by the early indigenous peoples: the Greeks and the Romans. And it is in these regions that *zeytinyağlı* dishes are most widespread.

Like other Eastern Mediterranean and Middle Eastern peoples, the Turks also have a passion for stuffing vegetables with herby rice or meat mixtures. These are known as dolma, which in Turkish means stuffed or filled, and the most popular vegetable dolma are made with eggplants, tomatoes, zucchinis

and peppers. If a vegetable is wrapped around a stuffing, such as cabbage, spinach or vine leaves, it is known as *sarma*. Meatless dolmas and *sarmas* are best served at room temperature or cold, and meat-filled versions are usually served warm. Both may be eaten with a yogurt sauce.

Given the seasonal nature of Turkish produce markets, it's not surprising that many vegetables are dried and pickled to be used during the winter months. Long garlands of dried eggplant, okra, peppers and chiles adorn the bazaars, and in villages they dangle from windows or balconies. *Turşu*—or pickled vegetables—are another standard pantry item. Made by immersing raw vegetables in a flavored pickling solution, they make a wonderful appetite stimulant at the start of many a meal.

Stuffed vine leaves, Istanbul-style

There are numerous versions of stuffed vine leaves to be found all around the Middle East and Mediterranean. According to Claudia Roden in *A New Book of Middle Eastern Food*, they were served at the court of King Khusrow II in Persia as early as the seventh century, subsequently spreading through the Muslim world and then the Ottoman Empire.

In Turkey, stuffed vegetables that are rolled, such as vine, cabbage or Swiss chard leaves, are known as *sarma*. This version is especially popular in the summer, when it is served at room temperature as part of a meze selection.

26-ounce jar preserved vine leaves or about 1 pound fresh vine leaves, washed

3 ounces olive oil

¼ cup pine nuts

1 large onion, finely chopped

1 level teaspoon ground allspice

½ teaspoon ground cinnamon

1 level teaspoon dried mint

¼ cup currants

9 ounces short-grain rice

sea salt

freshly ground black pepper

8 ounces Chicken Stock (page 41)

1 vine-ripened tomato, grated

2 tablespoons finely chopped dill

2 tablespoons finely chopped flat-leaf parsley leaves

1 lemon, sliced

7 ounces hot water

juice of 1 lemon

If using preserved vine leaves, soak them for 10 minutes, then rinse and pat dry. Fresh vine leaves should be blanched in boiling water for 30 seconds and refreshed in cold water.

To make the filling, heat half the oil in a heavy-based saucepan. Sauté the pine nuts for a few minutes over medium heat until golden brown. Add the onion and sauté until softened, then add the spices, dried mint, currants and rice and season with salt and pepper. Stir well and add half the chicken stock to the pan. Cook over a low heat, for 5 minutes, stirring occasionally. Add the remaining stock and cook for a further 5 minutes, or until the stock has been absorbed. Remove the pan from the heat and stir in the grated tomato and fresh herbs.

Line the bottom of a heavy-based casserole dish with a few vine leaves and slices of lemon. Arrange the remaining leaves over a work surface, vein-side up, and cut away the stems. Place a spoonful of the filling across the base of the leaf. Roll it over once, then fold in the sides and continue to roll it into a neat sausage shape. The *sarmas* should be around the size of your little finger—don't stuff them too tightly or they will burst during the cooking. Continue stuffing and rolling until all the filling has been used.

Pack the stuffed vine leaves into the casserole dish, layering them with more lemon slices, then pour in the hot water, lemon juice and remaining oil. Place a small plate on top of the *sarmas* to keep them submerged in the liquid, then simmer gently, covered, for 30 minutes. Check whether the *sarmas* are ready—if there is still liquid, return the dish to the heat and simmer for another 15 minutes, then check again.

Leave the *sarmas* to cool in the casserole dish. When ready to serve, turn them out onto a large platter.

SERVES 6–8

Baby carrots and leeks cooked in olive oil with orange peel and spices

To be honest it's not terribly Turkish to use wine in cooking, but I really love this method of slowly braising vegetables in an oil-rich, flavorsome pickling liquor. It works well for all sorts of vegetables, and you can vary the spices and aromatics to suit. Here I use orange, cardamom and coriander, which go particularly well with the carrots. You can strain, freeze and reuse the cooking liquor for other braised vegetable dishes.

Serve this versatile dish as part of a meze selection. It also makes a good accompaniment to grilled chicken or lamb, or to baked fish, such as Roasted Whole Baby Snapper with Almond and Sumac Crumbs (page 230).

10 baby carrots
4 small leeks, white part only
4 long red chiles
4 cloves garlic, peeled
long piece of peel from 1 orange
2 bay leaves
few sprigs thyme
½ teaspoon dried mint
5 cardamom pods
1 teaspoon coriander seeds, lightly crushed
½ teaspoon black peppercorns, lightly crushed
juice of 3 lemons
1¾ cups dry white wine
2 cups water
1¾ cups extra-virgin olive oil
½ teaspoon salt

Scrape the carrots, then trim off the stalks and cut them in half lengthwise. Split the leeks, keeping them attached at the root end, then carefully rinse under running water to remove any lingering dirt. Cut away the root end, then cut the leeks in half crosswise so they are around the same length as the carrots. Split each piece lengthwise. Split the chiles lengthwise, leaving them attached at the stalk. Use the point of a sharp knife to scrape out the seeds.

Put the carrots and leeks into a large, heavy-based, nonreactive saucepan. Add the remaining ingredients and stir well.

Press a piece of parchment paper, cut to the size of the pan, down over the vegetables. Bring to the boil, covered, then lower the heat and cook at a very gentle simmer for 25–30 minutes, or until the carrots are tender. Remove the pan from the heat and leave the vegetables to cool in the liquid.

When ready to serve, lift the vegetables from the poaching liquor to a platter—you may want to discard the peel and other larger herbs and spices. Strain the poaching liquor and refrigerate or freeze it for later use.

SERVES 4

Celery root, potatoes and bitter greens in oil

In Turkey, especially around the Aegean, there are literally hundreds of varieties of wild greens. Almost none of these are available commercially in Australia because we don't accord them the same value. If you know a forager, or have Greek, Turkish or Italian friends, they may be able to help you out with a secret supply, but otherwise bitter greens such as chicory and broccoli rapé work pretty well.

As with the recipe for Baby Carrots and Leeks Cooked in Olive Oil with Orange Peel and Spices (opposite), you can strain, freeze and reuse the cooking liquor for other braised vegetable dishes.

Serve warm or cold as part of a meze selection, with plenty of crusty bread for mopping up the juices.

¾ pound small kipfler potatoes, peeled
1 celery root (about 1 pound)
juice of 3 lemons
1¾ cups white wine
2 cups water
1¾ cups extra-virgin olive oil
1 sprig thyme
2 bay leaves
1 tablespoon coriander seeds, lightly crushed
1 teaspoon fennel seeds, lightly crushed
½ teaspoon black peppercorns, lightly crushed
½ teaspoon sea salt
1 red onion, cut into ½-inch dice
7 ounces rapé, roughly sliced
7 ounces chicory, roughly sliced
⅓ cup chopped dill

Cut the potatoes lengthwise into thickish slices. Peel the celery root and trim the sides to form a rough cube. Cut into five even slices, then cut each slice into sixths. Keep the celery root in a bowl of acidulated water to stop it discoloring.

Put the lemon juice, wine, water and oil into a large, heavy-based saucepan, and bring to the boil. Add the herbs, spices and salt and stir well. Add the celery root, potatoes and onion to the pan and simmer for 8 minutes. Add the greens and increase the heat. Boil vigorously for a few minutes until the greens have wilted. Reduce to a simmer, then press a piece of parchment paper, cut to the size of the pan, down over the vegetables. Simmer, covered, for 10–15 minutes, or until the potatoes and celery root are tender. Remove the pan from the heat and leave the vegetables to cool in the liquid.

When ready to serve, lift the vegetables from the poaching liquor to a platter—you may want to discard the larger herbs and spices. Strain the poaching liquor and refrigerate or freeze it for later use.
SERVES 4

Baby beets in an herb dressing

Dress the beets in this wonderfully sharp herb dressing while warm from the oven and serve at room temperature. They are equally good as a vegetable accompaniment to roasts, barbecues or grills or as part of a meze selection.

2 bunches baby beets (about 1⅓ pounds)
4 cloves garlic, roughly smashed
sea salt
1 tablespoon extra-virgin olive oil
2 shallots, peeled and finely sliced
½ teaspoon freshly ground black pepper
4 ounces feta, roughly crumbled

HERB DRESSING
1 clove garlic
1 teaspoon sea salt
juice of 1 lemon
2 tablespoons olive oil
2 tablespoons walnut oil
1 tablespoon dried oregano
¼ cup chopped flat-leaf parsley leaves
mixed herb leaves to garnish (optional)

Preheat the oven to 350°F. Wash the beets thoroughly to remove any grit, paying special attention to the area close to the stalks. Trim the roots and cut off the stalks, leaving about 1 inch attached. Place in a jelly-roll pan and scatter in the garlic cloves. Season lightly with salt, then add the oil and toss thoroughly. Cover the tray loosely with foil and roast for 30–45 minutes, until the beets are tender.

While the beets are cooking, start making the dressing. Crush the garlic with the salt, then whisk this with the lemon juice and oils.

Remove the pan from the oven and discard the garlic. When the beets are just cool enough to handle, peel them and cut them in half lengthwise. Place in a large bowl with the shallots and season with salt and pepper. Add the herbs to the dressing, whisk, and pour onto the beets. Check the seasoning, then add the crumbled feta and toss gently. Garnish with baby herb leaves, if using. Serve warm or cold.

SERVES 4

Zucchini Fritters with Dill (opposite)

Zucchini fritters with dill

These little fritters are a very popular meze dish in Turkey, and are often served at room temperature. They also make a great family supper, hot and crisp from the pan and served with lemon wedges and a yogurt-based sauce, such as *Cacık* or *Haydari* (page 54). Better still, they are a great way of using what otherwise can be a rather dull vegetable.

1⅓ pounds zucchini
sea salt
1 small onion, grated
1 small clove garlic, finely chopped
4 ounces feta, crumbled
¼ cup finely chopped dill
2 tablespoons finely chopped flat-leaf parsley leaves
2 eggs, well beaten
⅓ cup all-purpose flour
2 tablespoons rice flour
freshly ground black pepper
olive oil

Grate the zucchini coarsely and put into a colander. Sprinkle lightly with salt and toss, then leave for 20 minutes to drain. Rinse the zucchini briefly, then squeeze it to extract as much liquid as you can and pat dry with kitchen paper.

Mix the zucchini with the onion, garlic, feta, herbs and eggs in a large bowl. Sift on the flours, then season with pepper and stir to combine.

Heat a little oil in a nonstick frying pan over medium heat until sizzling. Drop small tablespoons of batter into the hot oil and flatten gently. Cook for 2 minutes on each side, or until golden brown. Drain on paper towels and serve piping hot.
MAKES 16

Creamy pepper and *pastırma* braise

A quick and easy dish that's good with all sorts of roasts and grills. Try it with Grilled Lamb Cutlets with Mountain Herbs (page 172) or any grilled kebabs. It would also be delicious served with Everyday Orzo Pilaf (page 128)—you can leave out the *pastırma* to make a tasty vegetarian meal.

2 ounces butter
1 large red onion, diced
3 long green peppers, seeded and diced
1 clove garlic, finely chopped
1 teaspoon coriander seeds, lightly crushed
1 vine-ripened tomato, skinned, seeded and diced
3 ounces heavy cream
sea salt
freshly ground white pepper
1 ounce *pastırma*, shredded
finely grated zest of ½ lemon
flat-leaf parsley leaves, shredded, to garnish

Melt the butter in a large, heavy-based frying pan. Add the onion, peppers, garlic and coriander seeds and sauté for 5 minutes, or until the vegetables start to soften. Add the tomato and cream to the pan and stir well. Simmer very gently for 8–10 minutes until the peppers are really tender. Taste and add salt and pepper if necessary, then stir in the *pastırma* and zest. Serve garnished with parsley.
SERVES 6

Crossing to Asia

[SALADS AND HERBS]

Dusk was falling and the market was full of shoppers stocking up for dinner.

Before there was Byzantium there was Chalcedon, a small colony perched on the southernmost shore of the Bosphorus at the threshold of Asia. It had been happily settled since ancient times, until Greek colonists arrived on the scene in the seventh century BC, establishing a bigger and better city on the opposite—superior—shore. They named this city Byzantium. These two colonies worked in partnership for the next few centuries to control trade through the Bosphorus, but the reality was that Chalcedon just wasn't as well positioned geographically. And so, as Byzantium grew to greatness, Chalcedon sank into obscurity.

Ancient Chalcedon is modern Kadiköy, in the Asian part of Istanbul. Even today it has less obvious charms than the European suburbs, being primarily a residential area with little evidence remaining of its ancient past. But we'd been advised to miss a visit to Kadiköy at our peril. For here, we were assured, was some of the best food to be had in the whole of Turkey.

So late one March afternoon, we met up with our friend Sedat at the Eminönü ferry terminal. The waterfront was thronged with commuters going about the business of daily life. In the jostling queue for the Kakidöy ferry, men in suits and thick knitted skullcaps rubbed up against students with dreadlocks and little old ladies in raincoats. Even though the sun was shining, everyone was bundled up in scarves, gloves and boots against the chill.

Swept on board the lumbering old ferry by the crowd, we clambered up the wide staircase to the top passenger deck. The ferry chugged off on its journey across the Bosphorus, and we had just enough time to enjoy a glass of hot *çay* from the wandering tea seller before we spied the grand old Haydarpaşa railway station looming up ahead. Then suddenly we had arrived. The ferry was docking and we stepped out onto Asian soil.

After negotiating the roaring traffic behind the ferry terminus we ducked down a narrow lane, emerging into a crowded street market. Dusk was falling and the market was full of shoppers stocking up for dinner. From all sides, we were offered tastes of honey or halvah; roasted chickpeas; slivers of tasty white Turkish cheese; green, pink, brown and black-hued olives; and the famous Istanbul mussels stuffed with dill-flavored rice.

It was hard not to be tempted, but we were set firmly on course for Çiya where we'd been invited to dinner with legendary Turkish chef Musa Dağdeviren. It turned out that Çiya is actually a cluster of three small restaurants: a *sofrası*, which specializes in soups, salads and stews; a *kebab köfteci*, or bread and meat restaurant; and a third that seems to do a mix of everything. The Çiya restaurants have earned wide and lavish praise for their menus of authentic regional dishes, sourced from villages all around Turkey—the sort of food, we'd been told, that you just don't find on other menus around town.

We were warmly welcomed by Musa and his wife Zeynep, who offered glasses of a refreshingly sour-sweet sumac sherbet as we took our seats. Zeynep, who manages the three busy restaurants, was small and bursting with energy. Musa was tall and lean with a healthy-looking mustache and a charming, gentle manner. But there was also an intensity gleaming in his coal-black eyes, and it soon became apparent that here was a man with a mission.

Over our sherbet, and with Sedat translating, Musa began to tell us about his life, his restaurants and his passion for what he calls "the forgotten peasant dishes of Anatolia." He's not interested in the stuff churned out by traditional Turkish restaurants, but in the cooking that people do in their own homes in villages around the country.

"The thing that really holds my imagination is the food that poor people make from almost nothing," he said. "Anyone can cook fancy meals with expensive ingredients. I think it's far more beautiful to see someone cook a delicious meal from weeds and tree roots, or use lentils if there's no meat or to make a soup just from yogurt and cracked wheat."

While Musa talked, dishes were arriving on the table thick and fast. We crunched on tiny pickled peppers and sipped a delicate yogurt soup brimming with young green garlic shoots. There was a salad of wild thyme, followed by braised artichokes stuffed with rice, mint, pine nuts and currants, and tiny pea-sized *köfte* dumplings in an intensely flavored tomato sauce.

In his gently insistent way Musa continued, "For the last twenty years or so I've been travelling everywhere around the rural parts of Turkey, going into people's homes and cooking with them, learning about the ingredients they use, watching what they do, and also trying to understand the ritual and method that goes with the food they cook."

He laughed, "When I find a new dish that excites me, I go a bit mad! What I've done, really, is to make the restaurants into my own personal test kitchen where I try to re-create the recipes I find from my research and travels."

It was impossible to stop eating. More dishes had arrived—tender lamb kebabs grilled with Turkish truffles, which we stuffed into hot, chewy, 'house-made' bread.

He rolled up pieces of crisp, wafer-thin *lahmacun* smeared with a spicy meat paste and offered them around, before continuing. "But I'm a realist, too. I know that a lot of traditional peasant recipes use ingredients that are very localized. There are literally hundreds of wild greens that grow around the Aegean coastline, for instance, that people in the rest of Turkey know nothing about. And there's no point making winter dishes from Antep, using the solid fat from the sheep's tail in the traditional way that they do, and offering it to urbanite Istanbullus. It would give them a heart attack—literally!"

Musa's genius seems to be knowing how to preserve the essence of a dish and adapting it to new surroundings, without slavishly re-creating dishes in a way that would otherwise be esoteric at best, and utterly impractical at worst.

It was impossible to stop eating. More dishes had arrived—tender lamb kebabs grilled with Turkish truffles, which we stuffed into hot, chewy, "house-made" bread. There was a pilaf from eastern Anatolia, thick with shreds of chicken and tiny currants; next came grilled intestines stuffed with savory cracked wheat and finally a casserole of tiny chunks of lamb, grapes and chickpeas from central Anatolia.

We learned that Musa serves more than a thousand different dishes at his restaurants every year and rarely repeats the same dish twice. He makes fifty or more meat kebabs, over a hundred kinds of pilaf made from rice or grains and has a seemingly endless repertoire of soups, salads and stews. It's a massive investment of time and labor and it was no surprise to hear that he has a small army of chefs in the kitchen, working from six in the morning until midnight.

Musa served us an exquisite dessert made from fermented fig seeds and cultured cream, followed by a selection of tastes from a platter of vividly colored candied fruits. There were slices of citron and bitter orange, sugary pumpkin smeared with tahini paste and two other, less readily identifiable objects. Musa leaned forward, black eyes gleaming wickedly, "What do you think these are?" he challenged us. We tasted each item a little apprehensively, and discovered we were eating candied tomatoes, their centers soft as jelly; and even more improbably, candied olives, dense and chewy, with a curiously appealing salty sweetness.

By the time we'd sipped down a much-needed digestif of spicy *za'atar* tea—made from wild thyme—it was close to midnight and we realized the restaurant was empty. We'd been listening to this compelling, dazzling, exhausting man for more than five hours and had only scratched the surface of his extraordinary knowledge. As we said our warm goodbyes and headed out to catch the last ferry back to Europe, Greg muttered happily, "I'd come back to Turkey for this food alone."

Gypsy salad

A favorite Turkish salad using raw vegetables, which make it wonderfully crunchy. Sometimes gypsy salads are made with grated hard white cheese, but I prefer to use a tangy yogurt dressing instead. The dried apricots aren't traditional, but I love their soft, chewy sweetness against the crunch of the vegetables.

2 vine-ripened tomatoes, skinned and diced

1 Lebanese cucumber, peeled, seeded and diced

1 small red onion, peeled and diced

4 dried apricots, diced

3 baby carrots, diced

1 long yellow pepper, diced

1 clove garlic, crushed

½ teaspoon sea salt

4 ounces Greek-style yogurt

1 tablespoon extra-virgin olive oil

juice of ½ lemon

1 red serrano chile, seeded and finely shredded

1 teaspoon ground cumin

freshly ground white pepper

Put the tomatoes, cucumber, onion, apricots, carrots and yellow pepper into a large bowl and toss gently.

Crush the garlic with the salt. In another bowl, whisk the yogurt with the garlic and salt and remaining ingredients to make a dressing. Pour on enough to coat the vegetables and toss gently.

SERVES 4

Tomato salad with tarragon, aged feta and sumac dressing

Use really tasty tomatoes for this salad: I like to use a selection of the heirloom tomatoes that are becomingly increasingly available from upscale markets or farmers' markets, but ripe tomatoes on the vine will do well too. You can buy barrel-aged feta from good Mediterranean food stores. It's much firmer than young feta, and has a sharp, earthy flavor. If you can't find barrel-aged feta, substitute a hard, aged goat cheese.

2 shallots, peeled and sliced into wafer-thin rings

3 tablespoons shredded French tarragon

3 tablespoons Sumac Dressing (page 113)

4 heirloom or vine-ripened tomatoes, skinned and thickly sliced

sea salt

freshly ground black pepper

4 ounces barrel-aged feta, crumbled

Soak the shallot rings in ice water for 10 minutes, then pat dry with kitchen paper. In a small bowl, toss the shallots with the tarragon and enough dressing just to moisten. Tumble the sliced tomato onto a serving platter and season lightly. Scatter on the shallots and feta, then drizzle with a little more dressing and serve.

SERVES 4

Tomato Salad with Tarragon, Aged
Feta and Sumac Dressing (opposite)

Belgian endive and radicchio salad with Caesar dressing, *pastırma* and soft-boiled eggs

Pastırma, Turkey's highly spiced and garlicky version of pastrami, is often served for breakfast with eggs, the bland richness of the yolks offsetting the meat's strong flavor beautifully. *Pastırma* works brilliantly with this creamy Caesar-style dressing too; for a change, you could grill or fry it like bacon. Ask for the *pastırma* to be sliced wafer-thin.

4 free-range eggs
4 Belgian endive, outer leaves removed
1 small radicchio, roughly torn
½ cup flat-leaf parsley leaves
1 large shallot, peeled and finely sliced
freshly ground black pepper
2 ounces *pastırma*, finely sliced

CAESAR DRESSING
2 free-range eggs, lightly poached
1 clove garlic, finely chopped
4 anchovy fillets
juice of 1 lemon
splash of white-wine vinegar
1 tablespoon Dijon mustard
7 ounces olive oil
7 ounces vegetable oil
sea salt
freshly ground black pepper
¼ cup finely grated parmesan

To make the dressing, pulse the eggs, garlic, anchovies, lemon juice, vinegar and mustard in a food processor, then gradually drizzle in the oils, a little at a time, ensuring each amount is incorporated before adding more. Season with salt and pepper and if necessary thin with a little warm water until the dressing is the consistency of light cream. Stir in the parmesan.

If you've taken the eggs straight from the refrigerator, put them into a bowl of hot tap water for 5 minutes to bring them to room temperature. Bring a saucepan of water to the boil. Carefully lower in the eggs and cook for 5½ minutes. Remove from the water and refresh briefly under cold running water.

While the eggs are cooking, cut the Belgian endive into quarters lengthwise and arrange in a large shallow serving bowl. Scatter in the lettuce, parsley and shallot and pour on enough dressing to coat the leaves. Season with pepper. Peel the eggs and halve them carefully, then add to the bowl. Drape slices of *pastırma* over the salad and serve immediately.
SERVES 4

Brain salad with parsley and black olive dressing

Poached brains are a popular meze dish in Turkey, but they often don't look terribly appealing, as they tend to be served cold and unadorned. They have a wonderful mild, creamy flavor and texture that really comes alive with a tangy dressing. If you like, serve them with thin slices of sourdough toast.

One of the great joys of lamb's brains is that they are blissfully easy and relatively unmessy to prepare, which may surprise some. An initial soaking dispels any lingering blood, after which the brains need only to be poached briefly. No peeling required!

4 sets of lamb's brains
cold salted water or milk
1 lemon, cut into quarters
1 cinnamon stick
4 cloves
½ onion
1 quart water
1 quantity Parsley and Black Olive Dressing (page 115)

Soak the brains in cold salted water overnight, or in milk for 2 hours.

Place the lamb's brains in a large nonreactive saucepan with the aromatics and water. Bring to the boil, then skim and simmer for 2 minutes. Remove the pan from the heat and allow the brains to cool in the liquid. When they are cold, remove them from the pan and split each set in half. Pat dry with paper towels.

Slice the brains thickly, arrange on a serving plate and spoon on the dressing.

SERVES 4

Green Olive, Walnut and
Pomegranate Salad (opposite)

Green olive, walnut and pomegranate salad

A stunning salad from southeast Turkey where all the ingredients grow in abundance. I love the balance of sweet, salty and chile-hot, and the ruby-red pomegranate seeds look gorgeous against the muted khakis and greens of the other ingredients.

¾ cup walnuts

½ cup pitted green olives, washed and coarsely chopped

¼ cup unsalted shelled pistachios, coarsely chopped

½ cup pomegranate seeds

2 small shallots, peeled and finely diced

1 red serrano chile, seeded and finely diced

1 tablespoon shredded flat-leaf parsley leaves

1 tablespoon olive oil

1 tablespoon walnut oil

splash of pomegranate molasses

juice of ½ lemon

sea salt

freshly ground black pepper

Preheat the oven to 350°F. Scatter the walnuts onto a jelly-roll pan and roast for 5–10 minutes until a deep golden brown. Pour the nuts into a tea towel and rub well to remove as much skin as possible. Chop the walnuts coarsely and toss in a sieve to remove any remaining skin and dust.

Combine all the ingredients in a large bowl and toss gently. Leave to stand for 5 minutes or so before serving, to allow the flavors to meld.

SERVES 4

Grated celery root salad

Celery root is a popular and versatile winter vegetable that the Turks make good use of in soups, dips, braises and salads. I've combined it here with Belgian endive, peppers, chiles and feta in a tangy dressing; it makes a tongue-tingling and refreshing winter salad to serve alongside grilled chicken, lamb or a good thick steak. The salad should be eaten within 30 minutes or so of preparation for best results.

1 celery root

1 small clove garlic

sea salt

2 long yellow peppers, shredded

1 purple Belgian endive, shredded

1 small red onion, finely sliced

1 long red chile, seeded and shredded

2 tablespoons shredded flat-leaf parsley leaves

2 tablespoons shredded mint leaves

½ teaspoon dried mint

1 tablespoon champagne vinegar

2 tablespoons extra-virgin olive oil

freshly ground black pepper

3 ounces feta, roughly crumbled

Peel the celery root and trim off the ends. Cut the celery root in half, then scoop out any soft, pulpy flesh from the center and discard it. Grate the celery root into a bowl of lightly acidulated water.

Crush the garlic with ½ teaspoon salt. Combine garlic with the remaining ingredients, except for the feta, in a large bowl. Drain the celery root and dry it thoroughly on paper towels, then add it to the bowl and toss everything well. Taste and adjust the seasoning, then put onto a serving platter and top with the feta. Serve straight away.

SERVES 4

Shepherd's salad

This is the classic Turkish "garden" salad that you find in restaurants and homes all around the country. It's a bit like the Lebanese salad *fattouche*, using commonly available ingredients that many people have growing in their gardens.

1 long yellow pepper

1 long cucumber

2 long green chiles, seeded and shredded

2 vine-ripened tomatoes, skinned and cut into large dice

1 small red onion, peeled and cut into large dice

6 radishes, sliced

1 cup flat-leaf parsley leaves

2 tablespoons chopped dill

1 romaine lettuce, shredded

juice of ½ lemon

2 tablespoons extra-virgin olive oil

sea salt

freshly ground black pepper

Quarter the pepper lengthwise, scraping out the seeds and removing the membrane, then slice. Quarter the cucumber lengthwise, then scoop out the seeds and slice. Toss all the ingredients in a large serving bowl and taste and adjust the seasoning.
SERVES 4

Meze

Turkish cooking is perhaps best known for the seemingly endless little meze dishes, either offered at the start of a meal or extended to make up an entire meal lasting many happy hours. It's a well-known and distinctive category, yet surprisingly difficult to define, as just about anything can be served as a meze.

Although meze dishes will vary with the season and the locale, one defining characteristic is the abundance of choice. There may be a selection of *ezme* (mashed vegetables mixed with garlic and yogurt) or yogurt dips like *cacık* or *haydari* or small dishes of gleaming olives and *dolmas* (stuffed vegetables). Near the sea, enticing little fish dishes of braised squid or fried smelt, stuffed mussels or grilled sardines will be offered. A meze nearly always includes cubes of *beyaz peynir*—soft white feta cheese, sprinkled with fresh herbs and olive oil—and just about anything that might be termed a salad.

Delicious seasonal salads will be made with whatever is available—such as the ubiquitous shepherd's salad of chopped tomatoes, cucumbers, peppers and onion. Other salads might be made with legumes, such as lentils or white beans, or with bulgur wheat softened with a simple dressing of olive oil and lemon juice. *Zeytinyağlı* (vegetables cooked in olive oil) are served cold and are very popular. Broad beans, artichokes, eggplant or zucchini are often prepared in this way, and along the Aegean you'll find an extraordinary selection of wild greens that are gently wilted and served with fruity olive oil and a splash of lemon juice.

Another defining characteristic of the meze table is the rakı that is drunk as an accompaniment. The Turks would find it hard to imagine eating meze without rakı as the two are inextricably linked. The tradition, believed to date back many centuries, began with small tasty dishes being offered in taverns to merchants and travelers to soak up the alcohol—very similar to the Spanish tradition of tapas. Despite the conversion of the Turks to Islam, the meze tradition survived—which either says a lot for the appeal of the rakı or of the food! Today some of the best meze can be found in *meyhane* restaurants.

Turkish spoon salad

One of my very favorite Turkish salads, this almost has the consistency of a gazpacho soup and definitely needs to be served with a spoon. The secret of its success is to dice the ingredients individually first, then chop them together to very fine and even dice. This salad has a wonderful balance of heat from the chiles and sweetness from the molasses. Serve it with kebabs and offer plenty of Turkish bread to mop up the juices.

The chile paste used here is readily available from Turkish food stores.

2 very ripe vine-ripened tomatoes, skinned and finely diced

1 long red pepper, seeded and finely diced

2 long red chiles, seeded and finely diced

1 small Lebanese or Persian cucumber, peeled, seeded and finely diced

1 large shallot, peeled and finely diced

2 tablespoons finely chopped flat-leaf parsley leaves

½ teaspoon dried mint

1 heaped teaspoon hot Turkish red pepper paste

½ teaspoon pomegranate molasses

1 teaspoon red-wine vinegar

¼ cup extra-virgin olive oil

sea salt

freshly ground black pepper

pomegranate seeds to garnish (optional)

Place the diced tomatoes, pepper, chiles, cucumber and shallot on a large chopping board. Use a very sharp, large knife to chop them all together. You are aiming for well-integrated, even and fine dice. Scrape into a large bowl and add the herbs, pepper paste, molasses, vinegar and 1 tablespoon of the oil, then season with salt and pepper. Stir throughly and leave for 20 minutes to macerate.

Just before serving, put the salad into a colander and drain for a few moments to remove some of the excess liquid—you want the salad to be wet, but not swimming in liquid. Pour out onto a shallow serving platter, then drizzle on the remaining oil and scatter over the pomegranate seeds, if using. Serve right away.

SERVES 4

Chopped romaine salad with green herbs

This salad is a great accompaniment to all sorts of grilled meats, and is especially good with kebabs.

2 romaine lettuces, outer leaves discarded

handful of arugula leaves, stems removed

2 green onions, finely green

2 tablespoons chopped dill

2 tablespoons chopped flat-leaf parsley leaves

1 tablespoon chopped mint leaves

1 small clove garlic

½ teaspoon sea salt

¼ cup extra-virgin olive oil

juice of ½ lemon

½ teaspoon dried mint

freshly ground black pepper

Shred the lettuce leaves, then toss gently in a large bowl with the arugula, green onions and herbs.

Crush the garlic with the salt and whisk with the remaining ingredients to make a dressing. Taste and adjust the seasoning before dressing the salad.

SERVES 4

À la Turque dressing

This full-flavored dressing suits bitter salad leaves or warm vegetable salads. Try it, too, with fish or seafood, or over warmed beans or legumes.

½ cup water

1 tablespoon white-wine vinegar

1 teaspoon honey

1 teaspoon pomegranate molasses

2 small shallots, very finely diced

1 small clove garlic, very finely diced

1 long green chile, seeded and finely diced

½ vine-ripened tomato, seeded and finely diced

1 teaspoon dried mint

2 tablespoons chopped dill

pinch of hot paprika

sea salt

½ teaspoon freshly ground black pepper

juice of 1 lemon

½ cup extra-virgin olive oil

In a small saucepan, combine the water and vinegar with the honey and molasses. Warm the pan gently to dissolve the honey, then add the shallots, garlic and chile. Simmer for a minute, then pour into a large bowl and leave to cool.

Add the tomato, herbs and paprika and season with salt and pepper. Whisk in the lemon juice and oil, then taste and adjust the seasonings if necessary. Pour into a sealable jar. The dressing will keep, refrigerated, for up to a week.

MAKES 1¼ cups

Sumac dressing

Sumac berries have a wonderful lemony tartness and are very popular in Turkey and the Middle East. You'll find them in Turkish or Middle Eastern food stores. This dressing is used in the tomato salad on page 102 but can also be used with bitter leaves such as Belgian endive or radicchio.

⅓ cup sumac berries
½ cup warm water
7 ounces extra-virgin olive oil
juice of ½ lemon
1 teaspoon superfine sugar
drizzle of pomegranate molasses
sea salt
freshly ground black pepper
1 sprig thyme
1 clove garlic, crushed

Crush the sumac berries roughly in a mortar. Put into a small bowl and pour on the warm water. Leave to infuse for 45 minutes, then strain through a fine cloth into a measuring jug and reserve 3 ounces.

In a bowl, whisk the sumac water with the oil, lemon juice, sugar and molasses. Season with salt and pepper and add the thyme and garlic. Leave to infuse for 20–30 minutes, then strain into a sealable jar. The dressing will keep, refrigerated, for up to 3 weeks.
MAKES 1¼ cups

Tomato and chile dressing

This wonderfully zesty dressing marries well with grilled seafood. It's a particularly good match with grilled shellfish.

3 vine-ripened tomatoes, skinned, seeded and diced
2 red serrano chiles, seeded and finely diced
1 clove garlic, finely diced
2 tablespoons superfine sugar
juice of 2 lemons
5 ounces olive oil
3 ounces walnut oil
sea salt
freshly ground white pepper

Whiz all the ingredients except for the oils, salt and pepper to a fine, smooth puree in a food processor. With the motor running, gradually add the oils until they are fully incorporated. Check the seasoning and add salt and pepper to taste. Pour into a sealable jar. The dressing will keep, refrigerated, for up to 5 days.
MAKES 2 cups

Pomegranate and tomato dressing

This dressing takes on a different feel, depending on the season. A jar of pomegranate molasses in the cupboard means I can make the dressing year-round to use with freshly shucked oysters, warm vegetable salads or brushed onto the barbecue. When pomegranates are in season, I use the fresh juice and seeds instead: follow the recipe below, substituting ¼ cup freshly squeezed pomegranate juice for the molasses and increasing the quantity of oil to 9 ounces.

4 ounces red-wine vinegar
2 tablespoons pomegranate molasses
1 cup extra-virgin olive oil
3 shallots, halved
1 clove garlic, halved
4 sprigs thyme
1 vine-ripened tomato, seeded and finely diced
½ teaspoon sea salt
generous grind of pepper

Whisk the vinegar and molasses in a small bowl, then stir in the oil. Add the shallots, garlic, thyme and tomato and season with salt and pepper. Cover and leave for 6 hours or overnight, so that the flavors mingle and intensify. Strain through a fine sieve into a sealable jar. The dressing will keep, refrigerated, for a couple of weeks.
MAKES 1¾ cups

Circassian yogurt dressing

One of my favorite herbs, fresh coriander, is rarely used in Turkish cooking, except in Circassian dishes. I developed this gorgeous creamy dressing as a way of combining coriander with my other favorite ingredient, yogurt. It's tangy, aromatic and a bit spicy, and redolent of the ancient spice routes.

Serve this dressing with vegetable salads, grilled chicken or even as a dip with raw vegetables and toasted flat bread.

4 cardamom pods
1 teaspoon black peppercorns
1 teaspoon caraway seeds
2 cups coriander leaves
3 long green chiles, seeded
4 cloves garlic
¼ teaspoon sea salt
splash of water
⅔ pound Greek-style yogurt

Crush the cardamom, peppercorns and caraway seeds with a mortar and pestle, then sift to remove the husks.

Wash and dry the coriander. Blend the coriander, crushed spices, chiles, garlic, salt and water to a puree in a blender. Put into a bowl and stir in the yogurt to form a smooth, pale-green dressing. If it's too thick, loosen with a little water.
MAKES 1¾ cups

Dill and lemon dressing

This dressing is often served with Creamy Fava Bean Pâté (page 60) as a meze dish. It's also extremely good with grilled white fish or seafood, barbecued chicken or quail, and all sorts of cold salads and vegetable dishes.

5 ounces extra-virgin olive oil

juice of 1 lemon

1 tablespoon champagne vinegar

⅓ cup water

2 teaspoons finely chopped dill

generous pinch of dried mint

sea salt

freshly ground black pepper

Whisk all the ingredients in a bowl. Taste and adjust the seasonings if necessary. Pour into a sealable jar. The dressing will keep, refrigerated, for up to a week.

MAKES 1⅓ cup

Parsley and black olive dressing

This dressing is a little similar to an Italian salsa verde, full of strong salty flavors, but made creamy with the addition of chopped egg.

I like to serve it with grilled fish—shellfish, in particular—and it's delicious with the creamy texture and mild flavor of poached brains (page 105).

⅓ cup extra-virgin olive oil

2 tablespoons apple vinegar

⅓ cup pitted and coarsely chopped kalamata olives

1 cold hard-boiled egg, peeled and coarsely grated

1 small shallot, peeled and finely chopped

1 clove garlic, roughly crushed

⅓ cup shredded flat-leaf parsley leaves

freshly ground black pepper

In a large bowl, whisk the oil and vinegar. Add the remaining ingredients, then whisk well to combine. Taste and adjust the seasonings if necessary. Use straight away.

SERVES 4

Land of fairy chimneys

[GRAINS AND LEGUMES]

We flew into central Anatolia, Turkey's rural heartland, on a bright clear morning. The plane from Istanbul had taken us over a wilderness of craggy mountains, darkly hidden lakes and a vast, icy plateau.

We flew into central Anatolia, Turkey's rural heartland, on a bright clear morning. The plane from Istanbul had taken us over a wilderness of craggy mountains, darkly hidden lakes and a vast, icy plateau. Gazing down, it was easy to imagine that gray wolves still roamed the rugged landscape. Easy, too, to picture the rampaging hordes of Turkic warriors, who rode into Anatolia a thousand years ago from their own windswept steppe-lands farther east.

And now we were making our descent into Kayseri, an ancient trading city situated almost slap-bang in the middle of Turkey. Leaving the city's charms for another day, we jumped into a rental car and sped off toward our destination: the famously strange and twisted topography of Cappadocia.

The forty-minute drive took us through remote, dun-colored plains, dotted here and there with little huddles of black-eared goats. Above us the sky was a brilliant blue and in the distance the snow-capped peak of Mount Erciyes was clearly visible. It was called the White Mountain by the Hittites, who occupied the region from 1800 to 1200 BC, and the rose-pink ash from this still-active volcano formed the region's fantastical rock formations.

As we sped farther on, the bare broad landscape began to change, erupting into folds and furrows, winding hills and plunging valleys. The fertile volcanic earth was a deep cocoa brown and in the shadows small patches of ice still clung to the ground. In summer this region is transformed into a lush market garden, but now, in the

Formed by centuries of erosion of the soft volcanic tuff, these knobbed pillars burst priapically from the corrugated hillsides and deep ravines.

early spring, the land was bleak and bare. Small tidy fields were as yet uncropped with wheat, potatoes and pumpkins. Gnarled black vines striped the hillsides, and little orchards of fruit trees were spiky against the blue sky, but in the summer their branches would be laden with cherries, peaches and plums.

Our first stop was in the village of Ürgüp, to check into our tiny hotel, the Sacred House. It had been lovingly created in a refurbished medieval mansion, and, like other dwellings in the area, many of the rooms were carved deep into the soft volcanic rock. All were delightfully decorated with antique furniture, textiles and knickknacks; it was all we could do to drag ourselves away from the sun-splashed courtyard and welcoming glasses of homemade cherry wine—but we still had fairy chimneys and cave churches to explore before bedtime.

"Fairy chimneys," we agreed, is a coy euphemism for what must surely be the gods' idea of a dirty joke. Formed by centuries of erosion of the soft volcanic tuff, these knobbed pillars burst priapically from the corrugated hillsides and deep ravines. But as we hurtled through the eccentric-looking countryside the snigger factor quickly subsided. We wound down the car windows and gazed out at the play of light across the cliffs and curves. What seemed from a distance to be uniformly dull gray rock was, close up, a riot of soft pinks, chestnut browns and mustard-yellow striations. In places, the foreground flattened out before a vast Wild West backdrop. Around another corner we plunged back into a mad profusion of cones, turrets and valleys, where pigeons swooped around myriad carved dovecotes.

The highlight of Cappadocia is near Göreme, where settlements of early Christians hid in the hillsides, hollowing a cluster of thirty or more monastic cells and chapels, bedchambers, refectories and wine cellars into the steep valley. Apart from a coach-load of Korean tourists the place was deserted, and we wandered lazily from church to tiny church, ducking inside to admire the superb frescos. Untouched by sunlight, many still retain their gorgeous glowing colors. They've fared less well at the hand of humans, though, and many of the faces of Christ, the disciples and saints have had their eyes roughly scratched away by superstitious religious vandals.

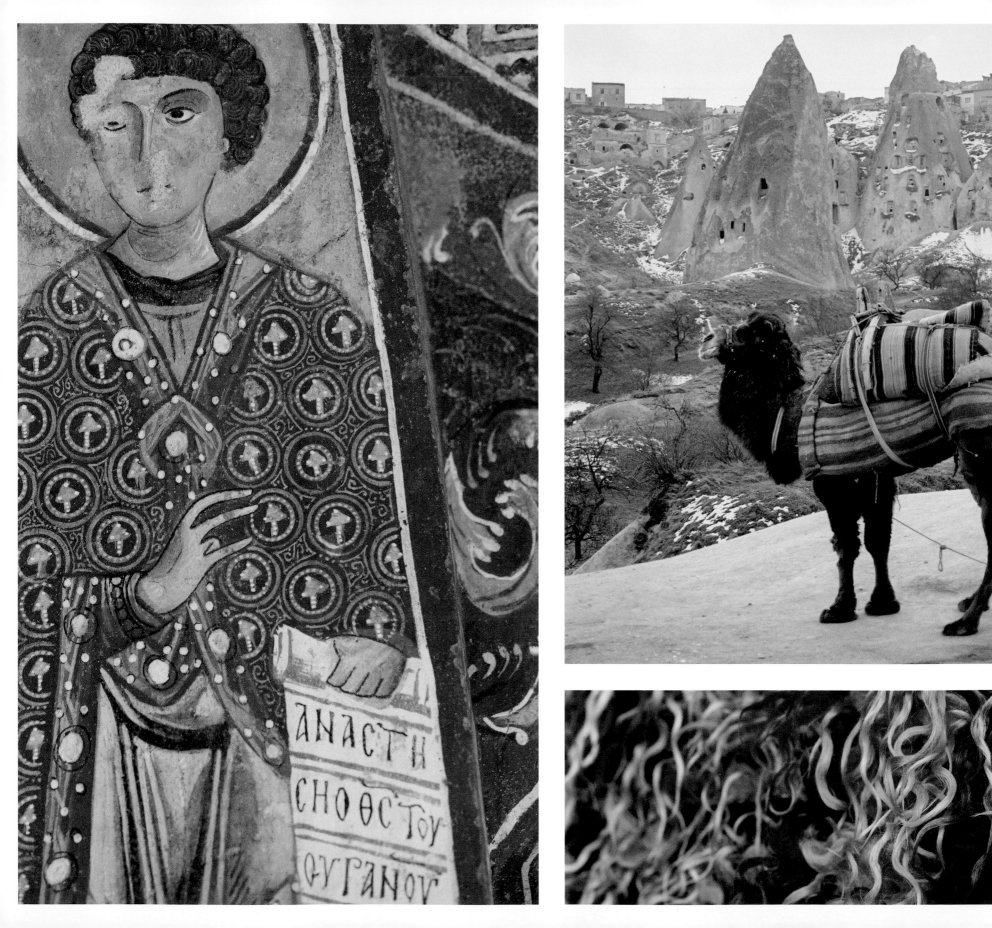

Around another corner we plunged back into a mad profusion of cones, turrets and valleys, where pigeons swooped around myriad carved dovecotes.

Despite the desecration, the power of Göreme is undeniable. It's impossible not to be moved by the thought of these early communities hiding from persecution and holed up against the elements in their damp, dark caves in the depths of snowy winter. They must surely have been a gentle, spiritual people, creating images of exquisite beauty and simplicity from the deep reds and ochre and brilliant blues of their paintbox.

We ate that evening at Sömine, reputed to be Ürgüp's best restaurant. A fire blazed in the central stone fireplace and the room was cozy and welcoming after a chilly walk to the restaurant. Our long day of sightseeing had left us ravenous and we scoffed down a succession of delicious meze dishes with puffs of golden bread, hot from the wood-fired oven. There were stuffed vine leaves as skinny as my finger and a spiral-shaped oversized fried *mantı* (dumpling). A grilled vegetable salad was tangy with *pekmez* (grape molasses) made from Cappadocian grapes. Greg watched the chefs in the kitchen making pilaf from the locally grown *burgul* wheat, which we ate with the house speciality *testi kebab*—a casserole of lamb and vegetables, slow-cooked in a sealed clay pot. This, it seemed, was the touch of theater that all tourist restaurants seem to embrace: a chosen diner at each table gets to smash the top off the pot and release the fragrant steam. But the meal was none the worse for it and the dish itself was tender and tasty. A few glasses of pale, melon-scented local white wine had washed it all down nicely, and we ambled back to the Sacred House through the snow-streaked streets in a glow of good humor.

A little while later, as I lay between crisp cotton sheets, snuggled up in the antique four-poster bed, a small lump of rock fell from the ceiling onto my pillow in a sprinkling of cave dust. I switched off the bedside light and the room was plunged into a blackness that was almost palpable. Outside in the icy night I heard the wind blowing up and my mind wandered back to those monks, huddled into their bleak cave bedrooms, with the wolves howling in the mountains beyond. A fleeting sense of panic shivered down my spine, and I lay awake in the dark listening to the sound of my beating heart.

Our long day of sightseeing had left us ravenous and we scoffed down a succession of delicious mezze dishes with puffs of golden bread, hot from the wood-fired oven.

Everyday orzo pilaf

The idea of cooking rice with little broken bits of vermicelli noodles is commonplace in the Middle East. On our travels around Turkey, we were fascinated to see this method used frequently to make pilaf, mainly using rice-shaped orzo pasta instead of the noodles. At Sömine restaurant in Cappadocia I spent some time watching the specialist pilaf chef at work. The first part of the process involved heating a substantial amount of butter to a foaming nut-brown. The orzo pasta was tossed in the butter, and stirred all the time, until it began to color. Now that I've tried it myself at home, I understand it's a fine line between achieving the desired toasty, nutty flavor and burning the butter. You need to turn and toss the pasta continuously, and move the pan on and off the heat to control the temperature. But it's worth the effort!

This buttery, fragrant pilaf is a good everyday accompaniment to all sorts of grilled meats, casseroles and vegetable dishes.

9 ounces long-grain or basmati rice
2 cups Chicken Stock (page 41) or water
2 ounces butter
1 teaspoon extra-virgin olive oil
¼ cup orzo pasta
pinch of sea salt

Put the rice into a large bowl and rinse well under cold running water, working your fingers through it to loosen the starch. Drain off the milky water and repeat until the water runs clear. Cover the rice with cold water and leave to soak for 10 minutes. Drain the rice and rinse a final time.

Bring the stock to the boil, then lower the heat and keep at a simmer.

Melt the butter and oil in a heavy-based saucepan. Add the orzo pasta and sauté over a medium heat, stirring continuously, until the butter foams and the orzo starts to color. You may need to move the pan away from the direct heat from time to time to ensure the butter doesn't burn.

Add the drained rice to the pan and stir it gently for a minute, so that all the grains are coated with butter. Stir in the simmering stock and salt. Bring to the boil, then cover with a tight-fitting lid and cook over a very low heat for 15–17 minutes. The grains should all look plump and separate and the surface will be dented with little holes. Remove the pan from the heat, then slide a clean, folded tea towel under the lid and leave it to stand for 15–20 minutes.

To serve, tip the rice onto a serving platter and fluff the grains up with a fork.
SERVES 4–6

Tomato pilaf

This is another favorite home-style Turkish pilaf, although its success does depend on using really tasty tomatoes. Please do not use canned tomatoes, as the dish will taste salty and metallic.

7 ounces long-grain or basmati rice
¾ pound vine-ripened tomatoes, skinned and roughly chopped
Chicken Stock (page 41) or vegetable stock
2 ounces butter
1 shallot, finely diced
1 teaspoon tomato paste
1 teaspoon grated lemon zest
1 sprig thyme
sea salt
freshly ground black pepper

Put the rice into a large bowl and rinse well under cold running water, working your fingers through it to loosen the starch. Drain off the milky water and repeat until the water runs clear. Cover the rice with cold water and leave to soak for 10 minutes. Drain the rice and rinse a final time.

Pulse the tomatoes to a rough puree in a food processor. Measure the volume and add enough stock to make it up to 1¾ cups. Put the tomato stock into a saucepan and bring to the boil. Lower the heat and keep at a simmer.

Melt the butter in a heavy-based saucepan. Add the shallot and sauté over a low–medium heat, stirring continuously, until it starts to soften. Add the tomato paste, zest and thyme and stir for another minute.

Add the rice to the pan, season with salt and pepper and pour in the simmering tomato stock. Return to the boil, stir briefly, then cover with a tight-fitting lid and cook over a very low heat for 15 minutes. The grains should all look plump and separate and the surface will be dented with little holes. Remove the pan from the heat, then slide a clean, folded tea towel under the lid and leave it to stand for 15–20 minutes.

To serve, put the rice onto a serving platter and fluff the grains up with a fork.
SERVES 4–6

Pistachio pilaf with spinach and herbs

This is a lovely vibrant-green pilaf, full of herbs and crunchy pistachios. It makes a particularly good accompaniment to grilled fish or chicken dishes—and I would always serve it with yogurt on the side.

7 ounces long-grain or basmati rice
1¾ cups Chicken Stock (page 41) or water
3 ounces butter
1 onion, finely diced
1¼ pounds spinach leaves, washed and shredded
sea salt
freshly ground black pepper
3 ounces unsalted shelled pistachios, roughly chopped
½ cup shredded mint leaves
½ cup shredded flat-leaf parsley leaves
½ cup chopped dill

Put the rice into a large bowl and rinse well under cold running water, working your fingers through it to loosen the starch. Drain off the milky water and repeat until the water runs clear. Cover the rice with cold water and leave to soak for 10 minutes. Drain the rice and rinse a final time.

Bring the stock to the boil, then lower the heat and keep at a simmer.

Melt half the butter in a heavy-based saucepan. Add the onion and sauté over a low–medium heat, stirring continuously until it starts to soften. Increase the heat, then add the spinach and stir well until any moisture has evaporated. Add the rice to the pan, then season with salt and pepper and pour in the simmering stock. Return to the boil, stir briefly, then cover with a tight-fitting lid and cook over a very low heat for 12 minutes.

In a small saucepan, melt the remaining butter. Add the pistachios and sauté over a medium heat, stirring continuously until the butter foams and the nuts start to color. Put the browned nuts into the pan of rice with the herbs. Don't stir! Replace the lid and return the pan to a very low heat for 5 minutes.

Remove the pan from the heat and use a fork to fluff up the grains and stir through the herbs and nuts. Taste and adjust the seasoning. Cover the pan with a clean, folded tea towel, then replace the lid and leave it to stand for 15–20 minutes. To serve, put the rice onto a serving platter and fluff the grains up with a fork.

SERVES 4–6

[From left] Tomato Pilaf (page 129),
Pistachio Pilaf with Spinach and
Herbs (opposite)

Sticky date pilaf with golden pine nuts and almonds

The chefs at Topkapı Palace used to vie to see who could create the most luxurious pilaf, cramming in nuts, spices and fruit as well as meat, seafood or poultry. I think the sultans would have loved this rich, fragrant pilaf: the sweetness of the dates is balanced by the exotic mix of spices, and the fried pine nuts and almonds add plenty of crunch.

9 ounces long-grain or basmati rice
2 cups Chicken Stock (page 41)
2 ounces butter
6 fresh medjool dates, pitted and diced
½ teaspoon freshly ground black pepper
½ teaspoon ground allspice
½ teaspoon ground cinnamon
pinch of hot paprika
pinch of sea salt
long strip of peel from ½ orange
2 tablespoons shredded flat-leaf parsley leaves

NUT GARNISH
2 tablespoons olive oil
½ cup flaked almonds, roughly chopped
⅓ cup pine nuts, roughly chopped
¼ teaspoon ground cinnamon
pinch of sea salt

Put the rice into a large bowl and rinse well under cold running water, working your fingers through it to loosen the starch. Drain off the milky water and repeat until the water runs clear. Cover the rice with cold water and leave to soak for 10 minutes. Drain the rice and rinse a final time.

Bring the stock to the boil, then lower the heat and keep at a simmer.

Melt the butter in a heavy-based saucepan. Add the dates, pepper and spices and stir briefly. Gently stir in the rice, so that all the grains are coated with the spiced butter. Pour on the simmering stock and add the salt. Stir, then bring to the boil and add the peel. Cover with a tight-fitting lid and cook over a very low heat for 15–17 minutes. The grains should all look plump and separate and the surface will be dented with little holes. Remove the pan from the heat, then slide a clean, folded tea towel under the lid and leave it to stand for 15–20 minutes.

To make the nut garnish, heat the oil in a small frying pan and sauté the nuts for a few minutes until evenly colored, then tip into a sieve to drain. Sprinkle on the cinnamon and salt and shake the sieve so the nuts are evenly coated.

When ready to serve, remove the peel from the pilaf and stir through the parsley, using a fork to fluff up the grains. Tip the rice onto a serving platter and scatter on the nuts.

SERVES 4–6

Rice and grains

Turkey is unquestionably a wheat-oriented cuisine. Wheat crops make up the major portion of the country's agricultural production, and its cultivation and use in food production date back many centuries to the Central Asian steppes, in the period before Turkic tribes migrated west into Anatolia. And yet one of the most famous Turkish dishes around the world is the rice pilaf.

Rice is an ancient crop, and it's generally thought that it originated in the hot, humid foothills of the mountainous region between China and India. Around 2,000 years ago, rice had spread through India to ancient Persia, where it was cultivated with great success. From Persia it was spread by the Arabs to Spain, while migrating Turkic tribes took it with them into Anatolia.

For many centuries in Anatolia, the bulk of the population consumed wheat as their staple grain, either made into bread or in the form of bulgur—cracked wheat. Rice was generally considered to be food of the wealthy, eaten on celebratory occasions. It was during the Ottoman period that pilaf reached its zenith, as chefs competed to create ever more luxurious versions: laden with dried fruits and nuts, enriched with butter, tinted with saffron and scented with exotic spices or flower waters, or made more substantial with the addition of meats, variety meats, shellfish, game or vegetables.

The word *pilaf* is of Persian origin and encompasses a variety of dishes made of cooked grains or legumes. Although rice pilaf is eaten all around Turkey, rice is still largely an imported product. Most rural Turks, especially in parts of central and eastern Anatolia, still favor locally grown bulgur wheat for making their pilafs. With its nutty flavor and slightly chewy texture, bulgur pilaf is as delicious as its more sophisticated rice cousin.

Whether made from rice or bulgur wheat, Turks take the business of making pilaf very seriously. As often seems to be the case with Turkish cooking, there are a number of "rules" associated with making pilaf, which frequently differ, depending on who you talk to. But one thing is a given: to make pilaf you need to invest time in learning about the basic ingredient. Bulgur wheat is a sturdier, more forgiving grain than rice, and merely needs to be soaked briefly and rinsed before cooking. When it comes to rice, though, it's another story, as the grain behaves differently depending on the variety. Some types—short-grain in particular—are naturally starchier, while older rices tend to be more absorbent. Turks tend to favor long-grain rice for making pilafs (we find basmati to be ideal), and use short-grain rice for making stuffings, soups and puddings; pilafs served hot are usually made with butter, if served lukewarm or cold they will be made with olive oil.

During our experimenting we found two steps that were critical to making a good rice pilaf. First, you do need to wash the rice before cooking it—this is especially true if you make pilaf using short-grain rice. All Turkish housewives devote considerable time to soaking and washing the grains to remove as much excess starch as possible. Next, don't skimp on the steaming time. After the rice has finished cooking, we always slip a tea towel under the lid of the saucepan and leave it to steam for a good fifteen minutes or so. The tea towel absorbs the steam and leaves you with delectably fluffy grains of rice.

Pilaf pie

Known as *perdeli* or "veiled" pilaf because of its pastry covering, this elegantly domed pie makes a good dinner party dish, ideally served with a green salad and *Cacık* (page 54). It requires a fair amount of time and patience to assemble, although most of the work can be done ahead of time.

The classic recipe uses chicken with a buttery nut pilaf, but you can vary this by adding herbs, pine nuts, currants or other dried fruit. And, of course, if you happen to have some leftover pilaf—of any variety—you could always turn it into a pilaf pie.

1 pound puff pastry
1 egg yolk, beaten with a splash of water

POACHED CHICKEN
one 2¼ pound chicken
1 small onion, cut into quarters
1 stick celery
1 sprig thyme
2 bay leaves
1 small cinnamon stick
½ lemon
½ teaspoon white peppercorns

PILAF
2 cups chicken stock (reserved from the poached chicken)
9 ounces long-grain or basmati rice
2 ounces butter
1 large shallot, finely diced
2 tablespoons barberries or currants
sea salt
freshly ground black pepper
2 tablespoons olive oil
3 ounces blanched almonds, roughly chopped
2 ounces unsalted shelled pistachios, roughly chopped
¼ teaspoon ground cinnamon
pinch of sea salt

To poach the chicken, put the bird and all the aromatics into a heavy-based saucepan and pour on enough water to cover. Bring to the boil, skimming away any fat and impurities that rise to the surface, then lower the heat immediately. Cover the pan and simmer very gently for 20 minutes. Turn off the heat and leave the chicken to cool in the stock. Remove the chicken from the stock and reserve for later. Strain the stock, measuring 2 cups for the pilaf.

Put the rice into a large bowl and rinse well under cold running water, working your fingers through it to loosen the starch. Drain off the milky water and repeat until the water runs clear. Cover the rice with cold water and leave to soak for 10 minutes. Drain the rice and rinse a final time.

Bring the stock to the boil, then lower the heat and keep at a simmer. Melt the butter in a heavy-based saucepan. Add the shallot and barberries and sauté over a low–medium heat until they soften. Add the rice and stir well. Season with salt and pepper and pour in the simmering stock. Return to the boil, stir briefly, then cover with a tight-fitting lid and cook over a very low heat for 15 minutes. The grains should all look plump and separate and the surface will be dented with little holes. Remove the pan from the heat, then slide a clean, folded tea towel under the lid and leave it to stand for 15–20 minutes. The pilaf can be prepared to this point ahead of time.

When ready to assemble the pie, preheat the oven to 400°F and grease a jelly-roll pan.

To finish the pilaf, remove the meat from the chicken, discarding the skin and bones. Shred the meat by hand into chunks and add to the rice. Heat the oil in a small frying pan and sauté the nuts for a few minutes until evenly colored, then put into a sieve to drain. Sprinkle on the cinnamon and salt and shake the sieve so the nuts are evenly coated, then add to the pilaf and fork well so all the ingredients are evenly distributed.

On a floured work surface, roll out the pastry to form a 16–18-inch square. Lift carefully onto the jelly-roll pan. Tip the pilaf into the center of the square and shape into a neat dome. Bring the four corners of the pastry square up over the dome of rice and pinch them together at the top. Pinch the excess pastry together tightly and trim as close to the surface of the pie as you can to make four secure "seams." (You may need to seal the edges with a little of the egg glaze before you pinch the sides together.) From the pastry trimmings, cut a small disk of pastry and use it to cover the join at the top of the pie.

Brush the pie all over with the egg glaze and bake for 30–40 minutes, or until the pastry is crisp and golden.

SERVES 6–8

Golden seafood pilaf

This dish makes a luxurious main course, the ground fennel and fresh mint giving it a distinctive Turkish edge. Serve with Hot Red Pepper Paste (page 59) for a wonderful chile hit.

9 ounces long-grain or basmati rice
2 cups Chicken Stock (page 41)
2 tablespoons olive oil
1 large shallot, finely diced
15 strands saffron
½ teaspoon ground fennel seeds
pinch of sea salt
12 mussels, scrubbed and bearded
6 red mullet fillets, halved crosswise
6 raw jumbo shrimp, split and cleaned
generous pinch of freshly ground black pepper
1 large vine-ripened tomato, seeded and diced
2 tablespoons chopped dill
2 tablespoons chopped mint leaves
2 ounces butter

Put the rice into a large bowl and rinse well under cold running water, working your fingers through it to loosen the starch. Drain off the milky water and repeat until the water runs clear. Cover the rice with cold water and leave to soak for 10 minutes. Drain the rice and rinse a final time.

Bring the stock to the boil, then lower the heat and keep at a simmer.

Heat the oil in a heavy-based saucepan. Add the shallot, saffron and fennel and sauté over a low–medium heat until the shallot softens. Gently stir in the rice, so that all the grains are coated with the oil. Pour on the simmering stock and season lightly with salt. Stir, bring to the boil, then cover with a tight-fitting lid and cook over a very low heat for 10 minutes.

Remove the lid and add the mussels, pushing them down into the rice. Distribute the fish and shrimp evenly over and between the mussels. Season lightly with salt, then add the pepper, scatter on the tomatoes and herbs, and dot with pieces of butter.

Replace the lid and steam for 5 minutes. Remove the pan from the heat, then slide a clean, folded tea towel under the lid and leave it for 10 minutes.

To serve, put the rice onto a serving platter. Stir gently so that the seafood and herbs are evenly distributed.

SERVES 4–6

Artichoke and barberry bulgur pilaf with fried mussels

Pilafs made with bulgur wheat are especially popular in southeastern Turkey. We enjoyed many different versions during our stay in Gaziantep—although none with seafood. But I think the delicate nutty flavor and slight chewiness of the grain work beautifully with these crunchy fried mussels. Just make sure you use coarse bulgur and not the fine variety, which is better used for salads and *köfte*.

3 artichokes

7 ounces coarse bulgur

2 tablespoons olive oil

1 large shallot, finely diced

1 clove garlic, finely chopped

1 long red chile, seeded and shredded

2 tablespoons barberries or currants

½ teaspoon paprika

½ teaspoon freshly ground black pepper

1 vine-ripened tomato, seeded and diced

¼ cup chopped dill

1 teaspoon dried mint

1¼ cups Chicken Stock (page 41)

generous pinch of sea salt

FRIED MUSSELS

35 mussels, scrubbed and bearded

3 ounces Chicken Stock (page 41)

3 cloves garlic

vegetable oil for deep-frying

7 ounces beer

⅔ cup self-rising flour

pinch of baking soda

pinch of sweet paprika

½ teaspoon dried mint

2–3 ice cubes

all-purpose flour

Trim the outer hard leaves from the artichokes and cut in half lengthwise through the stalk. Use a sharp knife to remove the choke, then drop the trimmed artichokes into acidulated water.

To make the pilaf, soak the bulgur in cold water for 5 minutes. While it's soaking, heat the oil in a heavy-based saucepan. Add the shallot, garlic, chile, barberries, paprika and pepper and sauté over medium heat for a few minutes until the shallot softens. Slice the artichokes thinly and add them to the pan. Sauté for 3–4 minutes, then add the tomato and herbs.

Bring the stock to the boil, then lower the heat and keep at a simmer. Drain the bulgur and squeeze it to remove any excess water. Add to the pan with the salt. Stir in the simmering stock, then bring to the boil, cover with a tight-fitting lid and cook over a low heat for 12 minutes. Remove the lid, increase the heat and cook until the liquid has been completely absorbed. Taste and adjust the seasoning if necessary.

While the pilaf is cooking, prepare the fried mussels. Put the mussels into a large saucepan with the stock and garlic. Cover the pan and bring to the boil, then cook over a high heat for about 4 minutes, shaking the pan from time to time, until the mussels open. Discard any that refuse to open.

To fry the mussels, heat the oil to 400°F in a large saucepan or deep fryer. Whisk the beer, self-rising flour, baking soda, paprika and mint to make a light batter. Add the ice cubes, which keep the batter cold and help make it really crisp. In batches of six, dust the mussels lightly with all-purpose flour, then dip them into the batter and fry for 2–3 minutes, or until golden brown. Be careful as the oil will splutter and spit a lot. Using a slotted spoon, remove the mussels to drain on paper towels—keep them warm while you fry the remaining mussels.

To serve, tip the pilaf onto a serving platter, then stack the fried mussels on top.
SERVES 4–6

Freekeh pilaf with lamb, wild greens, chickpeas and sweet spices

Freekeh is a relative newcomer to Western kitchens, although it has been used in Turkey and around the Middle East for millennia. Freekeh is made from whole wheat grains that are harvested while still immature and green. They are fire-roasted, which burns the chaff but leaves the young kernels intact and imparts a rich, smoky flavor.

You do need to spend a bit of time sorting through and cleaning freekeh wheat, as there are often bits of debris and tiny stones lurking. You'll probably have to soak and rinse it several times to ensure you get rid of any foreign matter. It may seem like too much effort, but its smoky, almost meaty flavor is unique and worth it.

Serve this dish with a bowl of creamy yogurt alongside.

7 ounces freekeh

3 tablespoons olive oil

1 large red onion, diced

2 cloves garlic, chopped

2 long green chiles, seeded and shredded

½ teaspoon hot paprika

2 teaspoons sweet paprika

1 heaped teaspoon ground cumin

1 tablespoon pomegranate molasses

14 ounces lamb (from the leg), cut into ¾-inch cubes

long strip of peel from ½ lemon

few sprigs thyme

one 14-ounce can chopped tomatoes

3½ cups Chicken Stock (page 41)

pinch of salt

½ teaspoon freshly ground black pepper

1 bunch chicory, leaves only, roughly sliced

¾ pound cooked chickpeas

juice of ½ lemon

¼ cup shredded flat-leaf parsley leaves

Pick through the freekeh to remove any debris and grit, then rinse it thoroughly under running water and leave to drain.

Heat the oil in a heavy-based casserole dish. Add the onion, garlic, chiles and spices and sauté over a medium heat until the onion starts to soften. Add the molasses and then the lamb and increase the heat. Sauté for a few minutes until the lamb starts to color and any moisture evaporates.

Stir in the freekeh, peel, thyme, tomatoes and stock, then season. Bring to the boil, skimming away any fat and impurities that rise to the surface, then lower the heat immediately. Cover the pan and simmer very gently for 45 minutes, skimming from time to time. Add the chicory and the chickpeas and cook for another 15 minutes, stirring from time to time to ensure nothing catches. If the lamb isn't really tender by this time, continue cooking for up to another 30 minutes, again stirring from time to time.

When the lamb is tender, remove the pan from the heat and add the lemon juice and parsley. Serve straight away.

SERVES 6

Spicy *kısır* salad

In Lebanon and Syria they have tabbouleh; in Turkey they have *kısır*. The ingredients in *kısır* vary from town to town, but in the southeast of the country it is usually enlivened with spicy red pepper paste and pomegranate molasses. While Arabic tabbouleh is, in essence, a herb salad flecked with bulgur, Turkish *kısır* is staunchly grain-based. Both salads, though, make a great addition to a meze table, and are best eaten scooped up in little lettuce leaves.

Don't be tempted to increase the amount of boiling water here: it doesn't look like a lot of liquid, but the bulgur will soften further in the juice from the tomatoes and the dressing.

You'll find the red pepper paste used here in Middle Eastern food stores.

7 ounces fine bulgur
½ cup boiling water
1 tablespoon tomato paste
1 teaspoon hot Turkish red pepper paste
juice of 1 lemon
1 teaspoon pomegranate molasses
¼ cup extra-virgin olive oil
1 long green chile, seeded and finely chopped
3 large vine-ripened tomatoes, chopped
5 green onions, finely chopped
1 cup flat-leaf parsley leaves, chopped
1 cup mint leaves, chopped
sea salt
freshly ground white pepper
baby lettuce leaves to serve

Soak the bulgur in the boiling water for 15 minutes, then put into a large bowl.

Add the pastes, lemon juice, pomegranate molasses and oil to the bulgur. Use clean hands to work the grains so that the pastes and liquid are evenly distributed and the bulgur is tinted a pretty pale pink. Add the chile, tomatoes, green onions and herbs and mix well. Taste and adjust the seasoning by adding salt and pepper and more lemon juice or pomegranate molasses if required.

Mound the salad onto a serving platter and garnish with baby lettuce leaves. Alternatively, use wet hands to form the mixture into walnut-sized balls and serve them nestled in the lettuce leaves.

SERVES 6–8

Spiced pumpkin *köfte* with walnut and feta stuffing

Köfte are a large and varied group of dishes that are probably best described as "ground." They can be made with ground meat or vegetables and flavored with different spices. Some include bulgur or bread crumbs or rice. They come in myriad shapes and forms and can be molded around skewers or shaped into patties or ovals, large or small. Some *köfte* are stuffed; others are eaten wrapped in lettuce or vine leaves. Some *köfte* are eaten raw; others are fried or baked.

These are loosely based on the Turkish stuffed *köfte* or *içli köfta*, but are made with lightly spiced pumpkin rather than the traditional minced lamb, so they are softer and more delicate. The sharp feta stuffing is the perfect counterpoint to the sweet pumpkin.

You'll find the red pepper paste used here in Middle Eastern food stores.

1 small butternut pumpkin (about 2¼ pounds)
3 tablespoons olive oil
1 red onion, finely diced
1 tablespoon hot Turkish red pepper paste
1 teaspoon ground cumin
1 teaspoon sweet paprika
9 ounces fine bulgur
generous pinch of salt
2 eggs, lightly beaten
vegetable oil for deep-frying

WALNUT AND FETA STUFFING
⅔ cup walnuts
6 ounces feta
2 tablespoons chopped flat-leaf parsley leaves
½ teaspoon freshly ground black pepper
1 tablespoon extra-virgin olive oil

Preheat the oven to 400°F. Use a large heavy knife to trim the ends from the pumpkin and quarter it lengthwise. Scoop out the seeds and discard them. Rub the pumpkin pieces lightly with a little of the oil, then roast them on a jelly-roll pan for 30–40 minutes, or until tender.

Heat the remaining oil in a large heavy-based saucepan. Stir in the onion, pepper paste, cumin and paprika and sweat over a low heat for 15–20 minutes.

When the pumpkin is cooked, scrape the flesh into a food processor and pulse to a fine purée. Stir the pumpkin purée into the sautéed onion mixture and bring to a simmer.

Rinse the bulgur, then add it to the pumpkin purée and season with salt. Remove the pan from the heat and leave to stand for 10 minutes, then put the mixture into a bowl and leave to cool in the refrigerator.

While the pumpkin mixture is chilling, make the walnut and feta stuffing. Preheat the oven to 350°F. Scatter the walnuts onto a baking tray and roast for 5–10 minutes until a deep golden brown. Pour the nuts into a tea towel and rub well to remove as much skin as possible. Chop the walnuts coarsely and toss in a sieve to remove any remaining skin and dust. Combine the stuffing ingredients in a bowl and use a fork to mash everything together.

When ready to make the *köfte*, mix the eggs into the chilled pumpkin mixture. Take a small lump of the mixture and mold it in your hand to make a smooth ball. Use a finger to make an indentation in the mixture and work it to hollow out the middle. Stuff a generous teaspoon of the stuffing into the hollowed-out *köfte*, then pinch the edges together to seal. Arrange the prepared *köfte* on a tray, and refrigerate until ready to cook.

To fry the *köfte*, heat the oil to 400°F in a large saucepan or deep-fryer. Fry four *köfte* at a time for 2–3 minutes, or until a deep golden brown. Be careful as the oil will splutter and spit a lot. Using a slotted spoon, remove the *köfte* to drain on paper towels—keep them warm while you fry the remaining *köfte*. Serve immediately.

MAKES 24

Little *köfte* dumplings in minted yogurt sauce

Köfte dumplings are a firm Turkish favorite and we ate countless versions on our travels. Sometimes they were served like meatballs, smothered in sauce or in a soup. Sometimes they were as tiny as chickpeas, and served as a garnish to a thick yogurt dip. These babies are the latter kind, and the secret to their success is to blend the mixture to a smooth, homogeneous paste.

Pekmez, or grape molasses, is available from Turkish food stores.

KÖFTE DUMPLINGS
4 ounces fine bulgur
²⁄₃ pound chilled lean lamb, cubed
1 small onion
½ teaspoon ground allspice
¼ teaspoon ground cinnamon
¼ teaspoon chile powder
1 tablespoon *pekmez*
sea salt
freshly ground black pepper

YOGURT SAUCE
2 tablespoons olive oil
1 onion, finely chopped
1 clove garlic, finely chopped
1 pound Swiss chard leaves, roughly chopped
1 red serrano chile, seeded, scraped and finely chopped
½ teaspoon ground allspice
1 cup Chicken Stock (page 41)
juice of 1 lemon
1 pound Greek-style yogurt
½ teaspoon cornstarch
3 tablespoons water
1 egg, lightly beaten
2 ounces butter
½ teaspoon sweet paprika
½ teaspoon dried mint

To make the dumplings, soak the bulgur in plenty of cold water for 15 minutes to soften it. Use your hands to squeeze out as much water as you can.

Pulse the chilled lamb in a food processor until it comes together as a smooth, homogeneous paste, then put into a bowl. Whiz the onion to a puree in the food processor and add to the lamb with the bulgur, spices and *pekmez*, then season with salt and pepper. Use clean hands to mix everything to a soft smooth paste. You may need to add a little cold water to help bind everything together. Refrigerate the bowl for 30 minutes to make the paste easier to work with.

Take a grape-sized lump of the paste and roll it between your hands to make as smooth a ball as you can (wet hands will make this easier). Arrange the prepared dumplings on a tray, and refrigerate until ready to cook.

Bring a large saucepan of water to the boil and poach the dumplings, ten at a time, for 10 minutes. Use a slotted spoon to remove the dumplings and drain on paper towels.

To make the sauce, heat the oil in a large saucepan and sauté the onion and garlic until they soften. Add the Swiss chard, chile, allspice, stock and lemon juice and cook over a gentle heat for about 20 minutes, or until the Swiss chard is tender.

To stabilize the yogurt, beat it in a large bowl until smooth. Mix the cornstarch with the water and add to the yogurt with the egg. Stir well, then pour this into the hot Swiss chard mixture. Lower the heat and cook, stirring in one direction only, for about 10 minutes, or until the sauce has thickened. Add the dumplings and simmer gently for a further 5 minutes, or until they are warmed through.

When ready to serve, melt the butter in a small frying pan. Add the paprika and mint and heat until foaming. Ladle the hot sauce into warmed serving bowls and swirl on the foaming butter. Serve right away.

SERVES 8

Crunchy red lentil *köfte* with fresh mint

The inspiration for these little *köfte* comes from Yorem Mutfak, a lovely home-style restaurant in Gaziantep. Rather unusually, the owner and chef is a woman, the charming and friendly Hatice Yildirim, who told us she'd been cooking for twenty-five years. We fell in love with these patties immediately; they are spicy with a lovely crunch from the bulgur. Hatice served them on baby lettuce leaves with wedges of lemon and green onions as part of a meze selection. You'll find the red pepper paste used here in Middle Eastern food stores.

2 ounces butter
1 small red onion, finely chopped
1 tablespoon tomato paste
1 tablespoon mild Turkish red pepper paste
1 heaped teaspoon ground cumin
4 ounces red lentils
1½ cups water
½ cup fine bulgur
2 tablespoons shredded mint leaves
1 heaped teaspoon dried mint
sea salt
freshly ground black pepper
juice of 1 lemon
3 ounces extra-virgin olive oil
1 romaine lettuce, washed
6 baby salad onions

Melt the butter in a heavy-based saucepan over a medium heat and add the onion, tomato paste, pepper paste and cumin. Sauté for a few minutes until the onion starts to soften, then add the lentils and water and bring to the boil. Lower the heat and simmer gently for 10 minutes, or until the lentils are tender and have absorbed two-thirds of the water. Stir in the bulgur and fresh and dried mint and season to taste with salt and pepper. Remove the pan from the heat and leave to stand for 5 minutes, then stir in half the lemon juice and 2 tablespoons of the oil. Put the mixture onto a tray to cool.

When ready to serve, whisk the remaining lemon juice and oil to make a dressing and season with salt and pepper. Form the cooled lentil mixture into little patties and use your thumb to make an indentation in the surface of each. Arrange the *köfte* on a platter with the lettuce leaves and onions, then drizzle over the dressing.
SERVES 4–6

Underground cities

[LAMB AND VARIETY MEATS]

It seemed that Cappadocia's geological attractions were not limited to its surreal landscape; there was also an extensive network of interlinked prehistoric cave communities carved deep beneath the earth's surface.

T he day dawned, cool but without a cloud on the horizon, and we breakfasted heartily on soft, flaky *açma* rolls served with tangy local ewe's butter, dark intensely flavored honeycomb and preserves made from last summer's apricots and plums.

Thus fortified, we headed off on the road south toward the mysterious-sounding "underground cities." It seemed that Cappadocia's geological attractions were not limited to its surreal landscape; there was also an extensive network of interlinked prehistoric cave communities carved deep beneath the earth's surface.

Derinkuyu was our destination, one of a handful of the cities to have been excavated safely enough for visitors. Hittite artifacts date some of the simpler caves back 3,000–4,000 years. Over the centuries they became more elaborate and extensive and were carved deeper and deeper into the earth—down to 250 feet, in places. Almost entirely invisible from the surface, these tunnels and caves were the ideal hiding place for communities who were vulnerable to attack. Early Christian communities were believed to have sought refuge here from Roman persecution and, later, from marauding Arab tribes.

At Derinkuyu we found ourselves hunched over in a narrow, back-breaking tunnel, descending inexorably down, away from the comforting daylight. Off either side of the tunnel, passages wound away into darkness. Rooms led into further rooms, and every now and then a ventilation shaft sent dim rays of hazy light down into the depths. There were ancient kitchens and ovens, winepresses, storage rooms, dormitories and dining rooms and even, we were startled to discover, stables.

The thought of living in this maze of narrow, damp darkness gave us the heebie-jeebies—this particular adventure is definitely not for the claustrophobic. But it did give us boundless respect for the poor persecuted communities that were forced, surely out of sheer desperation, to hide here for months on end, deep within the earth.

Back on the surface, in the glorious, reviving sunlight, we felt the urge to celebrate life. We'd arranged to have lunch in the small village of Ayvalı, back toward Ürgüp, and the Yazgan family were expecting us. Yusuf and Nurhoyat and their son Okan run a small traditional pension in an old village house and they welcomed us with the usual Turkish warmth and enthusiasm.

The old stone house was built into the side of a shallow valley and Nurhoyat had set the simple wooden table for lunch on a vine-shaded terrace. We had a sweeping view over the flat rooftops, domes and cupolas of the small village below. Pigeons, from their nesting boxes, swooped in and around the balustrade, while we sat quietly for a few moments enjoying the warm sunshine.

Okan took us over to the outdoor kitchen to show us the family's *tandır* oven. Although many people tend to think of Turks as being the masters of grilled dishes— they invented the kebab, after all—in this wild and remote part of the country, with its extremes of temperature, they favor slow-cooking in clay-pit ovens—*tandır* style.

Under the ground in Derinkuyu we'd seen ancient versions of these pit ovens hollowed into the cave floors. This was a more elaborate version, carved in stone and half-raised above the ground. Nurhoyat lifted the lid for us to peer down inside. At the bottom were two tall vase-like pots, one containing lamb, the other beans, and on the oven walls we spotted the telltale round charred marks where circles of dough had been pressed to bake flat bread.

Okan brought out a series of little dishes for us to eat: first there were crunchy long pickled peppers, mild, and tangy with vinegar. Next came a rich tomato soup, its surface gleaming with sizzling butter and flecked with chile and mint, accompanied by some of that flat bread, hot from the *tandır* oven. Nurhoyat's stuffed vine leaves were as skinny as a pencil, and made with leaves picked from their own grapevines, Okan told us. We scooped up creamy *haydari*, a dip made from homemade yogurt and

dill and crumbly *gömlek peyniri*, a white cheese that Okan's family matured for a few months in a clay pot to develop its flavor.

And then out came the main dishes, the clay pots of steaming *tandır* lamb and *fasulye* (beans). Nurhoyat had started preparing both dishes early that morning, so by now they'd been quietly slow-cooking away at the bottom of the *tandır* oven for nearly five hours. Both were simple peasant-style dishes, uncomplicated by layers of spices and herbs. The lamb was meltingly tender and juicy in a light tomato stock that was thick with onion, garlic and peppers. The beans were soft and flavorsome— a sort of home-style version of baked beans.

To end the meal, there were apricots from Nurhoyat's garden. Sun-dried on the roof, they'd been stored underground through the winter months before being simmered in the *tandır* oven with a little local grape juice. They were sticky and dark as treacle, with an intense muscat flavor; Nurhoyat served them warm, split open and stuffed with chopped walnuts and a spoonful of thick clotted cream.

By now the sky was becoming a deep, late-afternoon gold, and the shadows were lengthening. We said our thanks and farewells to Okan and his family, fumbling with our few words of Turkish. As we wandered contentedly down the hillside to where our car was parked, the muezzin's call from the village mosque started up and, turning, we saw a little group of men wending their way up the hill to prayer.

The next morning saw us broaching the outskirts of Kayseri, Turkey's most central city. Its key position on ancient trade routes meant that it has always had a thriving economy, most prominently and prosperously under Roman rule (its name derives from Caesarea) and later during the reign of the Seljuks, when it played second city to their nearby capital, Konya.

As we struggled through the midday traffic the only obvious sign of Kayseri's history was the sixth-century citadel in the center of the city. It seemed otherwise to be a busy modern town, complete with a brand-new streetcar line and freshly laid concrete walkways. We had read that Kayseri was famous throughout Turkey for two unrelated products: its fine carpets and *pastırma*, a sort of precursor to pastrami. Naturally enough, it was the latter that we'd come to investigate.

As we rounded a corner
we stumbled upon a row
of shops draped with strings
of reddy-orange sucuk
sausages, their windows
stacked high with nuggets
of pastırma.

Just inside the citadel walls we ventured into Kayseri's Grand Bazaar. Dating from the 1800s, we learned that it had been recently reroofed and renovated. There was plenty of carpet-selling going on in the main part of the bazaar, but we were more interested in tracking down the butcher shops. It didn't take long. As we rounded a corner we stumbled upon a row of shops draped with strings of reddish-orange *sucuk* sausages, their windows stacked high with nuggets of *pastırma*.

We were familiar with *pastırma*, having seen it in the northern Syrian town of Aleppo, just over the border from the southeast of Turkey, and now, it seemed, we were in *pastırma* heaven! The name itself is Turkish—meaning "pressed meat"—and legend says that it originated with the Turkic horsemen of Central Asia, who packed it into their saddlebags, where it would, literally, be pressed by their thighs as they rode.

With that rather unappetizing image in our mind we ventured into a few shops to sample the wares. One butcher told us that his family had been *pastırmacilik*— *pastırma* butchers—for many generations. Using a massive razor-sharp cleaver he rapidly sliced a few wafers for us to sample. As we chewed on the spicy beef, the butcher told us there were more than twenty types of *pastırma*. Pointing out a few, he identified the most expensive—cut from the fillet and sirloin—and then several from the leg, shank and shoulder. Chuckling as he demonstrated on his own body, he explained that secondary cuts like the flank, neck and brisket produce lesser-quality *pastırma*.

Irrespective of cut, all the meat is treated the same way. After being thoroughly air-dried it is smothered in a thick bright-red paste called *çemen*, and left to cure. It's the *çemen* that gives *pastırma* both its distinctive oxblood-red color and its strong, pungent flavor: it's made from crushed fenugreek, cumin, garlic and hot paprika. We noticed little tubs of it in the window, sold as a savory paste for spreading on bread. I bought a little tub to try later, stuffing it into my shoulder bag as we walked back to the car. It was indeed delicious, but it didn't take me long to regret that decision. A month later, back home in Australia, my bag still reeked of the stuff!

Spicy çiğ köfte

Raw *köfte* are popular around the Middle East, where they are known as *kifta nayee*, or *kibbeh nayee* when made with bulgur wheat. They are most often made with lamb, combined with finely chopped onion, spices and herbs, to make what is, in essence, an Eastern steak tartare. In Turkey, *çiğ köfte* are a specialty of the southeast and we ate a wonderful spicy version in Gaziantep, which is famous for the use of hot red chiles and peppers in its cooking.

It's essential to get really top-quality fresh meat for this dish. It is also important to chill the meat prior to use for the best results. Chopping it by hand will give a better texture, but it's laborious. Please use a meat grinder, not a food processor, as the latter will produce a gluggy paste. Alternatively, an accommodating butcher may grind your chosen lamb for you.

Serve the köfte with triangles of flat bread. I also like to add a dollop of Strained Yogurt (page 54), although it's not very Turkish to do so.

¾ pound chilled lean lamb or beef (from a prime cut such as the leg or rump)
4 long red chiles
2 shallots, very finely diced
2 tablespoons shredded mint leaves
2 tablespoons shredded flat-leaf parsley leaves
1 teaspoon dried mint
1 teaspoon sweet paprika
¼ teaspoon smoky paprika
sea salt
freshly ground white pepper
2 ice cubes
4 butter lettuce leaves, washed
2 tablespoons extra-virgin olive oil
lemon wedges to serve

Trim the meat of all fat, sinew and connective tissue. Roughly dice the meat and chop it by hand, or put it through a meat grinder twice, to achieve a smooth paste.

Roast the chiles over the naked flame of your stove, or under a broiler, until charred, then slip into a plastic bag to cool. When cool enough to handle, peel away the blackened skin. Split the chiles lengthwise, then scrape out the seeds and chop the flesh finely.

Tip the meat into a large bowl and add the chiles, shallots, herbs and spices, then season with salt and pepper. Add the ice cubes to the bowl and mix well with clean hands. (As the ice melts it will bind everything into a very smooth, sticky paste.) Divide the paste into four and shape into balls, then refrigerate until ready to eat.

To serve, arrange the lettuce leaves on four plates. Place a *köfte* on each and use your thumb to make an indentation on the surface. Drizzle in a scant teaspoon of the oil and serve with lemon wedges.

SERVES 4

Içli köfte

These are the most sophisticated of the huge range of *köfte*, combining a crunchy external "shell" made of ground lamb and bulgur wheat and a tasty stuffing of spiced lamb and pine nuts. They will be familiar to anyone who loves Lebanese food as the torpedo-shaped dumplings known as *kibbeh*. Serve as part of a meze selection, with plenty of yogurt alongside.

9 ounces fine bulgur
1 onion, very finely diced
¾ teaspoon ground allspice
½ teaspoon ground cinnamon
1 teaspoon sweet paprika
¼ teaspoon hot paprika
½ teaspoon freshly ground black pepper
sea salt
1½ pounds lean lamb (from the leg or shoulder), ground twice
1 ice cube
1 cup vegetable oil

PINE NUT AND LAMB STUFFING
⅓ cup olive oil
1 small onion, finely diced
¼ teaspoon ground allspice
3 ounces pine nuts
7 ounces lean lamb (from the leg or shoulder), ground
sea salt
freshly ground black pepper
2 tablespoons chopped flat-leaf parsley leaves

Put the bulgur into a small bowl and pour on just enough cold water to cover it. Leave for 5 minutes, then put into a sieve and squeeze out as much water as you can using your hands. Put the bulgur into a large bowl with the onion and spices, then season with salt and knead to a paste. Leave for about 5 minutes to allow the bulgur to soften and absorb some of the flavorings.

Add the lamb to the bowl with the ice cube and knead it thoroughly into the bulgur mixture. As the ice melts it will bind everything into a smooth, sticky paste. Refrigerate the mixture for 30 minutes to make the paste easier to work with.

Meanwhile, make the stuffing. Heat half the oil in a heavy-based frying pan. Sauté the onion and allspice over a low heat for 5 minutes until the onion has softened. Add the pine nuts and increase the heat. Sauté, stirring continuously, until the pine nuts are golden brown. Put into a bowl and set aside.

Wipe out the pan, then add the remaining oil and heat over a medium–high heat. Add the lamb, then increase the heat and sauté for around 5 minutes, breaking up any lumps with a wooden spoon. When any liquid has evaporated, add the onion and pine nut mixture, then season with salt and pepper and stir through the parsley. Put into a bowl and leave to cool.

To make the *içli köfte*, take a small lump of the chilled bulgur and lamb paste in the palm of your left hand and roll it into a smooth ball. Use the forefinger of your right hand to make an indentation in the lump and start to shape it into a hollow shell (reverse hands if you're left-handed). Try to make the walls of the shell as thin and even as you can. Fill the shell with about a teaspoon of the stuffing. Wet the edges of the opening with cold water and pinch shut. Use your fingers to shape the ends gently into the traditional torpedo shape. Arrange the stuffed *köfte* on a tray, then cover and refrigerate.

When ready to cook the *içli köfte*, heat the oil in a large, heavy-based frying pan or even a wok. Fry the *köfte*, a few at a time, turning them around in the oil until a deep golden brown all over. Drain on paper towels and serve hot.

SERVES 4

Butcher's *köfte kebabs*

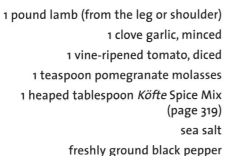

In Turkey when spiced ground meat is shaped into long sausages around skewers for grilling, it becomes *şiş köfte* (*şiş* is the Turkish word for skewer). Almost every town in Turkey has its own version of *köfte* kebabs, flavored with different combinations of spices and herbs, and many butchers will sell their own homemade *köfte* mixture. The following is a simple and tasty version that everyone will adore. If you can, try to find the long flat skewers—the meat is far less likely to fall off these than the regular round ones.

1 pound lamb (from the leg or shoulder)
1 clove garlic, minced
1 vine-ripened tomato, diced
1 teaspoon pomegranate molasses
1 heaped tablespoon *Köfte* Spice Mix (page 319)
sea salt
freshly ground black pepper
warmed flat bread to serve

SOFT HERB SALAD
1 cup shredded flat-leaf parsley leaves
1 cup shredded mint leaves
1 small red onion, finely sliced
juice of ½ lemon
drizzle of extra-virgin olive oil
sea salt
freshly ground black pepper
½ teaspoon ground sumac

Trim the lamb of any connective tissue and sinew, but leave the fat. Cut the meat into manageable chunks and grind it twice. Knead the ground lamb with the garlic, tomato, pomegranate molasses and spice mix for 2–3 minutes to combine thoroughly, then season with salt and pepper. Cover and refrigerate for 20 minutes to allow the flavors to develop.

When ready to cook, heat a griddle or barbecue to its highest setting. With wet hands, divide the seasoned ground lamb into four equal portions and mold each one around a flat metal skewer into a long sausage shape.

To make the salad, toss the herbs and onion in a bowl. Whisk the lemon juice, oil, salt, pepper and sumac in a small bowl to make a dressing, then set aside.

Cook the *köfte* on the griddle or barbecue for 2–3 minutes on each side, or until golden brown and cooked through. Serve the *köfte* on warmed flat bread with the dressed salad alongside for everyone to help themselves.
SERVES 4

Antep pistachio kebabs

Gaziantep—known colloquially as Antep—is famous throughout Turkey for its superb pistachio nuts. They feature prominently in many local dishes, even in these tasty kebabs.

Serve the kebabs on warmed flat bread with Soft Herb Salad (page 161) alongside.

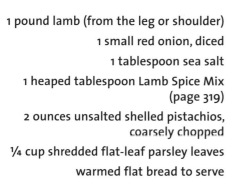

1 pound lamb (from the leg or shoulder)

1 small red onion, diced

1 tablespoon sea salt

1 heaped tablespoon Lamb Spice Mix (page 319)

2 ounces unsalted shelled pistachios, coarsely chopped

¼ cup shredded flat-leaf parsley leaves

warmed flat bread to serve

Trim the lamb of any connective tissue or sinew, but leave the fat. Cut the meat into manageable chunks and grind it twice. Knead the ground lamb with the onion, salt and spice mix for 2–3 minutes to combine thoroughly. Cover and refrigerate for 20 minutes to allow the flavors to develop. Add the pistachios and parsley and knead briefly to combine evenly.

When ready to cook, heat a griddle or barbecue to its highest setting. With wet hands, divide the seasoned ground lamb into four equal portions and mold each one around a flat metal skewer into a long sausage shape.

Cook the *köfte* on the griddle or barbecue for 2–3 minutes on each side, or until golden brown and cooked through. Serve on warmed flat bread with salad.

SERVES 4

Şiş kebabs

Şiş is the Turkish word for skewer, and this method of spearing meat—on any kind of makeshift skewer—and cooking it over an open fire is one of the very earliest cooking methods. Its popularity around Turkey dates back to the nomadic Turkic tribes, who migrated out of the eastern and central steppes and into Anatolia from the seventh century onward.

Şiş kebabs can be made from almost any meat or poultry, cubed or minced, and are often interspersed on the skewer with tomato, pepper, onion and eggplant. However, as the meat and vegetables take different lengths of time to cook, I prefer to keep them separate.

Here the kebabs are served the traditional way, with warmed flat bread, *Cacık* (page 54) and a salad—the Soft Herb Salad (page 161) is the perfect match for the spiced meat.

1 pound lamb (from the leg or shoulder)
1 heaping teaspoon ground cinnamon
1 heaping teaspoon ground allspice
1 teaspoon hot paprika
1 teaspoon ground nutmeg
½ teaspoon freshly ground black pepper
⅓ cup extra-virgin olive oil
sea salt
warmed flat bread to serve
1¼ cups *Cacık* (page 54)

Trim the lamb of any fat and connective tissue, then cut it into ¾-inch cubes. Combine the spices and oil in a bowl, then add the lamb and toss gently to coat. Leave for 45 minutes to marinate.

When ready to cook, heat a griddle or barbecue to its highest setting. Thread six cubes of lamb onto each of eight flat skewers, packing the meat close together; this way the meat will cook brown and crisp on the outside, but remain a little pink inside. Cook for 4–5 minutes, turning frequently and seasoning with salt as you go.

Remove the skewers from the grill. The idea is for everyone to wrap their own kebabs in flat bread with salad and a drizzle of *cacık*.
SERVES 4

Rabbit kebabs in lettuce leaves

Before they converted to Islam, the nomadic Turks survived in the steppes by hunting animals such as hare and rabbit, deer, horse and even camel, as well as by farming sheep. Although they brought their varied meat diet with them to Anatolia, the evidence is contradictory as to how much of it survived the Ottoman era. Today lamb is without a doubt the most commonly eaten meat in Turkey, with beef and chicken bringing up the rear. But we like to imagine a little group of nomads huddled around a campfire grilling rabbit kebabs on their journey ever farther west into the desolate plains of central Anatolia.

2¼ pounds rabbit hind legs, boned
1 teaspoon ground cinnamon
1½ teaspoons ground cumin
1½ teaspoons ground coriander
½ teaspoon ground allspice
½ teaspoon freshly ground black pepper
¼ teaspoon hot paprika
⅓ cup extra-virgin olive oil
4 small vine-ripened tomatoes, cut into quarters, or 2 small onions, cut into quarters
sea salt
butter lettuce leaves to serve
Whipped Feta Dip (page 58) to serve

Trim the rabbit meat of any fat and sinew, especially around the paw end, then cut it into ¾-inch cubes. Combine the spices and oil in a bowl, then add the rabbit and toss gently to coat. Leave for 30 minutes to marinate.

When ready to cook, heat a griddle or barbecue to its highest setting. Thread six cubes of meat onto each of eight flat skewers, with a piece of tomato at either end. Cook for 4–5 minutes, turning frequently and seasoning with salt as you go.

Remove the skewers from the grill and serve them on the lettuce leaves. The idea is for everyone to garnish their own kebabs with a dollop of feta dip and to eat them wrapped in the lettuce, instead of bread.
SERVES 4

Spicy liver kebabs with onion and sumac salad

Eating liver kebabs for breakfast is a regional eccentricity of southeastern Turkey—especially of Şanlıurfa and Gaziantep, so we rose with the birds one morning to sample *ciğer* kebabs for ourselves. Following our noses and the intense blue smoke from the grill, we joined a surprisingly large crowd of men outside Ciğerici Haydar. Threaded on a long, flat skewer with chunks of solid lamb's tail fat to keep the liver moist, the kebabs proved to be spicy and delicious. We ate them wrapped in flat bread with parsley, onion and an extra sprinkling of chile and could imagine how satisfying they'd be on a snowy winter's morning.

You'll find the red pepper paste used here in Middle Eastern food stores.

1 lamb's liver (about 1 pound)
1 tablespoon ground sumac
1 tablespoon ground cumin
1 teaspoon freshly ground black pepper
¼ teaspoon hot paprika
1 teaspoon hot Turkish red pepper paste
⅓ cup extra-virgin olive oil
sea salt
flat bread to serve
lemon wedges to serve

ONION AND SUMAC SALAD
½ cup shredded flat-leaf parsley leaves
1 small red onion, finely sliced
1 romaine lettuce, shredded
juice of ½ lemon
sea salt
1 teaspoon ground sumac

Use your fingers to remove the membrane from the liver, then cut out any little tubes with a small sharp knife. Cut the trimmed liver into even ¾-inch cubes. Combine the spices, pepper paste and oil in a bowl, then add the liver and toss gently to coat. Leave for 30 minutes to marinate.

To make the salad, toss all the ingredients in a large bowl.

When ready to cook, heat a griddle or barbecue to its highest setting. Thread eight cubes of liver onto each of eight flat skewers, packing the liver close together; this way the liver will cook brown and crisp on the outside, but remain a little pink inside. Cook for 15–20 seconds on each side—no more than a minute in total—and season with salt as you go.

Remove the skewers from the grill and serve them on flat bread. The idea is for everyone to wrap their own kebabs in flat bread, garnish with salad and add a squeeze of lemon.
SERVES 4

Skewered lamb's sweetbreads with cumin, chile and sumac

Turks are far less squeamish than many about eating every bit of the animal. *Kokoreç* (grilled intestines) are a popular street snack, while *işkembe çorbası* (tripe soup) is a famous hangover cure. Variety meats butchers are a common sight around the produce markets, with garlands of intestines, sheep's heads, and every conceivable organ proudly on display.

Sweetbreads are perhaps less of a challenge, and I love them for their creamy texture and delicate flavor. I like to serve them with Everyday Orzo Pilaf (page 128).

You'll find the red pepper paste used here in Middle Eastern food stores.

1½ pounds lamb's sweetbreads, trimmed of surrounding fat

milk

1 lemon, cut into quarters

1 stick celery

½ onion

1 stick cinnamon

4 cloves

1 teaspoon ground sumac

1 teaspoon ground cumin

½ teaspoon freshly ground black pepper

¼ teaspoon hot paprika

1 tablespoon hot Turkish red pepper paste

⅓ cup extra-virgin olive oil

sea salt

1 clove garlic

7 ounces Greek-style yogurt

1 tablespoon extra-virgin olive oil

freshly ground white pepper

Soak the sweetbreads overnight in enough milk to cover them.

When ready to cook the sweetbreads, rinse them well, then pat dry and use a sharp knife to trim away any membrane and remaining fat. Put the sweetbreads into a large saucepan with the lemon, celery, onion, cinnamon and cloves, then cover with cold water. Bring to the boil, then skim and simmer for 5 minutes. Remove the pan from the heat and drain the sweetbreads. Leave to cool, then cut into even ¾-inch cubes.

Combine the spices, pepper paste and oil in a bowl, then add the sweetbreads and toss gently to coat. Leave for 10 minutes to marinate.

When ready to cook, heat a griddle or barbecue to its highest setting. Thread eight cubes of sweetbread onto each of eight flat skewers. Cook for 20–30 seconds on each side—no more than 2 minutes in total—and season with salt as you go.

When ready to serve, crush the garlic with ¼ teaspoon salt, then whisk with the yogurt and extra-virgin olive oil to make a dressing. Taste and season with more salt and the white pepper if required. Serve the sweetbread skewers on a pilaf with the dressing on the side.

SERVES 4

Crumbed lamb's tongues with almond *tarator*

This is my interpretation of a brilliant dish I tasted at the fashionable Changa restaurant in Istanbul. The menu there is overseen by New Zealand fusion-maestro Peter Gordon, who travels to Turkey every few months to change dishes on the menu and to seek inspiration from the local produce markets. Peter's menu is modern and eclectic and it incorporates wonderful Turkish touches. I was especially delighted by a dish of crumbed lamb's tongues that he served with a hot garlicky aioli.

I like to serve my version as a starter, and to accompany the crispy crumbed lamb's tongues with Almond *Tarator* (page 63) and perhaps Pickled Cucumbers with Fennel (page 314). Another option would be to partner them with Whipped Feta Dip (page 58).

I like to use lamb's tongues for this recipe, but you could also use veal or ox tongue—the cooking time here won't alter. Ask your butcher to pickle whichever tongues you choose; it improves the flavor and helps maintain the rosy-pink color when you cook them.

1¾ pounds pickled lamb's tongues (about 8)
2 sticks celery, cut into chunks
2 small carrots, cut into chunks
1 onion, cut into quarters
1 small leek, cut into chunks
2 cloves garlic
2 bay leaves
few sprigs thyme
1 teaspoon black peppercorns
½ cup grated parmesan
⅓ pound fresh bread crumbs
2 tablespoons sesame seeds
2 free-range eggs
all-purpose flour
sea salt
freshly ground black pepper
olive oil for frying
lemon wedges to serve
1 quantity Almond *Tarator* (page 63) to serve

Rinse the tongues well, then put them into a large, heavy-based saucepan and cover with cold water. Bring to the boil, then put into a colander to drain.

Return the tongues to the rinsed-out saucepan and add the vegetables, garlic, herbs and peppercorns. Pour on enough cold water to cover, then bring to the boil and lower the heat immediately. Simmer gently, covered, for 1½–2 hours, or until the tongues are tender. Check the pan from time to time and top up with more water if needed—the tongues should always be covered with water. When cooked, allow the tongues to cool in the cooking liquid until easy to handle. While still warm, carefully peel away the skin and any excess fat. Refrigerate the peeled tongues in the cooking liquid overnight, or for a minimum of 8 hours.

Remove the chilled tongues from the cooking liquid and pat dry. Use a sharp knife to trim the back (root) of the tongue and to slice away any gristly muscle tissue and excess fat from the underside. If using lamb's tongues, cut in half lengthwise. If using veal or ox tongue, cut into slices crosswise.

When ready to cook the tongues, mix the parmesan, bread crumbs and sesame seeds in a shallow bowl. Lightly beat the eggs with a little water in another shallow bowl. Set up a production line of the flour, egg wash and crumb mix. Season the tongues lightly with salt and pepper, then dip each one into the flour, then the egg and finally the crumbs.

Heat the oil in a heavy-based frying pan and fry the tongues for 1–2 minutes on each side until golden brown. Serve them hot from the pan with lemon wedges and the *tarator*, and accompany with pickles or a salad.

SERVES 4

Shepherd's spinach

A simple, rustic dish that makes a tasty family meal. It is delicious served with plenty
of buttered bread to mop up all the sauce.

3 ounces unsalted butter

1 onion, finely chopped

1 clove garlic, finely chopped

1 teaspoon dried mint

¼ teaspoon hot paprika

¼ teaspoon sweet paprika

1 tablespoon tomato paste

½ pound lean lamb (from the leg or shoulder),
ground or finely chopped

3 ounces short-grain rice

1 cup water

2¼ pounds spinach, washed, trimmed and
roughly shredded

Melt the butter in a large, heavy-based saucepan. Add the onion, garlic, dried mint and
spices and sauté gently for about 5 minutes, until the onions are soft. Add the tomato
paste and lamb and increase the heat. Cook for another few minutes until the lamb is
evenly colored and the liquid has begun to evaporate.

Stir the rice into the pan, then add the water and bring to a boil. Lower the heat,
then cover the pan and simmer gently for 15 minutes. Add the spinach to the pan, using
a large spoon to stir it in gently. Cover and cook for a further 5 minutes.

SERVES 4–6

Sour–sweet lamb *yahni* with black-eyed peas and almonds

In Turkish cookery, *yahni* dishes correspond most closely to good old-fashioned stews. They are winter warmers, and the meat tends to be browned in butter first for extra lusciousness. Accompany this dish with a plain pilaf.

4 ounces black-eyed peas

⅓ cup dried sour cherries

1¾ pounds lamb (from the leg or shoulder)

2 ounces unsalted butter

1 tablespoon extra-virgin olive oil

8 pearl onions, cut in half

3 cloves garlic, finely chopped

¼ cup apple vinegar

1 tablespoon honey

2 large vine-ripened tomatoes, skinned, seeded and diced

1 red serrano chile, finely chopped

1¾ cup Chicken Stock (page 41)

few sprigs thyme

1 teaspoon ground coriander

¼ teaspoon ground allspice

3 tablespoons vegetable oil

2 ounces sliced almonds

¼ cup shredded flat-leaf parsley leaves

Soak the black-eyed peas overnight in cold water.

Soak the sour cherries in a little cold water for an hour. Meanwhile, drain and rinse the black-eyed peas. Trim the lamb of any fat and sinew and cut into 1-inch cubes.

Heat the butter and olive oil over a medium heat in a large, heavy-based casserole dish. Brown the lamb all over, then add the onions and garlic and sauté for a few minutes. Increase the heat and add the vinegar and honey. Let the pan bubble vigorously for a few minutes, then lower the heat and add the black-eyed peas, tomatoes, chile, stock, thyme and spices. Stir well, then cover the pan, lower the heat and leave to simmer very gently for 1–1½ hours or until the lamb is really tender and the sauce thick. About 10 minutes before the end of the cooking time, add the drained sour cherries.

Heat the vegetable oil in a heavy-based frying pan. Fry the almonds over a low heat until golden brown, then drain on paper towels.

When ready to serve, garnish the *yahni* with the fried almonds and parsley.

SERVES 4

Grilled lamb cutlets with mountain herbs

There's little to beat tender young lamb cooked on the barbecue to pink perfection. As a rule, Turks don't really like complicated marinades or sauces, preferring to keep the sweet flavor of the meat unadulterated. But brushing the meat with this fresh herb dressing toward the end of the cooking time adds just the right amount of complementary seasoning.

I like to accompany these cutlets with Spicy Eggplant Relish (page 311) and Tomato Salad with Tarragon, Aged Feta and Sumac Dressing (page 102).

Ask your butcher to cut double-thick cutlets, to ensure a rosy-pink center after grilling.

1 clove garlic
½ teaspoon sea salt
½ teaspoon freshly ground black pepper
1 small shallot, finely chopped
1 teaspoon finely chopped rosemary
4 sprigs dried oregano
½ teaspoon ground sumac
juice of 1 lemon
¼ cup extra-virgin olive oil
8 double lamb cutlets

Crush the garlic with the salt, then combine with the pepper, shallot, herbs, sumac and lemon juice in a bowl. Whisk in the oil to make a thick, pungent dressing. (This may not look like a lot, but don't worry as a little goes a long way.)

Heat a griddle or barbecue to its highest setting. Brush the cutlets very lightly with a little of the dressing, then cook for 2 minutes on each side for medium rare. Toward the end of the cooking time brush on a little more of the dressing.

Serve the cutlets hot from the grill with the remaining dressing on the side.
SERVES 4

Sultan's delight—lamb ragout with cheesy eggplant puree

Legend has it that this dish was served to the Empress Eugénie, wife of Napoleon III, on a visit to Istanbul in the 1860s. Keen to impress, the Sultan had many of his favorite dishes prepared for her, including this one. Apparently Eugénie enjoyed it so much that she dispatched her own French chef to the palace kitchens for the recipe. But the Sultan's chef was clearly not in the mood to give away his secrets, and he sent the interloper away saying, "an imperial chef needs only his heart, his eyes and his nose." He must have decided to share the recipe somewhere along the line, however, as this dish is now a favorite on restaurant menus around Turkey.

Traditionally the eggplant puree that accompanies this dish is made using a béchamel sauce, but as I'm not keen on gloppy flour-based sauces, I prefer to take a lighter approach. In Turkey they use the local *Kas gruyère* or *kaşar*, a mature yellow cheese, but you could also use a cheddar style. As this dish is fairly rich, it really only needs a simple green salad to accompany it.

You'll find the red pepper paste used here in Middle Eastern food stores.

1½ pounds lamb (from the leg or shoulder)
2 ounces unsalted butter
2 red onions, cut into 1½-inch dice
3 cloves garlic, finely chopped
2 teaspoons chopped oregano
1 teaspoon honey
2 large vine-ripened tomatoes, skinned, seeded and diced
1 tablespoon hot Turkish red pepper paste
1 teaspoon sea salt
½ teaspoon freshly ground black pepper
1–1¼ cups Chicken Stock (page 41)
flat-leaf parsley leaves, chopped, to garnish

CHEESY EGGPLANT PUREE
2 eggplants
⅓ cup heavy cream
3 ounces Gruyère or cheddar, grated
good pinch of ground nutmeg
sea salt
freshly ground black pepper
squeeze of lemon juice

Trim the lamb of any fat and sinew and cut into 1-inch cubes. Melt the butter in a large, heavy-based casserole dish over medium heat, then brown the lamb all over and remove from the pan. If necessary, add a little more butter to the pan, then add the onion, garlic and oregano and sweat over a low heat for about 5 minutes. Add the honey, then increase the heat and cook for another couple of minutes. Stir in the tomatoes, pepper paste, salt, pepper and stock, then bring to the boil. Stir well and return the lamb to the pan. Cover the pan, lower the heat and leave to simmer very gently for 1–1½ hours, or until the lamb is tender and the liquid has reduced to a thick sauce.

To make the eggplant puree, prick the eggplants all over with a fork and set them directly on the naked flame of your stove top. Set the flame to low–medium and cook for at least 15 minutes, turning constantly until the eggplants are charred all over and soft. Remove from the flame and place on a small wire rack in a sealed container or plastic bag so the juices can drain off. Allow the eggplants to cool for about 10 minutes. (If you don't have a gas stove, stand the eggplants under the broiler, set to high, turning them regularly until charred. You won't get quite the same smoky flavor, but the effect is reasonable.)

When the eggplants are cool, gently peel away the skin from the flesh, taking care to remove every little bit or the puree will have a bitter burnt flavor. Put the eggplants into a bowl of acidulated water and leave for 5 minutes—this soaks away any lingering bits of burnt skin and turns the flesh pale and creamy. Drain the eggplants in a colander and squeeze them gently to extract any moisture, then chop finely.

Bring the cream to the boil in a small saucepan and simmer for a couple of minutes to reduce slightly. Stir in the cheese and nutmeg, then season with salt and pepper and a squeeze of lemon juice. Add the chopped eggplant and beat lightly to combine. Taste and adjust the seasonings as required.

To serve, spoon the eggplant puree into the center of a warmed serving platter. Make a well in the center of the purée and spoon in the lamb. Garnish with parsley and serve straight away with a green salad.

SERVES 4

Meat

In Turkish cooking, as is generally the case in the Middle East, meat means lamb. Thousands of years ago, tribes of nomadic Turks roamed the Central Asian steppes on horseback, surviving by hunting game animals and birds and supplementing their sparse diet with wild vegetation and berries. Eventually they learned how to herd flocks of sheep to mountain pastures, so sheep became one of the first animals to be domesticated, bred for their woolly coats, milk and tallow fat as well as their meat.

This meat-oriented diet persisted as the nomadic Turks migrated out of the steppes and into Anatolia. Every part of the animal was eaten, from the head to the tail, and all the organs in between! A taste for variety meats endures to this day: *kokoreç* (grilled intestines) are a favorite street snack; brains, liver and kidneys all make popular meze dishes; and tripe soup (*işkembe çorbası*) has famous restorative properties.

The solid white fat from the oversized sheep's tail was traditionally used as a cooking fat called *kuyrukyaği*. Even today *kuyrukyaği* is still the preferred cooking fat in many rural parts of Turkey, although olive oil is more common along the Aegean and Mediterranean coastlines.

Many frequently used methods of cooking meat can be traced back to the nomadic Turks and, subsequently, the Ottoman armies. Being constantly on the move, there would be little time in the evenings to set up camp and gather firewood for cooking, so meat was generally cut into very small pieces, threaded onto makeshift skewers and cooked over a quickly lit, fierce-burning fire. If camp was struck for several days, they would have time for slow-cooking in clay pots or cauldrons; victories were celebrated by roasting whole lambs in a deep pit known as a *tandır*.

Köfte kebabs, made from ground meat, evolved as an economic way of pounding or grinding somewhat tougher cuts of meat into a smooth palatable paste, flavored with herbs and spices. The paste was shaped into long sausages around skewers for grilling over hot coals, or formed into meatballs for frying. When wood was scarce or there was danger afoot, *köfte* would be eaten raw—*çiğ köfte*.

In times of abundance, hunks of meat were hung on the nomads' saddles to be tenderized by the rhythmic pounding of the horses' flanks in motion. The meat was then rubbed with spices and hung in the dry air to cure. It is thought that *pastırma*—a sort of Turkish pastrami—originated in this way.

Turkish lamb has a superb flavor. It is generally slaughtered young, and Turks will tell you that its flavor and texture are acquired from the wildflowers and herbs in the pastures where the lambs graze.

Slow-cooked lamb with quinces

We spent a wonderful afternoon and evening with Ayfer Unsal, the legendary
Turkish food writer. Ayfer is a wonderful cook and she prepared this superb dish
for us, explaining that her mother and grandmother used to brown the lamb over a
charcoal fire before slow-cooking it with the quinces. It's not necessary to peel the
quinces, as the skins disintegrate into the thick, cinnamon-spiced sauce.

Accompany this dish with Everyday Orzo Pilaf (page 128) or boiled new potatoes.
You'll find the red pepper paste used here in Middle Eastern food stores.

3½ pounds lamb shoulder chops
2 tablespoons olive oil
1 pound onions, very finely chopped
2 tablespoons tomato paste
2 tablespoons mild Turkish red pepper paste
1 tablespoon ground cinnamon
1 tablespoon ground allspice
1 tablespoon freshly ground black pepper
8 cloves
1 teaspoon sea salt
1½ tablespoons pomegranate molasses
3 small quinces
flat-leaf parsley leaves, shredded, to garnish

Trim the lamb chops of any excess fat. Heat the oil in a large, heavy-based casserole
dish over a medium heat. Brown the lamb chops all over, then remove from the pan
and set aside.

Add the onion to the pan, lower the heat and gently sweat for 15–20 minutes, until
very soft and lightly colored. Add the tomato and pepper pastes and all the spices to the
pan and stir well. Return the lamb chops to the pan and pour on enough boiling water
to cover everything generously. Stir in the salt and pomegranate molasses, then bring to
the boil. Cover the pan, lower the heat and simmer gently for 30 minutes.

Cut the quinces in half and peel and core them. Cut each half into four slices and add
to the pan. Cover the pan and cook for a further 30–40 minutes, until the sauce is thick
and fragrant and the lamb and quinces are both meltingly tender. Taste and adjust the
seasonings as required.

When ready to serve, garnish with parsley.

SERVES 4

The Aegean coast

[POULTRY AND GAME]

The western coast of Turkey has drawn travelers for centuries, keen to explore its extraordinary natural beauty and its famous ancient ruins.

Tempers and emotions were running high among our fellow travelers as we boarded the late-night plane to Edremit from Atatürk Airport. It was a Friday, and Istanbul's famously bad traffic had been magnified a hundred times by the fact that it was Mevlid-i Nebi, the Prophet's birthday. The roads were jammed with people heading home to their families for celebratory feasting, and we had made the flight by the skin of our teeth.

It was past midnight by the time we landed at the small country airport. Outside in the still blackness the chilly air was thick with the pungent smell of olives; it felt damp, dense and oily on our faces. We were in the Aegean region, Turkey's western shoreline— not just the land of the olive tree, but also the birthplace of European civilization.

The western coast of Turkey has drawn travelers for centuries, keen to explore its extraordinary natural beauty and its famous ancient ruins. In Greek and Roman times these shores were the center of the classical world and the site of some of its most revered cities. This was the land of Homer's heroes and the scene of legendary battles; it was the birthplace of Herodotus, the "father of history" and the place where Cleopatra met Antony.

We were staying in Ayvalık, a lively fishing town forty minutes south of Edremit. As we sped south along the highway we could just make out the shadowy shapes of olive groves that fringed the road. Suddenly the moon emerged from behind a bank of dark clouds, and there in the distance we glimpsed the Aegean Sea, shimmering silver in the pale moonlight.

Our friend Tara, an Istanbul resident for eighteen years, had invited us to stay in her old Greek-style house for the weekend. This was her hideaway from the big city, her pride and joy, and she'd spent the last ten years or so gradually renovating the once dilapidated building. Until ninety-odd years ago, Ayvalık was predominantly a Greek town and traces of this heritage are still clearly visible in the old Orthodox churches and traditional Greek stone houses, like Tara's, that climb up the steep hillside in the old part of town.

The next morning dawned gray, wet and cold. We peered gloomily out of the window at the sleeting rain, which seemed to make a mockery of Herodotus' claim to this being "the most beautiful sky and best climate in the world." On the upside, it was perfect weather for soup and our friend Tara knew just the place.

Bundled up against the chill we trudged down the steep cobbled streets to Ayvalık's broad harbor. Rain-lashed and iron gray, only a few diehard fishermen were out on their boats and the waterfront cafés were deserted. Tucked away in a backstreet, we ducked in out of the rain to Erdogan and Neslihan Kapukaya's small soup restaurant. Inside it was warm and snug, the windows fogged up from the collective breath of family groups happily slurping up the day's offerings.

A popular local haunt, the restaurant's specialty was indeed its soups. Neslihan, a rosy-cheeked, smiling woman, was standing behind the counter stirring a number of steaming cauldrons. Today's specials were: chicken broth, thick with vermicelli pasta; a sludgy brown lentil soup; a pale soup of veal brains, thickened with yogurt and egg yolks; and a hearty veal tongue and vegetable soup. Naturally we wanted to try them all!

We squeezed into a corner table and Erdogan came rushing up to greet Tara. Rattling off a few sentences in Turkish, Tara made the introductions. Erdogan was amused that we had come all the way from Australia to find ourselves in his small restaurant. Within moments, three little plates appeared on the table: a tangled mound of wild greens, glistening with oil, a bowl of thick garlicky yogurt and a dish of green olives. Next was the soup—all four varieties for us to try. And finally, thick slices of crusty white bread to mop it all up.

We were stunned to see so many different kinds of "wild greens" on display. As well as the varieties we recognized, there were the more exotically named golden thistle, feverfew and curledock, knotweed and glasswort.

The soups were garnished with wedges of lemon and on the table was a dish of finely ground chile flakes, a little jug of garlic water and another of vinegar. These are the traditional accompaniments for soup, intended to sharpen the flavor as well as the appetite of the diner. All were excellent: the brain soup, chock-full of slices of creamy variety meats, its mild flavor enhanced by Erdogan's suggestion of vinegar and garlic; the hearty tongue soup, thick with gelatinous shreds of meat as well as vegetables and rice; the chicken broth, clear and bursting with flavor; and the traditional lentil soup, properly brought to life by a squeeze of lemon and a dusting of chile.

By now the weather had improved—there were even welcome signs of sunshine breaking through the clouds—so we headed out to explore Ayvalık further. The narrow streets were filling with shoppers and we decided we needed to stock up on provisions ourselves. In the small marketplace we found more than twenty different varieties of local olives, and huge cans of olive oil. There were fresh white cheeses and creamy *kaymaklı* yogurt, another specialty of the region, with a thick "clotted" layer on its surface. We were stunned to see so many different kinds of "wild greens" on display. As well as the varieties we recognized, such as purslane and chicory, zahter and watercress, there were the more exotically named golden thistle, feverfew and curledock, knotweed and glasswort. To complete our purchases we bought soft, cheese-stuffed buns for the next day's breakfast, and a bottle of rakı for dinner.

We were dining that evening with another friend of Tara's, Hüsna Baba, who runs a popular *meyhane* restaurant tucked away in a shaded alleyway near Ayvalık's marketplace. Inside, the small front room was crowded with tables of men, their eyes fixed on a massive television set. But they looked over and greeted us with a friendly "*Merhaba*" as we came in out of the cold. To the rear was Hüsna Baba's small galley kitchen, and we breathed in the tantalising smell of frying fish. As honored guests we were seated in the second, larger room. Another long table was set for a group of scuba divers from the local diving school—regulars at Hüsna Baba's place.

Hüsna Baba was a small dapper man, with a sweet smile and big mournful eyes. After settling us in with glasses and ice for our rakı, he started feeding us. The menu was heavily oriented toward seafood, cooked in a simple, no-nonsense Mediterranean style. Hüsna Baba bought his fish fresh every day, straight off the boat, so the menu varied depending on the day's catch. That evening we feasted on little grilled *barbunya* (red mullet), calamari rings and tiny slivers of deep-fried mullet roe. A real treat was a dish of brilliant-orange sea urchin corals. We smeared the soft flesh onto white crusty bread, squeezed on a little lemon juice and tasted the briny flavor of the sea.

Later that evening the rakı had made us all mellow and the scuba divers at the next table were our new best friends. There had been several toasts to Turkey and Australia and the divers posed enthusiastically for photographs. As we said our good-byes one of the divers grabbed my arm. Leaning toward me, just a touch too eagerly, he whispered in my ear that somewhere out there, deep beneath the silvery Aegean waters, lay the lost city of Atlantis. It could have been the rakı talking, but actually I think he was just pulling my leg.

Pressed quail, liver and *pastırma* terrine with spiced almond butter

This is a fairly complex restaurant-style dish, but it is a wonderful way to use strongly flavored *pastırma*—Turkish air-dried beef—and makes a stunning dinner party starter. Ask your butcher nicely to bone the quail for you, unless you feel confident about doing it yourself.

I like to serve this with a herb salad dressed with a tangy vinaigrette dressing, garnished with pomegranate seeds if in season.

10 baby leeks
3 ounces olive oil
2¾ pounds chicken livers, cleaned of sinew, blood and fat
sea salt
freshly ground black pepper
4 quail, boned and left whole
¼ pound *pastırma*, very finely sliced

SPICED ALMOND BUTTER
2 ounces blanched almonds
¼ cup sesame seeds
2 heaped tablespoons ground coriander
1 heaped tablespoon ground cumin
½ teaspoon hot paprika
½ teaspoon sea salt
½ teaspoon freshly ground black pepper
7 ounces unsalted butter, softened
1 teaspoon thyme leaves

To make the spiced butter, dry roast the almonds in a frying pan over a low heat until golden brown, then pour onto a plate and repeat with the sesame seeds. Pulse the almonds and sesame seeds in a food processor until coarsely ground. Add the spices, salt and pepper and pulse until finely ground. Be careful not to overgrind or the mixture will become an oily paste. Pour the spice mix into a bowl and, using a fork, mash in the butter until smooth and homogeneous. Refrigerate until ready to use.

Trim the tops of the leeks neatly and rinse well to get rid of any lingering dirt. Steam the leeks until tender, then drain and leave to cool.

Heat a large, heavy-based frying pan over a high heat until almost smoking. Add a few tablespoons of the oil to the pan, followed by a third of the livers. Seal the livers all over until a good color—no more than 2 minutes in total, to keep them medium rather than overcooked—and season with salt and pepper. Remove the livers immediately to a wire rack and repeat with the remaining livers, adding more oil to the pan as required. Reserve the cooked livers until ready to assemble the terrine.

Season the quail lightly with salt and pepper. Heat a little more oil in another frying pan and sauté the quail, skin-side down, over a medium heat until lightly colored. Turn and sauté the other side for another 1–2 minutes, or until the quail are just cooked. Remove the quail from the pan, cut them in half and set aside.

When ready to assemble the terrine, melt the spiced butter gently, then stir in the thyme and keep in a warm place. Line a 12-inch cast-iron terrine mold with four layers of plastic wrap, leaving enough of an overhang to seal the finished terrine.

Arrange overlapping slices of *pastırma* across the base of the mold so the ends reach up the sides. Pack in enough chicken livers to cover the base and drizzle on about 4 tablespoons of the melted spiced butter. Place four pieces of quail along the length of the terrine, filling in the gaps with more chicken livers. Drizzle on another few

tablespoons melted butter. Arrange the leeks on top of this layer of chicken livers, running them end-to-end to fit the mold, then flatten and press them slightly. Drizzle with a little more spiced butter. Continue to form more layers using the remaining quail and chicken livers, drizzling in spiced butter as you go.

Pour any remaining butter over the final layer of the terrine and fold up the plastic wrap to cover and seal. Cut out a piece of polystyrene (or a few thick pieces of cardboard) just smaller than the mold and fit it inside the terrine. Set a 2-pound weight on the polystyrene (full cans will also do) and refrigerate for at least 6 hours.

After 6 hours remove the weights. When ready to serve, unwrap the terrine and invert it onto a serving plate, then cut into ¾-inch-thick slices.

SERVES 10–12

Circassian chicken

The origins of this slightly strange dish, one of the masterpieces of Ottoman cuisine, are unclear. Did the name come about as a kind of homage to the fair-complexioned Circassian lovelies that were brought from their homeland northwest of the Caucasus Mountains to the palace harem as concubines and wives to the sultans? Or is it because this dish uses fresh coriander, which is otherwise virtually unheard of in Turkish cooking but prevalent in the food of Circassia? Whatever the truth of the matter, for Westerners the best way to think of this dish is as a sort of pâté or spread to serve as a starter or as part of a meze selection. Serve it with hot buttered Turkish bread, triangles of toasted flat bread or Lavosh Crackers (page 249) and accompany with Pickled Cucumbers with Fennel (page 314).

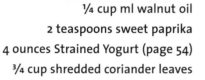

¼ cup ml walnut oil
2 teaspoons sweet paprika
4 ounces Strained Yogurt (page 54)
¾ cup shredded coriander leaves

POACHED CHICKEN
1 large free-range chicken breast on the bone
1 small onion, cut into quarters
1 stick celery
1 sprig thyme
2 bay leaves
½ lemon
½ teaspoon white peppercorns
1 red serrano chile, split lengthwise

WALNUT SAUCE
1 ounce unsalted butter
1 red onion, finely diced
4 cloves garlic
2 teaspoons sweet paprika
½ teaspoon hot paprika
2 slices stale sourdough bread, crusts removed
chicken stock (reserved from the poached chicken)
⅓ pound walnuts
1 teaspoon sea salt
¼ teaspoon freshly ground black pepper
squeeze of lemon juice

To poach the chicken, put the bird and all the aromatics into a large, heavy-based saucepan and cover with water. Bring to the boil, skimming away any fat and impurities that rise to the surface, then lower the heat immediately. Simmer very gently, covered, for 5 minutes. Turn off the heat and leave the chicken in the stock for 20 minutes.

Pull the chicken meat off the bone and shred it as finely as you can. Reserve for later. Strain the stock and reserve.

Meanwhile, heat the walnut oil and paprika in a small saucepan until just warm. Remove from the heat and leave to infuse for at least 30 minutes.

To make the walnut sauce, melt the butter in a heavy-based frying pan. Add the onion, garlic and both paprikas and sweat over a low heat for 10 minutes, until the onion is very soft.

Soak the bread in a little of the reserved chicken poaching stock. Squeeze it to remove as much moisture as possible and set aside.

Pulse the walnuts to fine crumbs in a food processor. Add the onion mixture and pulse to a smooth puree. Crumble in the bread, then add the salt, pepper and lemon juice and blend. With the motor running, trickle in enough of the reserved poaching stock to produce a mayonnaise consistency.

Pour the walnut sauce into a large bowl. Add the shredded chicken, strained yogurt and coriander and stir well to combine. Taste and adjust the seasoning.

To serve, place scoops of the pâté onto each of four serving plates. Use the back of a teaspoon to make an indentation in the surface and drizzle in a little paprika oil.
SERVES 4

Braised chicken with green chiles, *sucuk*, turnips and leek "noodles"

Sucuk is a spicy Turkish sausauge and can be found in Turkish or
Middle Eastern butchers and some specialist delis.

LEEK "NOODLES"

4 small leeks

3¼ cups Chicken Stock (page 41)

1 tablespoon extra-virgin olive oil

1 tablespoon lemon juice

sea salt

freshly ground black pepper

1 ounce unsalted butter

1 tablespoon extra-virgin olive oil

1¾ pounds boned free-range chicken thighs,
cut into chunks

sea salt

freshly ground black pepper

2 small turnips, peeled and cut into wedges

6 long green chiles, seeded and diced

1 large red onion, cut into large dice

1 vine-ripened tomato, seeded and
roughly chopped

1 clove garlic, sliced

1 teaspoon sweet paprika

1 bay leaf

4 ounces *sucuk*, sliced

1 cup leek poaching liquid (reserved from
making the "noodles")

squeeze of lemon juice

Trim the tops of the leeks neatly and rinse well to get rid of any lingering dirt. Pour the stock into a jelly-roll pan and add the leeks, then poach for 20 minutes, or until just tender. Drain and reserve the poaching liquid. Allow the leeks to cool.

When the leeks are cool enough to handle, use a sharp knife to cut them in half lengthwise and then into long, fine shreds. Put the shredded leeks into a bowl, then add the oil and lemon juice and season with salt and pepper.

Meanwhile, heat the butter and oil in a heavy-based casserole dish. Season the chicken pieces lightly with salt and pepper and sauté over a medium heat until golden. Add the vegetables, paprika, bay leaf, *sucuk* and ¼ teaspoon freshly ground black pepper, then stir briefly and add the leek poaching liquid. Bring to the boil, then lower the heat, cover and simmer for 10 minutes or until the turnips are cooked through.

When ready to serve, remove the pan from the heat and stir in the lemon juice, then taste and adjust the seasoning with salt and pepper, if necessary. Divide the braised chicken evenly between four warmed plates. Twirl the leek "noodles" into little swirling mounds on top of the chicken and serve immediately.

SERVES 4

Clay pot chicken with dates, *sucuk* and bulgur

In Turkish cookery there's a distinctive group of dishes known as *güveç*, which take their name from the earthenware pot in which they are cooked—in the same way that the tagine does in Morocco. In rural Anatolia the cooking pots may be sealed and buried in the ashes of a fire to cook slowly overnight—or, only slightly less romantically, in the local baker's oven. If you don't have a clay pot, a heavy-based cast-iron casserole dish will serve almost as well.

Güveç dishes encompass all sorts of meat or poultry cooked with legumes, vegetables and fruits. My addition of star anise is not remotely Turkish, but it adds a wonderful layer of aniseed flavor. This *güveç* is spicy with a lingering sweetness, so serve it with a light salad or braised wild greens. A dollop of yogurt would also be delicious.

Sucuk is a spicy Turkish sausauge and can be found in Turkish or Middle Eastern butchers and some specialist delis.

2 ounces unsalted butter
1 tablespoon extra-virgin olive oil
2 red onions, cut into thick rings
1 clove garlic, sliced
2 long red peppers, seeded and cut into rings
2 long green peppers, seeded and cut into rings
2 long green chiles, seeded and diced
1 heaped teaspoon ground cumin
1 level teaspoon ground cinnamon
generous splash of sherry
2 large vine-ripened tomatoes, skinned, seeded and diced
2 ounces bulgur, washed
1½ cups Chicken Stock (page 41)
1 stick cinnamon
2 star anise
few sprigs thyme
2 1-pound chickens
sea salt
freshly ground black pepper
1 tablespoon olive oil
2 ounces *sucuk*, sliced
4 medjool dates, seeded and cut into quarters

Preheat the oven to 400°F. Heat the butter and extra-virgin olive oil in a heavy-based casserole dish. Gently sweat the onions, garlic, peppers and chiles with the cumin and cinnamon for about 5 minutes, or until the vegetables soften. Add the sherry, tomatoes, bulgur, chicken stock, cinnamon, star anise and thyme and bring to the boil. Lower the heat, then cover and simmer gently for 5 minutes.

Meanwhile, cut the chickens into quarters and season lightly with salt and pepper.

In another heavy-based frying pan, heat the olive oil over a medium heat and brown the meat lightly all over. Add the *sucuk* and fry until golden brown on both sides. Transfer the poussins and *sucuk* to the casserole dish and tuck in the dates. Cover the pan and cook in the preheated oven for 20 minutes. Taste and adjust the seasoning and serve immediately.

SERVES 2

The Noah Vine

It may come as a surprise to learn that Turkey is the world's fourth-largest producer of grapes. The bulk of Turkish vines produce eating grapes, with most crops going to fresh table grapes or dried sultanas and raisins. Others go toward the manufacture of rakı, the national drink, but only a paltry 3 percent of total production is used for wine making.

Yet Turks are very keen to point out to visitors that their country was the birthplace of wine. The Bible tells us that after the flood, Noah planted a vineyard on the sunny slopes of Mount Ararat, becoming the world's first recorded vigneron. And it wasn't long before Noah became the world's first recorded drunkard, with the discovery that fermented grapes produce a delicious-tasting beverage with several happy side-effects.

This Biblical story has recently been given greater weight by archaeological discoveries of wine-making paraphernalia in the region that date back to the Neolithic period. There has been other corroborating evidence of early wine making in the nearby Zagros Mountains, in Titris Höyük in southeastern Turkey and in Hittite burial chambers near Ankara.

The discovery of these early artefacts has intensified the hunt for the "Noah Vine" in Turkey's Taurus Mountains. This elusive vine is generally regarded as the common ancestor for the many thousands of modern domesticated grape varieties in existence around the world today.

While Turkey may be the birthplace of wine, the country's wine industry today can perhaps best be described as still being in its infancy. Although early inhabitants, such as the Greeks, Romans and Byzantines, had a strong tradition of wine making, the arrival of Islam in the eighth and ninth centuries brought things to a halt. During the Ottomans' 600-year reign, Muslim subjects were prohibited from drinking wine, although minority Christian communities of Greeks and Armenians still produced wine in very small quantities.

The modern Turkish wine industry owes its existence to Kemal Atatürk's modernizing drive and the removal of Islam as a state religion. As a result, the 1920s saw a boom in viticulture and many of Turkey's oldest wine companies date back to this time. Over the course of the last eighty years or so, dozens of small wineries have sprung up around the country, although their contribution is relatively small. The large producers—Doluca, Kavaklidere and Kayra—are the biggest players, each with an annual production of more than 10,000,000 liters.

With its Mediterranean climate of cool wet winters and hot dry summers, Turkey certainly offers a perfect environment for growing wine. And with a population of seventy-five million, it would seem there is limitless potential to develop the industry. But the Turks do not seem to have taken to wine in a big way. It's hard to pinpoint the reason why the domestic consumption of wine remains at less than 1 liter per capita per annum. It's not because alcohol consumption and intoxication are frowned upon in what is a predominantly Muslim population—after all, most Turks seem perfectly happy to drink beer and rakı in very healthy quantities.

One thing for sure is that the industry is not being helped by Turkey's prohibitive taxes. The current government taxes home-produced wines at a whopping 63 percent of the wholesale price, and has recently reduced import tariffs on European wines, allowing a flood of foreign wines to wash through the country. In the face of such obstacles, it is hardly surprising that many of the larger Turkish wine producers are now focusing their marketing efforts on more receptive overseas markets, such as Europe, North America and even Japan.

For a visitor to the country, though, there is something delightfully exotic and enticing about sampling new indigenous grape varieties, with names such as *yapincak*, *sultaniye*, *bogazkere*, *okuzgozu* and *narince*, to name but a few. And it's even more exciting to think that with each sip you're tasting a little piece of ancient history.

Chicken in pistachio, sumac and sesame crumbs

I like to serve this crunchy, moist and flavorsome chicken with Shepherd's Salad (page 108), which provides another textural element via its combination of cucumber, peppers, radishes and tomatoes.

4 small free-range chicken breasts, skinned
2 free-range eggs
sea salt
freshly ground black pepper
all-purpose flour
⅓ cup olive oil
lemon wedges to serve

PISTACHIO CRUMBS
4 ounces fresh bread crumbs
1 tablespoon ground sumac
finely grated zest of 1 lemon
2 ounces unsalted shelled pistachios, coarsely chopped
¼ cup sesame seeds
⅔ cup finely grated parmesan

To make the crumbs, put the bread crumbs into a food processor with the sumac, zest and pistachios and pulse briefly—you don't want to break up the nuts too much. Add the sesame seeds and parmesan and pulse briefly to combine.

Preheat the oven to 350°F. Lightly flatten the chicken breasts to an even ½-inch thickness.

When ready to cook the chicken, lightly beat the eggs with a little water in a shallow dish to make an egg wash. Set up a production line of seasoned flour, egg wash and crumb mix. First dip the chicken pieces into the flour, then the egg wash and finally the crumb mix, patting them carefully all over.

Heat the oil in a heavy-based frying pan and sauté the chicken pieces, two at a time, until golden brown all over—this should only take a few minutes. Transfer to a jelly-roll pan and cook for 8–10 minutes in the center of the oven. Remove the chicken from the oven and allow to rest for a few minutes before serving with wedges of lemon.
SERVES 4

Roast chicken with pine nut and barberry pilaf stuffing

one 3 to 3½ pound free-range chicken
sea salt
freshly ground black pepper
2 tablespoons olive oil
1 cup Chicken Stock (page 41)
watercress to garnish

PILAF STUFFING
10 ounces short-grain rice
2½ cups Chicken Stock (page 41)
2 ounces unsalted butter
1 large red onion, finely diced
2 cloves garlic, finely diced
2 ounces pine nuts
½ teaspoon ground allspice
½ teaspoon ground cinnamon
⅓ cup barberries
sea salt
squeeze of lemon juice
⅓ cup unsalted shelled pistachios,
roughly chopped
½ cup shredded flat-leaf parsley leaves

To make the stuffing, put the rice into a large bowl and rinse well under cold running water, working your fingers through it to loosen the starch. Drain off the milky water and repeat until the water runs clear. Cover the rice with cold water and leave to soak for 10 minutes. Drain the rice and rinse a final time, then drain again.

Bring the stock to the boil, then lower the heat and keep at a simmer.

Melt the butter in a heavy-based saucepan. Add the onion and garlic and sauté over a low–medium heat, stirring continuously, until the onion starts to soften. Add the pine nuts and spices, then increase the heat and sauté until the nuts start to color. Add the barberries to the pan, followed by the simmering stock. Season with salt, then return to the boil, stir briefly, and cover with a tight-fitting lid. Cook over a very low heat for 15 minutes.

Put the cooked rice onto a shallow tray and sprinkle on the lemon juice, pistachios and parsley. Use a fork to fluff up the grains and leave to cool.

Meanwhile, preheat the oven to 400°F. Clean the chicken, removing any excess fat from around the cavity. Stand the chicken upright and season lightly inside with salt and pepper. Spoon around half the stuffing into the cavity, being careful not to overfill it, and secure the skin at the opening with a small skewer. Set the remaining rice aside. Season the chicken lightly with salt and pepper and rub with oil, then transfer it to a heavy-based jelly-roll pan. Pour in half the stock and roast for 20 minutes. Lower the oven to 350°F and roast for a further 40 minutes. Remove the chicken from the oven and leave in a warm place for 10 minutes to rest.

While the chicken is resting, reheat the remaining stock and pilaf in a saucepan over a gentle heat. Spoon out the stuffing from the chicken and add it to the pan. Mound the rice onto the center of a warm serving platter. Cut the chicken into quarters, stack it around the rice and serve garnished with watercress.

SERVES 4

Skewered sweet-spiced duck

With its fatty skin, duck lends itself very well to fiercely hot grilling. It's important to make sure that the skin is all facing the same way when you are skewering the meat; otherwise you'll end up with a mix of crisp skin and burnt flesh. I like to serve this sweet duck with Spicy *Kısır* Salad (page 141).

4 duck breasts
1 heaping tablespoon Poultry Spice Mix (page 319)
sea salt
warmed flat bread to serve

Trim the duck breasts of any excess skin and sinew. Slice each breast into four strips. Thread the duck strips onto long flat metal skewers, two strips per skewer, making sure the skin is all facing the same way. Pack the duck strips onto the skewer fairly tightly, so that the meat will cook brown and crisp on the outside but remain a little pink inside.

When ready to cook, heat a griddle or heavy-based frying pan over a high heat. Dust the kebabs lightly with the spice mix and cook for 2 minutes on each side—around 8 minutes in total. Season with salt while cooking.

Serve the duck kebabs on pieces of warmed flat bread and let everyone help themselves to salad.

SERVES 4

Duck *döner* kebab

This recipe is a playful interpretation of the ubiquitous *döner* kebab—spit-roasted layers of lamb that are sliced into warmed flat bread, topped with salad, rolled up and eaten as a filling snack-on-the-go all around the Middle East and eastern Mediterranean. Try serving it with Soft Herb Salad (page 161).

1 large clove garlic
1 teaspoon sea salt
1 teaspoon sweet paprika
1 teaspoon ground cinnamon
1 teaspoon hot paprika
½ teaspoon ground allspice
½ teaspoon ground nutmeg
½ teaspoon freshly ground black pepper
3 ounces olive oil
4 duck legs, boned
4 long red chiles
2 vine-ripened tomatoes, sliced
1 quantity Soft Herb Salad (page 161) to serve
warmed flat bread to serve

Crush the garlic with the salt, then combine in a bowl with the spices and ⅓ cup of the oil. Trim the duck of any excess fat and sinew, keeping each piece of meat whole, then toss gently in the marinade to coat. Leave overnight or for at least 2–3 hours to marinate.

When ready to cook, preheat the oven to 325°F. Heat a heavy-based jelly-roll pan on the stove top over a high heat, then add the remaining oil and sear the duck pieces, skin-side down, until colored. Turn and sear the other side. Place a chile on top of each duck leg, then transfer to the oven and cook for 30–40 minutes.

Remove the duck from the oven and transfer to a wire rack on a tray to catch the juices. Rest for 5–10 minutes. Meanwhile, add the tomatoes to the salad and toss gently.

Slice each piece of duck leg very thinly and serve, drizzled with the juices, on pieces of warm flat bread with the roasted chiles. Let everyone help themselves to salad.
SERVES 4

An island journey

[SEAFOOD]

The old two-story stone houses painted in brilliant pinks, lilacs and yellows seemed to tumble joyously, one on top of the other, down toward the harbor.

he next morning was Sunday, and the memory of the previous night's rakı indulgence still lingered. Luckily the day had dawned bright and sunny, so a brisk reviving walk was in order. We climbed the narrow cobbled street behind Tara's house to admire the view. From the peak of the hill we could see beneath us a jumble of twisting lanes and red-tiled rooftops. The old two-story stone houses painted in brilliant pinks, lilacs and yellows seemed to tumble joyously, one on top of the other, down towards the harbor. In the distance, the bay of Ayvalık stretched out in a broad, lazy curve. The deep turquoise waters were dotted with little islands, basking like seals in the sunshine, and farther away still, we could see the purple mountains of Lesbos rising out of the Aegean Sea.

Perched as we were on the edge of the Greek archipelago, with the reminder of Ayvalık's own Greek heritage sprawled below us, it was strangely disconcerting to hear the muezzin's prayer call start up from the nearby mosque. Since the sixteenth century Ayvalık had been predominantly a Christian town, and Greeks and Turks had coexisted perfectly happily on these peaceful shores, undisturbed by politics. It was only in the 1920s, in the aftermath of war, when the twin imperatives of nationalism and religion led to a series of population exchanges, that Greek Christian families vanished entirely from the region. Their hurriedly abandoned houses were soon occupied by bewildered Muslim families, themselves uprooted and "repatriated" from nearby islands and other more distant parts of the Greek mainland.

Down on the shore, the fishermen were busy making up for yesterday's weather-enforced absence. We wandered along the quay past brightly painted wooden fishing boats, watching the catch being hauled ashore. There were buckets of red mullet, silvery dory and sea bass, some late-season anchovies, tiny papalina and a few large stingrays. Farther on, we admired a pyramid of neatly stacked razor clams, each tidy bundle carefully wrapped in newspaper, ready for sale.

Our eyes were drawn to a huddle around two men in a tiny blue rowboat. They were working their way through a crate of spiky black sea urchins; fascinated, we watched as one man used a pair of oversized scissors to crack them open, a little like slicing the top off a soft-boiled egg. His partner was carefully spooning out the brilliant orange corals and slipping them into small jars to sell to their waiting customers. Noticing our interest, a young man standing next to us explained in faltering English that the sea-urchin catch is highly protected, and restricted to Ayvalık, where the trade is passed down from father to son. The spiky black *denizkestanesi* are pried off the rocks using long, flexible lightweight poles and the professional fishermen are careful to collect only the largest, mature sea urchins.

By now the waterside cafés were filling up with Sunday strollers out enjoying the sunshine. Tara told us that in the hot summer months Ayvalık becomes a busy resort town, primarily visited by Turkish vacationers. It seems that European tourists tend to prefer the fleshpots of Bodrum and Marmaris further to the south.

Today we were doing as the locals, and heading for a day out on Cunda Island; also known as Alibey. This is the largest in the Ayvalık Islands group, sitting just a short ferry ride offshore. In fact, it's also connected to the mainland by a causeway and bridge, so we took the more expedient option of a bus ride, jammed in with the other day-trippers from Ayvalık. On the way out of town we passed a tatty-looking olive oil factory, quieter now, out of season, but Tara told us that after the harvest, when the factory is working at full steam, the pungent smell of olive oil hangs over the whole town like a heavy cloud.

Cunda Island had the sleepy feel of a resort town out of season. After weeks of cold weather, people seemed keen to make the most of the spring sunshine and

all along the shore restaurants were setting up for a busy lunch trade. At Ada's Restaurant, an eager waiter proudly pointed out the day's fresh selection before seating us at a table in the dappled shade, right by the water's edge.

The sea air had sharpened our appetites and we were ready to attack lunch. Our friendly waiter brought a plate of new season's artichokes, braised in olive oil, and another of briny green samphire, redolent of the sea. Next, a feast of mussels: some stuffed in the shell with rice, others served as a cold tomatoey braise called *pilaki*, and finally, a platter of delectably crunchy fried mussels with a thick garlic dipping sauce. We munched contentedly in the warm sunshine, listening to the waves lapping gently at the quay. Between mouthfuls, Tara told us that Ada's husband caught much of the restaurant's fish himself, and she pointed him out, sitting on an upturned barrel mending his nets, cup of tea at his side.

Farther along the harbor, *dondurma* and *lokma* sellers were vying for attention, and we felt duty-bound to give them both our custom. Luckily we had just enough room after our fish lunch to enjoy pistachio ice cream in freshly made waffle cones and a little tub of syrup-soaked doughnuts, hot from the deep fryer.

Ready to explore more, we headed inland, away from the bustling waterfront, following a cobbled lane that led us gently up the hill toward an old Greek Orthodox church. Long abandoned by its Christian congregation, it had fallen into a state of disrepair; its

Through an open gateway we spied a
dainty white goat gazing curiously back
at us. And then an elderly lady appeared,
clutching in her arms a baby kid.

columns were crumbling and the stucco work was cracked and faded. As we turned the corner, the houses thinned out and the village quickly gave way to small fruit orchards and neat, densely planted plots of land. Farther away, the hillsides were covered with pine and olive trees and we could smell mint on the warm breeze.

From behind a high stone wall we heard a quavering voice calling out, "Come my pretty daughters, come my little girls!" and through an open gateway we spied a dainty white goat gazing curiously back at us. And then an elderly lady appeared, clutching in her arms a baby kid. She seemed surprised to see us, but invited us in to admire her brood.

Like many villagers, the old lady and her husband were largely self-sufficient. They grew their own wheat and vegetables; the goats provided milk, yogurt and cheese; the chickens produced eggs. When the weather was good, her husband was still, God willing, sprightly enough to go out fishing; otherwise they made do with a largely vegetarian diet. We were charmed by her smile and willingness to share her life with us, complete strangers that we were. She seemed equally fascinated by us, and did her best to ply us with gifts of honey and freshly laid eggs. Following Tara's example, we said our thanks and farewells in the traditional way, kissing the old lady's hand and touching it to our foreheads. As she waved us good-bye, she smiled her sweet smile and asked us to come back and see her again.

Stuffed mussels, Istanbul street-style

For us, a defining image of Istanbul will always be the great trays of gleaming blue–black mussels that are sold from vendors around the street cafés, markets and waterfront. They were exquisitely displayed, the shells open just enough to reveal their stuffing of plump orange mussel, herbed rice, pine nuts and currants. Always willing to make the most of this bounty, we also learned the elegant art of eating these mussels: you break off the top shell, squeeze on a little lemon juice, then use the loose shell as a scoop to spoon the delicious contents straight into your mouth.

There's also an art to opening live mussels, but it definitely gets easier with practice. Soaking the mussels in warm water first relaxes them, so that the shells open a little. You then insert a sharp knife between the shells along the flat edge and cut through the mussel where it is attached to the top, rounded end. The shells can then be pried open gently and filled with the traditional rice stuffing before cooking.

This is a great starter—for an extra-special presentation, lightly brush the shells with vegetable oil to give them a glossy sheen.

¼ cup currants
⅓ pound short-grain rice
30 mussels, cleaned and bearded
⅓ cup olive oil
2 ounces pine nuts
1 large onion, finely diced
2 cloves garlic, finely chopped
¼ teaspoon ground nutmeg
1 teaspoon ground cinnamon
1 vine-ripened tomato, grated
pinch of sea salt
boiling water
⅓ cup finely chopped dill
⅓ cup finely chopped flat-leaf parsley leaves
lemon wedges to serve

Soak the currants in a little warm water for 10–15 minutes, then drain.

Meanwhile, put the rice into a large bowl and rinse well under cold running water, working your fingers through it to loosen the starch. Drain off the milky water and repeat until the water runs clear. Cover the rice with cold water and leave to soak for 10 minutes. Drain the rice and rinse a final time.

Soak the cleaned mussels in a sink or large bowl of warm water for about 10 minutes.

Heat the oil in a saucepan. Fry the pine nuts, onion, garlic and spices on a medium–low heat for about 10 minutes until the pine nuts begin to color a light golden brown. Stir in the drained rice, tomato and currants and cook for 2 minutes. Season lightly with salt, then pour on enough boiling water to just cover the rice. Stir, then bring to the boil and cover with a tight-fitting lid. Cook over a very low heat for 15 minutes, or until the liquid has been absorbed. Put the rice into a shallow bowl, then fork through the herbs and leave to cool a little.

To prepare the mussels, use a small sharp knife and work over a large bowl to catch and reserve the juices. Hold each mussel by its narrow end, with the "pointed" edge facing outward. Insert the knife between the two shells near the large rounded top and cut through the mollusk where it is attached. You should then be able to pry the shells open, taking care not to break them—the idea is to open them slightly, not fully, and for the mussels to stay in their shells.

Strain the reserved mussel juice into a measuring cup and add water to make it up to about 2 cups if necessary, then pour this into a large, heavy-based saucepan. Stand a colander inside the pan. Spoon a generous amount of rice into each mussel, then squeeze the shells shut and wipe away any excess. Stack the mussels in the colander and cover with wet parchment paper. Weight the mussels down with a plate to keep them from opening too wide as they cook. Cover the pan and bring to the boil, then lower the heat and simmer for about 20 minutes.

Remove from the heat and let the mussels cool in the pan. When cold, refrigerate for at least 1 hour before serving chilled or at room temperature.

Stack the mussels onto a serving platter when ready to serve. To eat, break off the top shell, squeeze on a little lemon juice, then use the loose shell to scoop out the contents.

SERVES 4–6

Feta- and dill-stuffed sardines fried in chile flour

Sardines are hugely popular in Turkey, eaten fried, stuffed, wrapped in vine leaves or grilled over charcoal. I always think that their oily texture and flavor needs to be subdued by strong accompanying flavors. Here I use salty feta combined with chile and herbs—it works a treat. Enjoy them as a starter with a glass or two of chilled rakı.

8 sardines, filleted and butterflied
½ cup all-purpose flour
¼ teaspoon sweet paprika
¼ teaspoon hot paprika
3 tablespoons olive oil
sea salt
freshly ground black pepper

FETA AND DILL STUFFING
6 ounces feta, crumbled
1 long red pepper, roasted, peeled, seeded and diced
¼ teaspoon freshly ground black pepper
1 teaspoon finely grated lemon zest
½ teaspoon dried mint
2 tablespoons finely chopped dill
2 tablespoons shredded mint leaves
1 small red serrano chile, seeded and finely diced

To make the stuffing, combine all the ingredients in a bowl and mash with a fork to a smooth, homogeneous paste.

Open out the sardine fillets and lay them skin-side down on your work surface. Make a ¾-inch-long incision along the natural seam, cutting right through the skin. This will stop the fish from bursting open when you fry it. Smear a tablespoon of the stuffing along one side of the fish. Close the fish and squeeze gently to seal. Repeat with the remaining sardines.

Mix the flour and spices together. Heat the oil in a heavy-based frying pan. Season the sardines with salt and pepper, then dust them lightly with the seasoned flour. Fry the sardines, four at a time, over a medium heat for around a minute on each side, or until golden brown.
SERVES 4

Shrimp baked with *haloumi* in a clay pot

Traditionally *güveç* dishes are cooked in little earthenware pots buried in the ashes of an open fire or barbecue. Different herbs are used depending on the region, and along the shores of the Mediterranean the wild basil that grows in profusion adds a lovely spicy note. You could also use dill, parsley or oregano with success. The combination of shrimp and melted cheese makes this dish rather rich. It would make a light supper or lunch for four people, with a salad of bitter green leaves and plenty of crusty bread to mop up the sauce and melted cheese. You could also serve it as part of a meze selection for eight people.

Pekmez, or grape molasses, is available from Turkish food stores.

8 raw jumbo shrimp, peeled (heads and tails removed)

2 ounces unsalted butter

1 small red onion, diced

1 clove garlic, finely chopped

1 long red pepper, seeded and cut into ½-inch dice

1 long red chile, seeded and shredded

1 teaspoon coriander seeds, roasted and lightly crushed

1 teaspoon caraway seeds, roasted and lightly crushed

pinch of saffron strands

¼ teaspoon freshly ground black pepper

few strips of lemon peel

sea salt

2 teaspoons *pekmez*

2 large vine-ripened tomatoes, skinned, seeded and chopped

¼ cup roughly torn basil leaves

extra-virgin olive oil

1½ ounces *haloumi*, washed and finely grated

Preheat the oven to its highest setting. Use a sharp knife to butterfly the shrimp and carefully pull away the intestines.

Melt the butter gently in a heavy-based frying pan. Add the onion, garlic, pepper, chile, spices and peel and season lightly with salt. Sauté over a low heat for about 15 minutes, stirring frequently, until the vegetables are soft. Add the *pekmez* and cook for 5 minutes, then stir in the tomatoes and bring to a gentle boil. Gently add the shrimp and basil to the sauce, then put it all into a heavy-based casserole dish—or an earthenware pot if you have one. Sprinkle with extra-virgin olive oil, then scatter on the *haloumi* and bake in the oven for 3–5 minutes, or until the cheese is bubbling and brown.

SERVES 4

Marinated whiting with baby fennel braise

Marinating fish, whole or in portions, in olive oil, lemon and garlic is popular all around the Aegean and Mediterranean shores of Turkey. There are few things to beat this approach for simplicity and flavor, although do make sure you use spanking fresh fish.

In this recipe I've paired pan-fried fish with a braise of baby fennel, tomatoes and olives—the very essence of the Mediterranean. Adding snipped fennel fronds to the fish marinade imparts a hint of anise that complements the braise beautifully. Use other small fillets of fish, such as needlefish, or even strips of salmon or shrimp, if you like. For a dinner party you might like to cook a medley of different fish—just make sure they are all a similar size.

eight 4-ounce whiting fillets
4 baby fennel, long stalks attached
2 tablespoons olive oil
1 small red onion, finely sliced
1 teaspoon ground cumin
¼ teaspoon hot paprika
10 kalamata olives, pitted and roughly chopped
1 vine-ripened tomato, skinned, seeded and diced
⅓ cup water
sea salt
freshly ground black pepper

MARINADE
2 cloves garlic
1 teaspoon sea salt
finely grated zest of ½ lemon
2 tablespoons chopped fennel fronds
1 tablespoon extra-virgin olive oil

Combine the marinade ingredients in a shallow dish. Add the whiting fillets and turn in the marinade so they are evenly coated. Cover and refrigerate for 30 minutes, basting from time to time.

Preheat the oven to 400°F. Trim the ends of the fennel stalks neatly. Cut each bulb into quarters lengthwise. Heat the oil in an ovenproof frying pan or small, heavy-based jelly-roll pan. Add the fennel, onion, cumin and paprika and sauté over a medium heat for 3 minutes. Add the olives, tomato and water to the pan and season with salt and pepper. Transfer the pan to the oven and cook for 8–10 minutes or until the fennel is just tender. Return the pan to the stove top and cook on a high heat until the liquid has reduced and you have a thick braise.

Heat a heavy-based frying pan over a very high heat. Fry the fish, four pieces at a time, for a minute per side until lightly colored. Serve immediately on top of the fennel braise.
SERVES 4

The Fish Doctor's stew—with black pepper, lemon peel and mint

We ate several times at a wonderful seafood restaurant in Istanbul called Doğa Balık. The chef-owner is nicknamed "The Fish Doctor" for his knowledge of and skill in cooking seafood—as well as for his habit of wearing green surgeon's scrubs! This is my interpretation of one of his wonderful dishes.

The Fish Doctor's stew included turbot and sea bass, but you could also choose a selection of baby snapper, John Dory, whiting or black bream. Cooking the fish on the bone adds incomparably to the flavor of the finished dish.

Serve with a plain rice pilaf or boiled potatoes and a green salad.

two 14–18 ounces whole baby snappers, cleaned
two ⅔-pound whole whitings, cleaned
sea salt
freshly ground black pepper
3 tablespoons extra-virgin olive oil
2 large onions, very finely diced
2 cloves garlic, very finely diced
½ teaspoon dried oregano
1 teaspoon dried mint
3 bay leaves
long piece of peel from 1 lemon
few sprigs thyme
½ teaspoon red pepper flakes
1 cup Chicken Stock (page 41)
baby chives to serve

Preheat your oven to its highest temperature.

To prepare each snapper, cut away the head just below the gills. Snip off the side fins and cut the fish in half crosswise through the bone. To prepare each whiting, cut away the head, then cut the body into three pieces crosswise through the bone. Season well with salt and pepper.

Heat the oil gently in a heavy-based casserole dish. Add the onion and garlic and sweat very gently for a few minutes until they start to soften. Add the oregano, mint and bay leaves, peel and ½ teaspoon freshly ground black pepper, then cook over a low heat for another 5 minutes. Lay the pieces of fish on top of the onion mixture, then sprinkle on the thyme and red pepper flakes, add the stock and transfer to the very hot oven. Cook for 8 minutes, which should be long enough to color the fish and just cook it through. Remove the pan from the oven, sprinkle with snipped baby chives and take to the table straight away.

SERVES 4

The Fish Doctor

One of the most interesting people we met in Istanbul was İbrahim Soğukdağ, also known as "The Fish Doctor." İbrahim Bey is the chef-owner of the city's highly respected fish restaurant Doğa Balık, in Cihangir. Dubbed "The Fish Doctor" because of his penchant for wearing surgeon's scrubs, he is obsessed with seafood, a passion he dates back to his early childhood.

We sat down to chat with The Fish Doctor in his sunny rooftop restaurant, looking toward the Bosphorus in one direction and across the Golden Horn to the Old City in the other. With his serious manner and immaculately coiffed silver-gray hair, it did feel a little like an appointment with one's cardio-thoracic surgeon! But in the late afternoon sunshine he relaxed and mellowed as he told us about some of his earliest memories of eating fish as a four-year-old child. To this day he greatly prefers it to meat.

The Fish Doctor began his working life selling fish at market and shortly afterward, working from a tiny restaurant near the Eminönü waterfront, learning how to cook it. The catches in and around Istanbul are plentiful and he was soon discovering the best ways to prepare and cook turbot, bluefish, mackerel and *hamsi*—the local variety of anchovy—from the chilly waters of the nearby Black Sea. Simple cooking techniques, such as grilling or pan-frying, that allow the inherent flavor of the fish itself to shine through.

He also began researching traditional recipes for seafood stews, or for stuffing whole fish with wild herbs before baking.

The more The Fish Doctor learned about fish, the more he began to value its health-giving properties; over time, a new obsession arose, sparked again by childhood memories. He told us that the hillsides around Kastamonu, the Black Sea village where he grew up, are overrun with different types of wild greens, many specific to that region. In rural Turkey, especially in mountainous areas and along the Aegean coastline, wild greens form an important part of the local diet, but, for The Fish Doctor, gathering and eating this wild vegetation was a part of his childhood that had fallen away since moving to Istanbul.

A partnership between the bounty of the sea and the bounty of the hillsides seemed only natural to The Fish Doctor, and the name of his restaurant—*doğa*, meaning nature, and *balık*, meaning fish—reflects this happy marriage. He started bringing in produce from the Black Sea and Aegean and now, on any given day, his restaurant will have around thirty different types of wild greens and herbs on offer as part of a vast selection of meze. And on the several occasions we ate at Doğa Balık we tried a fair few. Wild nettles, purslane, chicory and borage were some of the more familiar names we tasted, but

others, such as feverfew, coltsfoot, knotweed and curledock, were like something from a medieval cookery book.

Above the meze display at Doğa Balık, there is a chart of the different varieties of wild greens, outlining their various health-giving properties. Clearly they were working their magic on The Fish Doctor himself as the next day we learned from one of the waiters that the tiny toddler we'd seen running around the restaurant tables was his eight-month-old son. Not bad for a man of his advancing years!

Fried fish sandwich

Admittedly, tucking into fried fish sandwiches at home doesn't have quite the same romance as eating them on the shores of the Bosphorus, but these are very tasty and would make a quick-and-easy weekend lunch.

2 tablespoons olive oil
1 teaspoon sea salt
½ teaspoon freshly ground black pepper
½ teaspoon sweet paprika
four ¼-pound catfish fillets
1 baguette
extra-virgin olive oil
2 tablespoons good-quality mayonnaise (optional)
1 romaine lettuce (inner leaves only), shredded
2 vine-ripened tomatoes, sliced
½ small red onion, finely sliced into rings
½ cup mint leaves
2 pickled green chiles, shredded
generous squeeze of lemon juice
lemon wedges to serve

Heat the olive oil in a heavy-based frying pan. Combine the salt, pepper and paprika and sprinkle over the fish fillets. Fry the fish, about 2 minutes on each side, until crisp and golden brown.

Meanwhile, split the baguette lengthwise and brush inside with extra-virgin olive oil and add the mayonnaise, if using. Fill the baguette with lettuce, then top with the tomato, onion, mint and chile. Place the hot fish on top and squeeze on the lemon juice. Press the baguette shut and use a very sharp, serrated knife to cut it into quarters. Serve wrapped in napkins with lemon wedges alongside.
SERVES 4

Roasted whole baby snapper with almond and sumac crumbs

Fish in Turkey is often served with nut *tarator* sauces, and I've included a couple of recipes for such sauces elsewhere in this book. For a change, this time I've turned the nuts into a crunchy coating for the fish.

Serve this dish hot from the oven with a salad or braised vegetables.

four ⅔-pound whole baby snappers, cleaned
sea salt
freshly ground white pepper
⅓ cup extra-virgin olive oil
4 long red, yellow or green peppers
4 cloves garlic, peeled
1 large red onion, cut into cubes
small handful of thyme sprigs
1 teaspoon dried oregano

ALMOND AND SUMAC CRUMBS
finely grated zest of 2 oranges
2 tablespoons olive oil
⅓ pound blanched almonds
2 cloves garlic
½ cup homemade dried bread crumbs
¼ cup sesame seeds
1 tablespoon ground sumac

To make the crumbs, leave the orange zest out on a plate to dry overnight or put it into a very low oven for 30 minutes. This will intensify the flavor.

Heat the olive oil in a heavy-based frying pan, then gently fry the almonds until golden brown. Remove and drain on paper towels. Add the garlic to the pan and fry gently until it just starts to color, then remove from the pan to drain with the almonds. Fry the bread crumbs, tossing, until just colored. Put all the fried ingredients into a blender. Wipe out the pan to remove any remaining oil and toast the sesame seeds until just colored, then add these to the blender with the sumac and dried zest and blend to form crumbs.

Preheat the oven to 325°F. To prepare each snapper, cut away the head just below the gills. Snip off the side fins and cut the fish in half crosswise through the bone. Season with salt and white pepper. Brush the fish pieces with half the olive oil and coat them with the crumbs.

In a bowl, tumble the peppers, garlic, onion and herbs with the remaining oil, so that everything is evenly coated, then put into a heavy-based jelly-roll pan. Arrange the crumbed fish on top and roast for 25–30 minutes, or until the fish is just cooked.
SERVES 4

The ruins of Pergamum

[DUMPLINGS, BREADS AND PASTRIES]

The spectacularly sited amphitheater unfolds fanlike in the steep slope of the hillside. We perched ourselves at the top and gazed out at the view, feeling just a bit dizzy in the midday sun.

We left Ayvalık in the cool early morning, bound for Bergama and the ruins of ancient Pergamum. On either side of the main road, gently rolling hills were thickly covered with olive trees, their leaves flashing silver-gray in the light breeze. As in ancient times, the olive makes a significant contribution to the local economy: around three-quarters of the region's farming land is used for the cultivation of close to two million trees. In fact, Ayvalık is known throughout Turkey as the olive capital and renowned for the excellent quality of its oil.

As we sped farther south, the landscape began to change. The hillsides became rockier, the vegetation more sparse and olive trees gave way to groves of cypress and pine trees. It wasn't long before we turned off the highway, heading inland toward the small modern town of Bergama, and, beyond it, the massive peak that rises up more than 300 yards from the plain.

Of all the ancient cities that are scattered along Turkey's western shores, Pergamum surely has the pick of the sites, with its dramatic views of the surrounding countryside and the glittering Aegean Sea in the distance. According to Homer, Pergamum was such an excellent lookout that Zeus popped over from Mount Olympus to check out the action in the nearby Trojan wars.

Archaeologists believe that the site was settled as early as the eighth century BC, but Pergamum's golden years were in the third and second centuries BC, when it was one of the most powerful and richest city-states in Asia Minor, rivalling Athens and Alexandria as a cultural center. Not much remains of Pergamum's former greatness and glories, it must be said, but we spent a happy few hours clambering among the

ruins and taking in the expansive view. By Roman times, the city had a population of more than 300,000, and helpful posters around the site show that it was laid out in a strictly hierarchical manner. Palaces and temples enjoyed pole position on the peak, and government buildings, shops and houses spread out farther down the hillside.

We wandered over to the spot where the massive altar to Zeus, with its famous frieze depicting the battle between the gods and the giants, once stood. The remains of the altar itself have been transported to Berlin as a kind of reward to the German archaeologists who were responsible for much of Pergamum's excavation. The altar has been reconstructed in the Berlin Museum and there were more helpful posters showing us how splendid it looks in its new location.

Pergamum is perhaps best remembered for its magnificent library, built by Eumenes II in the second century BC. The library reputedly held 200,000 volumes, a clear sign of Eumenes' pretensions to cultural grandeur. Legend tells us that the quality of the Pergamum library was viewed by Ptolemy of Egypt as such a threat to his own great library at Alexandria that he cut off the export supply of papyrus from the Nile. As a result, the ancient method of using animal skins to write on was revived and refined in Pergamum. It was known as *pergaminus*—pergamum paper—from which the English word *parchment* originated.

A little way down the hill past the library ruins is the spectacularly sited amphitheater, unfolding fanlike in the steep slope of the hillside. We perched ourselves at the top of its eighty-odd rows of stone seats and gazed out at the view, feeling just a bit dizzy in the midday sun.

The parking lot was filling up fast with tourist buses, which seemed a sign for us to head off for lunch. Dodging the attention of the ice-cream vendors near the ticket office, we pointed the car down the hill and maneuvred our way carefully along the steeply winding road back to Bergama.

After our exertions clambering around the hilly ruins, we felt the need for something substantial; however, the guidebooks were worryingly silent on the subject of Bergama's eating establishments. But a short while later, seated in a clean and tidy restaurant, we were tucking into generous bowls of *mantı* dumplings.

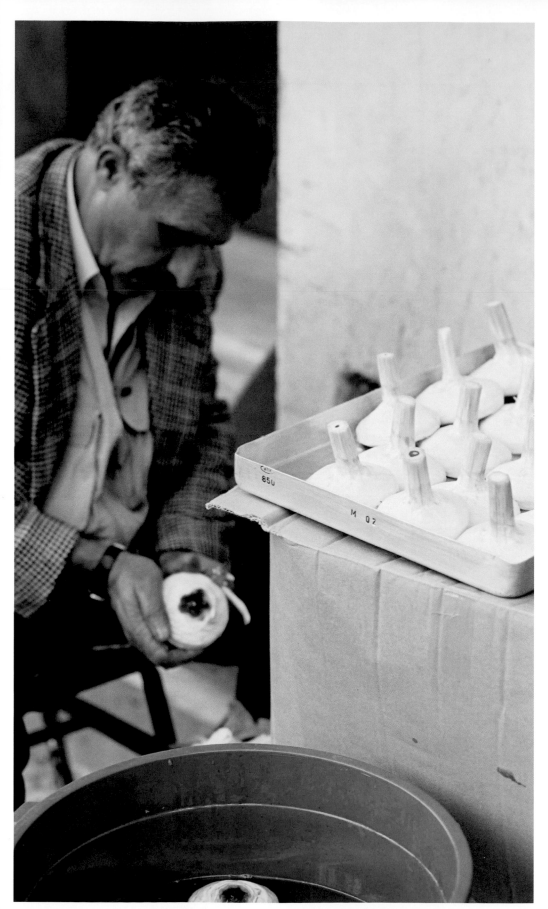

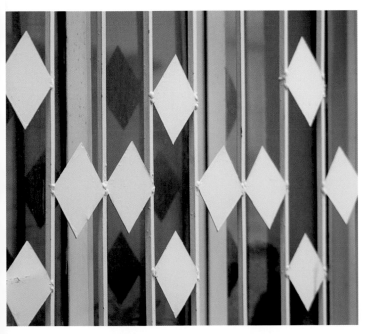

The very best *mantı* are
homemade, the pasta dough
slippery and soft under a creamy
blanket of garlicky yogurt.

We'd been quite surprised to discover that pasta is such a feature of Turkish restaurant menus, but a little research had revealed that *mantı* is one of the original dishes of the steppes, dating back, in all likelihood, to the nomadic Uyghur Turks in the mid-eighth century. The Uyghurs were strongly influenced by the culture of Northern China, and the same tradition of stuffing little dumplings can be seen in both cuisines to this day.

The Turks brought *mantı* with them when they migrated west into Anatolia, and although they're generally considered a specialty of eastern and southern Turkey, they now feature widely on restaurant menus around the country. The very best *mantı* are homemade, the pasta dough slippery and soft under a creamy blanket of garlicky yogurt. This version was a little on the chewy side, but on the surface of the yogurt was a delicious swirl of sizzling butter, spiked with dried mint.

Thus fortified we decided to walk off a few calories at Pergamum's other major attraction, the Asklepieum, on the outskirts of Bergama. The Asklepieum was a kind of ancient health spa, catering to stressed Roman officials and gladiators in need of a spot of pampering or purging. Much like today's spas, treatments included mud baths, mineral springs, massage and dietary advice, and even a spot of dream analysis.

The Asklepieum became world famous in the second century, largely thanks to Galen—the wonder doctor of his time. Physician to the stars, he treated gladiators and emperors, and more importantly made a significant contribution to modern-day medicine with his theories about the human circulatory and nervous systems.

Like visitors to this famous health center two millennia ago, we wandered down the broad colonnaded street toward the grand entrance foyer. Off an open forecourt were treatment rooms, a medical library, a temple to Asklepios, the god of healing, and a handsome amphitheater where waiting patients were entertained by plays and gladiatorial wrestling matches—the modern-day equivalent of the waiting-room television set.

We seemed to be the only visitors to the Asklepieum that afternoon and all was peaceful as we ambled past the sacred well, easily resisting the temptation to sip from its scummy waters. We paused for a moment in the sunshine; a few basking lizards scuttled out of sight under a fallen column and a small tortoise lumbered its way slowly through the daisies. Around us the grass was splattered with red poppies.

Making our way back along the colonnaded bazaar to the parking lot, we passed a cluster of souvenir stands and juice vendors offering freshly squeezed pomegranate juice. "Madam! Please madam! Have you had your vitamin C today?" they entreated. Our eyes were drawn upward to the Pergamum acropolis, high on the hillside. The white marble ruins gleamed in the sunlight and we couldn't help but think that in its golden years this would have been a pretty good place to live.

PİDE
1-KG. 1.50 YTL
1 - ADEDİ 134 GR.
1 Adedi 0.20 -YKR.

K.D.V. DAHİL

Mantı in yogurt with sizzling paprika butter

We spent a fascinating afternoon in Istanbul with Turkish food journalist Engin Akin, who showed us how to make the silky, soft dough that's used to make *mantı*, a sort of Turkish ravioli. We watched, fascinated, as Engin and her helpers made the tiny dumplings. "The smaller the better," Engin said. "Although, really, it's a sort of snob thing to make them so tiny!" We enjoyed the results for lunch in a traditional garlic-laden yogurt sauce drizzled with sizzling butter.

Although Turkish women deftly roll the dough into paper-thin fineness, if you have a pasta machine at home feel free to use it. Just work the dough through each setting until you reach the finest one. When made correctly, *mantı* dumplings are around the size of a grape, and it takes great patience and dexterity to shape and seal them with the traditional finish—but it's worth having a go!

7 ounces minced lamb
1 small onion, grated
sea salt
freshly ground black pepper
3 cloves garlic
14 ounces Greek-style yogurt
2 ounces unsalted butter
½ teaspoon hot paprika
½ teaspoon dried mint

MANTI DOUGH
14 ounces bread flour
2–3 large free-range eggs
1 teaspoon sea salt

To make the *mantı* dough, lightly beat two of the eggs, then put these into the bowl of an electric mixer with the flour and salt. Use the dough hook to work it to a stiff dough—if the dough is too stiff, add the remaining egg, lightly beaten. Knead for about 5 minutes, then put the dough onto a lightly floured work surface and knead by hand for a further 5 minutes or so until smooth and elastic. Place the dough in a lightly oiled bowl, then cover with plastic wrap and leave to rest for about 1 hour.

Divide the dough into pieces the size of a golf ball. Working with one piece at a time, roll the dough on a lightly floured work surface to form a large, paper-thin rectangle. Cut into strips around 1½ inches wide. Repeat with the remaining dough. Stack the strips on top of each other and cut into 1½-inch squares. (If you have a pasta machine, roll the dough through the settings, then trim the sheets to end up with 1½ inch squares.)

Combine the lamb and onion in a bowl, then season with salt and pepper. Place a chickpea-sized amount of filling in the center of each *mantı* square.

If you're brave enough to attempt the traditional shape, bring two opposite corners together over the filling and press to join at the top. Repeat with the other two corners, carefully moistening and pinching the side "seams" as you go to seal them. You should aim to end up with a four-cornered star-like shape. For an easier option, simply moisten the edges with a little water and fold the pastry over the filling to create little triangles, then squeeze to seal. Whichever shape you decide to make, ensure that the edges are sealed well so the filling doesn't come out as the *mantı* cook. Place the *mantı* on a lightly floured tray as you complete them and repeat until all the dough and filling has been used.

Crush the garlic with 1 teaspoon salt, then beat into the yogurt until well combined.

Bring a large saucepan of salted water to the boil. Drop in around half the *mantı*—they will rise to the surface within 1½–2 minutes as they are cooked. Use a large slotted spoon to transfer the cooked *mantı* to four warmed serving bowls. Repeat with the remaining *mantı*.

Spoon the garlic yogurt sauce over the warm *mantı*. Quickly sizzle the butter in a small frying pan, then add the paprika and mint and heat until foaming. Swirl the sizzling butter over the *mantı* and serve straight away.

SERVES 4

Shellfish *mantı*—Turkish ravioli in a crab and saffron broth

If you make your own pasta it's well worth having a go at making *mantı* traditionally (page 244). It's up to you whether you go all the way and learn how to produce the tiny, pleated dumplings as well. On the other hand, gyoza dumpling wrappers make a good substitute and are readily available from Asian grocers.

24 round gyoza wrappers or
1 quantity *Mantı* Dough (page 244)
3⅓ cups Crab Stock (page 41)
sea salt
2 tablespoons extra-virgin olive oil
¼ teaspoon sweet paprika
pinch of hot paprika
flat-leaf parsley leaves, shredded, to garnish

SEAFOOD STUFFING
⅔ pound raw shrimp meat, finely chopped
¼ pound raw crab meat, finely chopped
1 tablespoon chopped mint leaves
2 tablespoons chopped dill
½ teaspoon dried mint
1 long green chile, seeded and finely chopped
finely grated zest of 1 lime
2 hard-boiled free-range eggs, roughly chopped
1 tablespoon extra-virgin olive oil
drizzle of honey
sea salt
freshly ground black pepper

To make the stuffing, combine all the ingredients in a large bowl. Refrigerate for 30 minutes to chill thoroughly.

To make the *mantı*, put a teaspoon of filling into the center of each gyoza wrapper. Moisten the edges with a little water and fold over to make a half-moon shape. Use your fingers to press the edges together and seal well.

Bring the stock to a simmer in a large, heavy-based saucepan. Taste and adjust the seasoning by adding salt, if required. Reduce the heat to keep the stock at a very gentle simmer. Bring another large saucepan of salted water to the boil. Add the *mantı* to the water and poach for 4–5 minutes or until they are cooked and rise to the surface. Use a large slotted spoon to lift them out to drain in a colander.

Meanwhile, gently heat the oil and two paprikas to body temperature in a small saucepan. Tip the bright red oil into a small tea strainer lined with paper towels over a small bowl.

To serve, ladle the stock into four warmed bowls. Divide the *mantı* between the bowls and drizzle with a little of the paprika oil. Garnish with parsley and serve immediately.
SERVES 4

Soft *simit*

"Simiiiit!" The sight and sound of the *simitçi*—*simit* vendor—will be familiar to nearly all visitors to Turkey. His first round is in the morning, as he weaves his way through the streets pushing his *simit* cart or carrying a tray of the warm, sesame-encrusted bread rings on the top of his head. He'll be out again later in the day with a freshly baked batch, tempting shoppers with an afternoon snack.

No Turk in their right mind would ever dream of making their own *simit* at home. For a start they're just too readily available, and they take many long hours of rising. So instead, here's a recipe for a simpler version. These are almost scone-like, with a crisp shell and a slightly sweet, soft and moist interior. *Simit* are quite irresistible hot from the oven, spread liberally with butter and jam and enjoyed as an afternoon tea treat.

Simit are often distinctively flavored with *mahleb* (ground cherry kernels), but you can omit this if you can't find it in your closest Middle Eastern food store.

1 teaspoon dried yeast

heaping ¼ cup superfine sugar

approximately ½ cup warm water

3 free-range eggs

17 ounces bread flour

1 tablespoon sea salt

9 ounces unsalted butter (at room temperature), diced

2 teaspoons ground *mahleb* (optional)

1 cup sesame seeds

Dissolve the yeast and a generous pinch of the sugar in ¼ cup of the warm water and set aside in a warm place for about 10 minutes until frothy.

Lightly beat one of the eggs. Sift the flour and salt into a large bowl and stir in the remaining sugar. Make a well in the center and add the beaten egg with the butter, *mahleb* (if using) and yeast mixture. Use your fingers to work in the flour and enough of the remaining water to make a fairly stiff dough.

Put the dough onto a lightly floured work surface and knead briefly until just smooth, being careful not to overwork it. Transfer to a lightly greased bowl, then cover with a tea towel and leave to rest at room temperature for 30 minutes.

Preheat the oven to 350°F. Divide the dough into 22 portions, each around 1½ ounces. Roll each portion into a little log about 7 inches long. Shape the logs into rings, pressing the overlapping ends together to join. Lightly beat the remaining eggs in a shallow bowl, and put the sesame seeds into another shallow bowl. Dip one side of each *simit* into the egg mixture, then into the sesame seeds. Transfer each *simit* as you finish to two cookie sheets lined with parchment paper. When all the *simits* are ready, bake for 20 minutes until golden brown. Transfer to a wire rack and leave to cool. The *simits* will keep for 2–3 days in a sealed container.

MAKES 22

Black Sea corn bread

The Black Sea region is famous around Turkey for producing corn, as the wet, mountainous terrain is unsuited to growing wheat. Locals use corn to make cookies, sweet wafers, flat breads and leavened corn breads. But we also found versions of these pale-golden rustic loaves of "Black Sea corn bread" as far south as Gaziantep, near the Syrian border. It is a fairly dense and chewy bread with a mild corn flavor, and is excellent toasted.

2 teaspoons dried yeast
½ teaspoon sugar
3 ounces warm water
7 ounces polenta
15 ounces bread flour
1 tablespoon sea salt
1½ cups cold water
olive oil

Dissolve the yeast and sugar in the warm water and set aside in a warm place for about 10 minutes until frothy.

Sift the polenta, flour and salt into a large bowl. Make a well in the center and add the yeast mixture and cold water. Use your fingers to work in enough of the flour mixture to make a sloppy paste. Sprinkle lightly with a little more flour mixture, then cover the bowl with a tea towel and set aside in a warm place for 20–30 minutes to form a "sponge."

Mix the remaining flour mixture into the sponge with your hands and work to a smooth ball. Add a little more cold water if necessary. Transfer to an electric mixer fitted with a dough hook and knead on a low speed for 10–15 minutes, until very smooth and shiny. Transfer to a lightly oiled bowl, then cover with a damp tea towel and leave to rest at room temperature for 2 hours or until doubled in size.

Knock back the dough, then put it onto a floured work surface. Shape gently into a round and put onto a lightly oiled cookie sheet. Cover with a damp tea towel and leave for a further 30 minutes or so, until the dough has doubled in size again.

Preheat the oven to 425°F. Bake the corn bread for 35–40 minutes, until golden brown and it sounds hollow when you tap the bottom. Transfer to a wire rack and leave to cool completely.

MAKES 1 loaf

Lavosh crackers

Lavosh are reputedly of Armenian origin, and they are crisp and delicate with just a hint of dill. They come in many shapes, and may be sprinkled with sesame, caraway or poppy seeds. I like to make them into elongated triangles, which is easy to do by simply cutting a long rectangle in half from corner to corner. Lavosh are a great addition to any cheeseboard, and I also serve them with dips and spreads.

It's important that the dough is rolled out paper-thin, so that you end up with light and crispy crackers. If you happen to have a pasta machine, all the better—just feed the dough through each of the settings until you reach the finest one.

9 ounces all-purpose flour
1 teaspoon sea salt
1 teaspoon superfine sugar
½ teaspoon dill seeds
1 ounce unsalted butter
5 ounces milk
1 free-range egg
additional 1 tablespoon milk
sesame, caraway or poppy seeds

Combine the flour, salt, sugar and dill seeds in a large bowl and rub in the butter. Use your hands to mix in the milk until the mixture comes together as a ball of dough. Knead for 5 minutes, then cover with plastic wrap and leave to rest for a minimum of 1 hour or overnight.

Preheat the oven to 300°F and line a cookie sheet with parchment paper.

Cut the dough into quarters, and work with one piece at a time (keep the rest wrapped). On a lightly floured surface, roll out the dough until paper-thin, or use a pasta machine, working through the settings. Transfer the sheet of dough to your work surface, then cut it into long strips about 2¼ inches wide, and carefully transfer these to the prepared baking sheet. Lightly beat the egg with the extra milk, then brush each strip of dough with this. Sprinkle the dough with seeds of your choice and allow to air-dry for about 5 minutes.

Cut each strip into triangles, rectangles or squares and bake for 10–15 minutes until golden and crisp, then transfer to a wire rack to cool. Repeat with the remaining dough. When all the crackers are cold, store them in an airtight container.

MAKES 20

Turkish pizza dough

Turkish pizzas are one of the country's most popular snacks. They are baked in wood-fired ovens, resulting in a wafer-thin, crisp base. Toppings vary from region to region, but the most widely available is known as *lahmacun* (opposite), which is made with a paste of mildly spicy lamb (and is known as *lahme bi-ajeen* in Lebanon and Syria).

Three topping variations follow this dough recipe: one is a traditional ground lamb topping and the others are my own creations. Once you've got the hang of them, try some of your own ideas, too.

1 tablespoon dried yeast
¾ teaspoon sugar
2 tablespoons warm water
5 ounces Greek-style yogurt
¼ cup extra-virgin olive oil
10 ounces bread flour
½ teaspoon sea salt
olive oil

Dissolve the yeast and sugar in the warm water and set aside in a warm place for about 10 minutes until frothy. In another small bowl, whisk the yogurt and extra-virgin olive oil.

Sift the flour and salt into a large bowl. Make a well in the center and add the yeast and yogurt mixtures. Use your fingers to work in the flour and form a smooth ball. Transfer to an electric mixer fitted with a dough hook and knead on a low speed for 10–15 minutes until very smooth and shiny. Transfer to a lightly oiled bowl, then cover with a damp tea towel and leave to rest at room temperature for 2 hours or until doubled in size.

Preheat the oven to 425°F. Knock back the dough, then put it onto a lightly floured work surface. Divide the dough into 10 portions. Roll each portion into a round, 6 inches in diameter. Brush lightly with oil and spread with your choice of topping. Bake for 6–8 minutes (a convection oven may take as little as 4–5 minutes) and serve piping hot.
MAKES 10 small crusts

Lamb and smoky chile *lahmacun*

A Turkish-style pizza topped with lamb is quite traditional—this is called *lahmacun*. Try to find lamb that is not too fatty, but not too lean either. In Turkey the lamb is finely chopped by hand with onion, tomato and parsley. Sometimes garlic and red pepper flakes will be included in the mix, sometimes a teaspoon of pomegranate molasses. You can also serve *lahmacun* with a big dollop of yogurt on top, a sprinkling of extra chile flakes and a squeeze of fresh lemon. Chilled *ayran*—a yogurt drink—is the usual accompaniment for this snack in Turkey.

2 long red chiles

7 ounces ground lamb (not too lean)

1 small red onion, finely diced

1 vine-ripened tomato, seeded and finely diced

¼ cup chopped flat-leaf parsley leaves

½ teaspoon smoky paprika

1 teaspoon extra-virgin olive oil

sea salt

freshly ground black pepper

1 quantity Turkish Pizza Dough (opposite)

olive oil

Roast the chiles over the naked flame of your stove, or under a broiler, until charred, then slip into a plastic bag to cool. When cool enough to handle, peel away the blackened skin. Place the ground lamb on a large chopping board and put the chiles, onion, tomato, parsley, paprika and extra-virgin olive oil on top. Use a very large knife to chop and mix everything together until well combined. The topping should be the consistency of a smooth, fine paste. Season with salt and pepper.

Preheat the oven to 425°F. Knock back the dough, then put it onto a lightly floured work surface. Divide the dough into 10 portions. Roll each portion into a round, 6 inches in diameter. Bake for 6–8 minutes (a convection oven may take as little as 4–5 minutes) and serve piping hot.

MAKES 10

Chicken and pistachio pizzas

Chicken is not at all traditional as a topping for Turkish or Middle Eastern pizzas, but I think this is a shame! Here I combine a base of lightly spiced ground chicken with tarragon, which has a slight aniseed flavor, and chopped pistachio nuts, to give a satisfying crunch. The result is a light and tasty pizza, perfect for a summer lunch or snack.

7 ounces boned, skinned free-range chicken thighs, ground

1 large shallot, finely diced

1 clove garlic, finely diced

1 tablespoon Poultry Spice Mix (page 319)

2 tablespoons chopped Russian tarragon

sea salt

freshly ground black pepper

2 tablespoons extra-virgin olive oil

1 quantity Turkish Pizza Dough (opposite)

olive oil

¼ cup unsalted shelled pistachios, roughly chopped

¼ cup finely grated parmesan

Place the ground chicken on a large chopping board and put the shallot, garlic, spice mix and tarragon on top. Use a very large knife to chop and mix everything together until well combined. The topping should be the consistency of a smooth, fine paste. Season with salt and pepper and use your hands to mix in the extra-virgin olive oil.

Preheat the oven to 425°F. Knock back the dough, then put it onto a lightly floured work surface. Divide the dough into 10 portions. Roll each portion into a round, 6 inches in diameter. Brush lightly with oil and spread with topping. Mix the chopped pistachios with the parmesan and scatter on top. Bake for 6–8 minutes (a convection oven may take as little as 4–5 minutes) and serve piping hot.

MAKES 10

Haloumi, crème fraîche and spinach pizzas

1¼ pounds spinach leaves, washed
1 shallot, finely diced
1 small clove garlic, finely diced
finely grated zest of ⅓ lemon
½ teaspoon dried mint
⅓ pound *haloumi*, washed and finely grated
¼ cup crème fraîche
sea salt
freshly ground white pepper
1 quantity Turkish Pizza Dough (page 250)
olive oil

Bring a large saucepan of salted water to the boil and blanch the spinach leaves in batches. Refresh in cold water, then squeeze firmly to extract as much liquid as you can.

Place the spinach on a large chopping board and put the shallot, garlic, zest and mint on top. Use a very large knife to chop and mix everything together as fine as you can get it until well combined. Put the spinach mixture into a large bowl and stir in the *haloumi* and crème fraîche. Season with salt and pepper.

Preheat the oven to 425°F. Knock back the dough, then put it onto a lightly floured work surface. Divide the dough into 10 portions. Roll each portion into a round, 6 inches in diameter. Brush lightly with oil and spread with the spinach topping. Bake for 6–8 minutes (a convection oven may take as little as 4–5 minutes) and serve piping hot. MAKES 10

Pide—Turkish flat bread

We use this dough to make the soft, slightly chewy flat bread known as *pide* or Turkish bread. It's typically shaped into a large rectangle or oval, and the top is marked with parallel rows of indentations and sprinkled with black nigella or sesame seeds. The same dough is used to make the long, open-faced *pide* pies (see pages 255–56), with all manner of savory fillings.

1 tablespoon dried yeast
pinch of superfine sugar
1½ cups warm water
15 ounces bread flour
1 teaspoon salt
¼ cup extra-virgin olive oil
2 free-range eggs
3 tablespoons milk
nigella or sesame seeds

Dissolve the yeast and sugar in ½ cup of the warm water and set aside in a warm place for about 10 minutes until frothy. Use your fingers to work 3 ounces of the flour into the yeast to make a sloppy paste. Sprinkle lightly with a little more flour, then cover with a tea towel and set aside in a warm place for 30 minutes to form a "sponge."

Put the remaining flour and the salt into a large bowl. Make a well in the center and add the sponge, oil and remaining water. Use your fingers to work it to a soft, sloppy dough. Don't panic: it is meant to be very sticky!

Transfer to an electric mixer fitted with a dough hook and knead on a low speed for 10–15 minutes until very smooth and springy. Transfer to a lightly oiled bowl, then cover with a damp tea towel and leave to rest at room temperature for 1 hour or until doubled in size. (From this point you can proceed to bake the *pide* bread or filled *pide* boats. You can also refrigerate the dough until you are ready to use it. It will keep for around 24 hours, but take it out of the refrigerator a good 3 hours before you want to use it, to give it time to return to room temperature slowly.)

When ready to bake the bread, preheat the oven to its highest setting with two pizza stones or oiled cookie sheets in it. Divide the dough in two, then form into rounds and leave, covered, to rest for 30 minutes.

Mix the eggs and milk to make an egg wash. Place the dough on a lightly floured work surface. Use the heels of your hands to press and flatten each piece of dough out to an 8-inch oval. Brush the surface liberally with the egg wash. Dip your fingertips into the egg wash and mark rows of deep indentations across and down the length of the dough, leaving a narrow border.

Now comes the tricky bit. Lightly flour the hot pizza stones or cookie sheets. Lift on the *pides*, stretching them gently and evenly. Sprinkle with nigella or sesame seeds and bake for 8–10 minutes until crisp and golden brown.

MAKES 2

Cheese, egg and onion *pide* pies

The addition of an egg makes these *pide* pies wonderfully filling. Make an indentation along the length of the topping and allow the egg to run along it—this will ensure it cooks more evenly.

1 quantity *Pide* dough (opposite)

9 ounces *haloumi*, washed and finely sliced

5 ounces mozzarella, finely sliced

1 heaping teaspoon ground sumac

½ teaspoon freshly ground black pepper

½ teaspoon dried mint

4 shallots, finely sliced

1 tablespoon extra-virgin olive oil

1 free-range egg yolk

3 tablespoons milk

6 free-range eggs

sea salt

Cut the dough into six even portions and leave, covered, to rest for 30 minutes.

When ready to bake the *pide*, preheat the oven to its highest setting with two pizza stones or oiled cookie sheets in it.

To make the topping, mix the cheeses, spices, mint, shallots and oil in a large bowl.

Roll each portion of dough on a lightly floured work surface to form a long rectangle, around 14 x 4 inches. Scatter a sixth of the cheese topping down the *pide*, leaving a ¾-inch border around the edge. Make a shallow indentation in the topping down the middle of each *pide*. Quickly fold up the two long sides of the dough, bringing them up and over the topping, but without meeting in the middle. Squeeze the sides together at each end, twisting slightly, so that the *pide* looks like a long canoe. Mix the egg yolk and milk to make an egg wash, then brush the dough with a little of this. Carefully transfer two *pides* to the hot stones or cookie sheets and bake for 5 minutes.

Crack one of the eggs into a small bowl and break the yolk. When the 5 minutes is up, open the oven door and carefully slip the egg into one of the *pides* so it runs naturally along the length of the indentation. Repeat with the other *pide*. Bake for a further 2 minutes. Bake the remaining pides in two batches, repeating the step with the eggs. Eat hot from the oven sprinkled with a little sea salt.

MAKES 6

Spinach, raisin and feta *pide* pies

Spinach and feta is a classic combination, but the addition of raisins adds a sweet dimension that I love.

1 quantity *Pide* dough (page 254)
⅓ cup raisins, roughly chopped
9 ounces spinach leaves, washed
1 clove garlic
1 teaspoon sea salt
1 shallot, finely sliced
½ teaspoon ground nutmeg
½ teaspoon freshly ground black pepper
finely grated zest of ½ lemon
2 tablespoons extra-virgin olive oil
⅓ pound feta, roughly crumbled
1 free-range egg yolk
3 tablespoons milk

Cut the dough into six even portions and leave, covered, to rest for 30 minutes.

Soak the raisins in a little water for 15 minutes, then drain. Meanwhile, bring a large saucepan of salted water to the boil and blanch the spinach in batches. Refresh in cold water, then squeeze firmly to extract any liquid.

When ready to bake the *pide*, preheat the oven to its highest setting with two pizza stones or oiled cookie sheets in it.

To make the topping, crush the garlic with the salt and mix with the raisins, spinach, shallot, spices, zest, oil and all but 1 ounce of the feta in a large bowl.

Roll each portion of dough on a lightly floured work surface to form a long rectangle, around 14 x 4 inches. Scatter a sixth of the topping down the *pide*, leaving a ¾-inch border. Quickly fold up the two long sides of the dough, bringing them up and over the topping, but without meeting in the middle. Squeeze the sides together at each end, twisting slightly, so that the *pide* looks like a long canoe. Mix the egg yolk and milk to make an egg wash, then brush the dough with a little of this. Dot the open surface of each *pide* with some reserved feta. Bake in batches, two at a time—carefully transfer the pides to the hot stones or cookie sheets and bake for 7 minutes. Eat hot from the oven.

MAKES 6

Cheese, *sucuk* and olive *pide* pies

Sucuk is a spicy Turkish sausauge and can be found in Turkish or Middle Eastern butchers and some specialty delis.

1 quantity *Pide* dough (page 254)
9 ounces *haloumi*, washed and finely sliced
5 ounces mozzarella, finely sliced
18 kalamata olives, pitted and cut in half
1 long green pepper, seeded and chopped
2 tablespoons extra-virgin olive oil
sea salt
freshly ground black pepper
4 ounces *sucuk*, sliced
1 free-range egg yolk
3 tablespoons milk

Cut the dough into six even portions and leave, covered, to rest for 30 minutes.

When ready to bake the *pide*, preheat the oven to its highest setting with two pizza stones or oiled cookie sheets in it.

To make the topping, mix the cheeses, olives, green pepper and oil in a large bowl, then season with salt and pepper. Roll each portion of dough on a lightly floured work surface to form a long rectangle, around 14 x 4 inches. Scatter a sixth of the topping down the *pide*, leaving a ¾-inch border around the edge. Lay some of the *sucuk* down the center, then quickly fold up the two long sides of the dough, bringing them up and over the topping, but without meeting in the middle. Squeeze the sides together at each end, twisting slightly, so that the *pide* looks like a long canoe.

Mix the egg yolk and milk to make an egg wash, then brush the dough with a little of this. Bake in batches, two at a time—carefully transfer the *pides* to the hot stones or cookie sheets and bake for 7 minutes. Eat hot from the oven sprinkled with a little sea salt.

MAKES 6

Cheese, *Sucuk* and Olive *Pide* Pie
(opposite)

Gruyère and spinach *gözleme*

In markets and villages, especially in the summer months, you'll see women in traditional garb sitting cross-legged at low, broad tables rolling out large thin rounds of *yufka* dough. These are then stuffed and folded, oiled and cooked on a flat griddle to make *gözleme*, a famous Turkish snack. Hot and oozing with melted cheese, they are irresistible.

Gözleme are popular all around the country, although there can be some regional variations in the filling—I offer three of my own favorite fillings here.

Yufka pastry requires great skill and patience to make but thankfully is available ready-made from Middle Eastern food stores.

1¼ pounds spinach leaves, washed

1 shallot, finely diced

1 small clove garlic, finely diced

sea salt

freshly ground white pepper

2 sheets *yufka* pastry

7 ounces Gruyère, finely grated

melted unsalted butter

Bring a large saucepan of salted water to the boil and blanch the spinach leaves in batches. Refresh in cold water, then squeeze firmly to extract as much liquid as you can. Place the spinach on a large chopping board and put the shallot and garlic on top. Use a very large knife to chop and mix everything together until well combined. Season with salt and pepper.

Open out a sheet of *yufka* pastry so you have a large round on your work surface. Use a sharp knife to cut the pastry in half, then cut each half into three equal wedges. Stack them on top of each other and trim the curved edge straight. Repeat with the other sheet of pastry so you have a total of 12 small equilateral triangles.

Working with one triangle of pastry at a time, smear a generous tablespoon of the spinach mixture into the middle of the triangle, leaving a border around the edge. Top with some of the cheese, then brush a little melted butter on the triangle's points and fold in the points to form a small enclosed triangle. Repeat until all the pastry, filling and cheese have been used.

Heat a heavy nonstick frying pan over a medium heat. Brush the *gözleme* with a little more melted butter and fry for 2–3 minutes, turning once. Serve hot from the pan.
MAKES 12

Feta and dill *gözleme*

Feta and dill is a popular filling for *gözleme*, but you could also use ricotta or curd cheese instead of feta for a milder flavor.

9 ounces feta, grated
1 free-range egg, lightly beaten
1 shallot, finely diced
1 small clove garlic, finely diced
½ cup chopped dill
sea salt
freshly ground white pepper
2 sheets *yufka* pastry
melted unsalted butter

Mix the feta, egg, shallot, garlic and dill in a large bowl, then season with salt and pepper.

Open out a sheet of *yufka* pastry so you have a large round on your work surface. Use a sharp knife to cut the pastry in half, then cut each half into three equal wedges. Stack them on top of each other and trim the curved edge straight. Repeat with the other sheet of pastry so you have a total of 12 small equilateral triangles.

Working with one triangle of pastry at a time, smear a generous tablespoon of the feta mixture into the middle of the triangle, leaving a border around the edge. Brush a little melted butter on the triangle's points, then fold in the points to form a small enclosed triangle. Repeat until all the pastry and filling have been used.

Heat a heavy nonstick frying pan over a medium heat. Brush the *gözleme* with a little more melted butter and fry for 2–3 minutes, turning once. Serve hot from the pan.

MAKES 12

Pastırma and goat's cheese *gözleme*

Yufka pastry is available from Turkish and Middle Eastern food stores. It generally comes in large pastry rounds, which can be cut or trimmed to size and shape. Traditionally *gözleme* are made as rectangular parcels, but I think these triangles are more fun.

2 sheets *yufka* pastry

½ pound *pastırma*, very thinly sliced

8 ounces soft goat cheese, crumbled

1 tablespoon dried mint

1 teaspoon lemon zest

2 tablespoons extra-virgin olive oil

melted unsalted butter

Open out a sheet of *yufka* pastry so you have a large round on your work surface. Use a sharp knife to cut the pastry in half, then cut each half into three equal wedges. Stack them on top of each other and trim the curved edge straight. Repeat with the other sheet of pastry to total 12 small equilateral triangles.

Working with one pastry triangle at a time, arrange slices of *pastırma* in the center of the triangle leaving a border around the edge. Scatter on the cheese and sprinkle with a little mint, lemon zest and oil. Brush some melted butter on the triangle's points, then fold in the points to form a small enclosed triangle. Repeat until all the pastry, *pastırma*, cheese, mint and oil have been used.

Heat a heavy nonstick frying pan over a medium heat. Brush the *gözleme* with a little more melted butter and fry for 2–3 minutes, turning once. Serve hot from the pan.

MAKES 12

On the old Silk Road

[DESSERTS]

The goats, sheep and cows that graze in the nearby mountains produce the country's sweetest milk, and the wild orchids that contain salep also grow abundantly in the mountain pastures.

S edat had arranged for us to meet up with his friend Emine Serin in Kahramanmaraş, en route to our next destination, the southeastern city of Gaziantep. Emine was a schoolteacher at a nearby town and she spoke English. "Em's a free-spirit," Sedat had said, when we'd asked if she would be able to take time off from school to be our translator and guide for the next five days. "She'll be over the moon to have a break from school and an adventure with you."

Through a series of text messages we'd arranged to meet her in Yaşar Pastanesi, a well-known pastry shop in the city center. And over a cup of strong black tea and a plate of walnut baklava we began to get to know each other. Within a few minutes of our meeting, I could tell that Greg was smitten! Emine, a tall young woman with a lovely face and a gentle, eager manner, had taken the task of helping us with our food research seriously. She'd organized for us to meet the owner and chef at Mado restaurant, and we soon found ourselves sitting in a packed dining room on the outskirts of the city.

It was pitch-black and windy outside and we were eating, of all things, ice cream. But this was not just any old ice cream; it was *dondurma*, the famous Turkish "stretch" ice cream. We'd encountered something similar on our visits to Lebanon and Syria and had grown addicted to the smooth elastic texture and subtle flavor. Like its Middle Eastern cousin, *dondurma* is a pounded ice cream and that unique stretchiness comes from mastic (plant resin) and salep (an extract of orchid root).

Talk to any Turk, and they'll tell you that Maraş is the true home of ice cream. The goats, sheep and cows that graze in the nearby mountains produce the country's

sweetest milk, and the wild orchids that contain salep also grow abundantly in the mountain pastures. In fact, Maraş *dondurma* is more than just stretchy; the ice cream we were tasting was firm enough to be eaten with a knife and fork and was perhaps better described as hard and chewy.

Chef Osman Demiroz had just treated us to a whistle-stop tour of the gleaming Mado ice cream factory, located behind the restaurant, which churns out around 50 tons a week for transportation all around the country and even overseas. As well as the traditional mild-flavored salep variety, Mado also makes a wide range of other flavors, including pistachio, almond, sour cherry, mulberry and blackberry, as well as bizarre flavors like pumpkin.

Of course, this ultramodern factory product, impressive as it was, didn't have quite the same romance as the handmade stuff. But during the long hot summer months, *dondurma* really comes into its own: local ice creameries put on a show with traditionally garbed men wielding long hand-forged metal rods and working the ice cream in a deep skinny barrel. Massive blocks of it hang out the front of shops, taffy-like from hooks, waiting to be sawn off with a sharp knife.

After we'd finished our ice cream it was time to move on to our next destination—an hour farther south, down near the Syrian border. By the time we reached Gaziantep it was almost midnight but the traffic was still chaotic, especially in the narrow streets near the bazaar, where our hotel was located. It turned out that Anadolu Evleri was just around the corner from one of Gaziantep's most famous kebab restaurants, which was doing a roaring trade, even at that late hour.

Anadolu Evleri was a delightful boutique hotel, located down a winding alleyway and set behind a high stone wall. Owner Timur Schindel and his wife Dila had bought four old Anatolian houses in 2001 and renovated them to provide thirteen charming rooms—if slightly quirkily appointed. Mine was tucked in under the eaves at the top of the house; it had whitewashed walls, an antique brass bed and wooden beams set into the sloping ceiling.

I slept through the early prayer call the next morning, but was awakened instead by pigeons clucking and cooing outside my windows. We gathered for breakfast in a sunny dining room overlooking the central courtyard, or *hayat*. In the dappled morning sunshine we could better appreciate the light- and dark-patterned paving stones, the soft honey-colored stonework and the graceful arched windows of the buildings. Timur explained that these features are typical of old Gaziantep houses, and it fascinated us how similar it was to the architecture we'd seen in Aleppo, over the border in neighboring Syria.

It has to be said that Gaziantep—or Antep, as it's generally called—gets pretty short shrift in the guidebooks. From a tourist perspective it's not the most obviously appealing city. And yet Gaziantep dates back to Hittite times and it has a Roman citadel to explore. The city is located between Mesopotamia and the Mediterranean, at the intersection point of roads connecting the east to the south, north and west—and it was a key spot on the old Silk Road.

We'd heard that Antep food is a wonderful blend of Arabic, Armenian, Kurdish and Anatolian influences, and we were keen to start exploring the nearby markets. First, though, we had an appointment next door, at İmam Çağdaş.

We met with Burhan Çağdaş in his large airy restaurant, the fourth-generation owner of the business. It was late morning and the place was already filling up with families, groups of women and young couples. A few seemed to be tucking in to an early lunch, but most were swooning over plates of delectable pastries. It was these pastries we'd come to investigate, because, as well as being renowned for kebabs, İmam Çağdaş is famous in Turkey for its exquisite baklava.

Antep baklava is made almost exclusively from pistachios, yet another thing the city is famous for, and it even lends its name to the nut—*Antep fıstığı*. Burhan brought over a small wooden bucket of pistachios for us to inspect. They were a vivid emerald green and much larger than any we'd seen before. "These pistachios are of exceptional quality," said Burhan, doling out handfuls of the nuts for us to taste. "With ordinary pistachios, you get maybe 500–600 to a kilogram. The pistachios from Antep, there can be 130–200 to a kilogram."

We nibbled at the pistachios delicately, aware that in Australia they are almost as costly as the emeralds they resembled. 'Eat, my friends, eat!' urged Burhan, trickling more nuts into our hands and chuckling at our expressions. Suddenly he leaped to his feet. "Come!" he instructed, marching across the cool marble floor of the restaurant to an elevator tucked away next to the busy kitchen.

Up on the third floor, above the restaurant's dining rooms, we walked into an extraordinary scene. Half the vast space was enclosed behind glass, where, in a cloud of fine white dust, a team of young men worked around a massive, long table. Using long wooden rolling pins called *oklava*, they rolled out stacked sheets of *yufka* pastry into ever-thinner layers. As graceful as ballet dancers, the *yufka* rollers rose onto their toes, then, arms fully extended, sank down onto the pastry, pushing and stretching it out in front of them. The effect was delicate, rhythmic and mesmerizing—a sequence of rolling and lifting—the pastry itself, billowing in the air, as light as gossamer.

As graceful as ballet dancers, the *yufka* rollers rose onto their toes, then, arms fully extended, sank down onto the pastry, pushing and stretching it out in front of them.

Burhan smiled and continued, proudly, "This work is very skilled. The boys, they start here as young as seven or eight years old to learn how to become a *yufka* chef. It takes many years, but if they make it, it is a job that earns them respect … and they will have it for life."

In the room next door, more men were busy assembling the large trays of pastries for baking. Some were draping the tins with layers of translucent pastry; others were scattering great handfuls of ground pistachios before gently settling on the top layers. Little boys, whose job it was to carry the trays of prepared baklava to the massive wood-fired oven, scuttled around the perimeter of the room.

We moved over to watch two men supervise the baking process. They were also specialists, knowing exactly where in the oven to place the trays and for how long, pushing them around on the end of long paddles and then whisking them out at just the precise moment.

Next, the trays of baked baklava were moved along a mini-assembly-line of gas rings. Each tray was spun around on the flame to maintain the temperature, before being flung onto the workbench where an elderly man ladled boiling sugar syrup onto the still-hot pans. We could see the top layers of golden pastry "dancing," as the syrup bubbled up from the sides of the tin.

Burhan introduced us to the syrup-ladler—his father. Although well in his sixties, Talat Çağdaş came into the workshop every day, as he'd done all his life. Burhan told us that his father no longer works as a *yufka* chef, but oversees the final part of the process. As we watched Talat Çağdaş lift the ladles of boiling syrup we could see that the knuckles on his hands were swollen, his fingers gnarled and distorted by the relentless, repetitive work. As is so often the case, beauty is achieved only at a cost. In the same way that ballet dancers' feet are destroyed by their art, it seemed that the dance of the *yufka* rollers exacted its own terrible price.

Flower of Malatya

This is a bit of a play on one of my signature desserts, the Rose of Damascus. One of the wonderfully generous people we met on our Turkish travels was Emine Serin, a schoolteacher living in Malatya, the apricot capital of Turkey. This dish was created for her.

To form the pastry "petals," you'll need to find a teardrop-shaped pastry cutter, which are readily available from specialist food stores.

They come in various sizes, and I like to use one about 5 inches long. You'll also need a round pastry cutter that is about the same size as the "base of the tear drop.

Amardine sheets are essentially dried apricot paste and are available from Middle Eastern and Mediterranean food stores. *Pekmez*, or grape molasses, is available from Turkish food stores.

---

unsalted shelled pistachios, slivered

8 dried apricots, cut into ¼-inch dice and rolled in confectioners' sugar

handful of citrus blossoms (optional)

pekmez to garnish

APRICOT ICE CREAM

1¾ cups water

1 cup sherry

4 cardamom pods, seeds only

1 pound amardine sheets

7 ounces superfine sugar

2 ounces mild honey

8 free-range egg yolks

2½ cups thickened cream

1 teaspoon vanilla extract

4 ounces Candied Walnuts (page 317), crushed

PHYLLO PASTRY PETALS

10 sheets phyllo pastry

7 ounces clarified unsalted butter, melted

4 ounces confectioners' sugar

3 ounces mild honey, warmed

To make the ice cream, combine half the water with the sherry and cardamom seeds in a heavy-based saucepan. Bring to the boil, then lower the heat. Add the amardine sheets and simmer gently, stirring occasionally, until they dissolve into a thickish, smooth consistency. Remove from the heat and allow to cool.

Gently heat the rest of the water with the sugar and the honey, stirring occasionally until the sugar has dissolved. When the syrup is clear, increase the heat and bring to a rolling boil.

Meanwhile, whisk the egg yolks in an electric mixer until thick, pale and creamy. With the motor running, slowly pour the hot sugar syrup onto the egg yolks. Continue whisking for about 5 minutes, or until the mixture cools. You will see it bulk up dramatically into a soft, puffy mass. Fold in the cream and vanilla extract and chill the mixture in the refrigerator.

Fold the amardine puree into the chilled ice cream base, then pour into an ice cream machine and churn according to the manufacturer's instructions. When nearly set, add the walnuts, mix well and pour into two 10 x 8½–inch (no more than ¾ inch deep) trays lined with plastic wrap. Transfer to the freezer until ready to assemble the dessert.

To prepare the phyllo pastry petals, preheat the oven to 325°F. Line and butter two cookie sheets. Put a piece of phyllo on your work surface and brush it liberally with clarified butter and dust with confectioners' sugar. Repeat with two more layers, drizzling half the warm honey instead of the confectioners' sugar on the third phyllo sheet. Stack, brush and dust another layer, then repeat with a fifth and final layer, but do not dust with confectioners' sugar. Repeat this process with the remaining five sheets of phyllo pastry. You should now have two stacks of phyllo pastry, each comprising five layers.

Use a 5-inch teardrop-shaped pastry cutter to cut nine petals from each pastry stack—18 in total. Carefully transfer the pastry petals to the prepared cookie sheets and

cover with parchment paper. Put another tray on top to weigh down the flowers and keep them flat as they cook. Bake for 8–10 minutes, or until golden. Remove from the oven and leave to cool.

When ready to assemble, remove the ice cream from the freezer and turn out onto a chopping board, then peel away the plastic wrap. Use a pastry cutter to cut out 12 ice cream rounds.

To serve, place a pastry petal in the center of each plate so that it points upwards, and top it with ice cream, aligning the curved edges. Add another pastry petal so that it overlaps the first slightly but tends to the left. Add another ice cream round and finish with another petal, tending farther to the left. Serve sprinkled with the slivered pistachios, the apricot pieces and orange blossom and drizzle with a little *pekmez*.
MAKES 6

Chewy Turkish ice cream

This is our version of the famous "chewy" Turkish ice cream using *sahlab*, which comes from the root of a wild orchid that grows in the mountains of central Anatolia, and mastic, acacia tree resin. Both contribute to the thick chewy texture and the unique flavor. Pure *sahlab* is almost impossible to find, but you may well find powdered *sahlab* (for making hot milky drinks) in Middle Eastern stores. You won't be able to replicate the distinctive stretchiness completely, but using the powdered form will go some way toward achieving it.

4 cups whole milk
1¼ cups heavy cream
1 large grain mastic
8 ounces superfine sugar
heaping ¼ cup *sahlab* powder or
1 teaspoon pure *sahlab*
long strip of peel from 1 orange
long strip of peel from 1 lemon

Put the milk and cream into a large heavy-based saucepan.

In a mortar, grind the mastic with a pinch of the sugar, then add the *sahlab*. Stir in about 7 ounces of the milk mixture to dissolve the powders, then stir this into the saucepan with the rest of the milk mixture and the remaining sugar. Add the citrus peels and bring gently to the boil, then lower the heat. Simmer for 10–15 minutes, whisking continuously to stop the mixture from catching and burning on the bottom of the pan. It will thicken to the consistency of a light pouring cream.

Pour the mixture into a bowl and press a sheet of wax paper, cut to size, down onto the surface to prevent a skin from forming. When cold, put into an ice cream machine and churn according to the manufacturer's instructions.

MAKES 3⅓ cups

Pistachio halvah ice cream

As well as being the sand-colored, sesame-based confectionery with which Westerners are familiar, halvah is also a type of Turkish dessert made from semolina or flour. Turkish confectioners often have displays of huge blocks of halvah—many studded with nuggets of emerald-green pistachios. Because it is not too sweet, it works brilliantly in ice cream.

1 cup whole milk
1 cup heavy cream
1 vanilla pod, split
long piece of peel from 1 lemon
4 ounces superfine sugar
5 free-range egg yolks
2 ounces pistachio halvah
1 ounce unsalted shelled pistachios

Put the milk, cream, vanilla pod and peel into a large, heavy-based saucepan and heat gently. Meanwhile, whisk the sugar and egg yolks by hand in a large bowl until thick and pale. Pour on the hot cream and whisk in quickly. Pour the mixture back into the rinsed-out pan and cook gently until it thickens to a custard consistency. You should be able to draw a distinct line through the custard on the back of a spoon. Remove from the heat immediately and cool in a sink of iced water. Stir from time to time to help the custard cool down quickly. Remove the vanilla pod and peel. Refrigerate the custard until chilled.

Pour the chilled custard into an ice cream machine and churn according to the manufacturer's instructions.

While the ice cream is churning, crush the halvah in a mortar to even crumbs. Pulse the pistachios in a food processor to form coarse crumbs. When the ice cream is nearly churned, add the halvah and pistachio crumbs and churn in briefly.
MAKES 2½ cups

Yogurt and honey sorbet

This is a silky, smooth sorbet with a light tang and subtle sweetness. It makes a wonderfully refreshing end to a rich meal. Serve it drizzled with a little more honey, or with a salad of fresh berries or stone fruits.

1½ cups water
8 ounces superfine sugar
1 tablespoon light corn syrup
9 ounces Greek-style yogurt
⅓ cup crème fraîche
¼ cup heavy cream
2 tablespoons honey
2 tablespoons lime juice

In a small saucepan, gently heat the water, sugar and corn syrup until the sugar has dissolved. Increase the heat and bring to a gentle boil. Simmer for 3 minutes, then remove from the heat and leave to cool. When cool, refrigerate until chilled.

Whisk together the yogurt, crème fraîche and cream, then chill.

Stir the honey and lime juice into the cold syrup, then stir this into the chilled yogurt mixture. Put into an ice cream machine and churn according to the manufacturer's instructions.
MAKES 2 cups

[Clockwise from left] Pomegranate
and Vodka Sorbet (opposite), Pistachio
Halvah Ice Cream (page 285), Yogurt
and Honey Sorbet (page 285)

Pomegranate and vodka sorbet

Serve this very adult sorbet in cocktail glasses with an extra splash of icy cold vodka.

1 cup water
9 ounces superfine sugar
3 ounces light corn syrup
1¾ cup pomegranate juice (around 4 large pomegranates)
3 ounces vodka
juice of 1 lime

Combine the water, sugar and corn syrup in a heavy-based saucepan and heat gently, stirring occasionally, until the sugar dissolves. When the syrup is clear, increase the heat and bring to the boil. Simmer for 5 minutes, then remove from the heat and leave to cool.

Stir in the pomegranate juice, vodka and lime juice. Pour into an ice cream machine and churn according to the manufacturer's instructions.

MAKES 2½ cups

Sour-cherry sorbet

1 cup water
2 ounces liquid glucose
10 ounces superfine sugar
4 ounces dried sour cherries
1½ cups blood orange juice
juice of up to 1 lemon

Combine the water, liquid glucose and 7 ounces of the sugar in a heavy-based saucepan and heat gently, stirring occasionally, until the sugar dissolves. When the syrup is clear, increase the heat and bring to the boil. Simmer for 5 minutes, then remove from the heat and leave to cool.

Put the cherries into a heavy-based saucepan with the orange juice and remaining sugar. Heat gently until the sugar dissolves, then simmer for around 5 minutes, or until the cherries are soft. Remove from the heat and leave to cool.

Add the cold syrup to the cold cherry mixture and stir in 2 tablespoons lemon juice, then blend to a smooth puree in a blender. Strain through a fine sieve, then pour into an ice cream machine and churn according to the manufacturer's instructions. Toward the end of the churning time, taste the sorbet and add a little more lemon juice to taste if required.

MAKES 2½ cups

Milk pudding with *labne*, apricot and Turkish cotton candy

This is the classic milk pudding recipe, which I've tweaked by adding strained yogurt to give it a lovely tang.

Turkish or Persian cotton candy is the super-sophisticated cousin of the familiar fairground sugary confection. You'll find it in a range of different flavors in Middle Eastern food stores and some upmarket delis. As well as looking spectacular, its delicate texture and melting sweetness are irresistible to young and old alike.

4 grains mastic
4 ounces superfine sugar
⅓ cup cornstarch
1 quart whole milk
long strip of peel from ½ lemon
long strip of peel from ½ orange
2 tablespoons orange-blossom water
8 ounces Strained Yogurt (page 54)
orange-flavored Turkish or
Persian cotton candy to garnish

APRICOT PUREE
10 ounces amardine sheets
5 ounces water
2 ounces superfine sugar
1 tablespoon lemon juice

Grind the mastic with ½ teaspoon of the sugar in a mortar, then mix with the remaining sugar and cornstarch in a bowl. Stir in 3 ounces of the milk to make a paste.

Put the rest of the milk into a large, heavy-based saucepan, then whisk in the paste until smooth. Add the citrus peels and bring to the boil, whisking continuously, then lower the heat. Simmer for 4–5 minutes, whisking continuously to make sure it doesn't catch and burn.

Remove from the heat, then strain into a bowl and cool in a sink of ice water, whisking continuously so that the mixture becomes light and fluffy. When the mixture cools to body temperature, stir in the orange-blossom water, then fold in the strained yogurt. Spoon into serving glasses and refrigerate until chilled.

To make the apricot puree, put the amardine, water and sugar into a heavy-based saucepan and cook gently, stirring occasionally, until the amardine softens and dissolves to a thickish, smooth consistency. Put into a blender and whiz to a smooth puree. For an even smoother consistency, pass the puree through a fine sieve, if you like. Stir in the lemon juice.

Spoon a little of the puree onto the milk puddings and keep chilled until ready to eat. Serve garnished with a top-knot of cotton candy.
SERVES 8

Turkish coffee creams

If you enjoy cardamom-scented Turkish coffee, then you'll love these indulgent creamy *petit pots*.

2 ounces dark-roasted, plain Turkish coffee, finely ground
4 cardamom pods, lightly crushed
1 stick cinnamon
1 cup heavy cream
2 ounces best-quality dark chocolate, grated
5 free-range egg yolks
heaping ¼ cup superfine sugar

Moisten the coffee grounds with a little water and put onto a muslin square with the cardamom pods and cinnamon stick, then tie securely with kitchen string to make a bag. Put the cream into a heavy-based saucepan with the muslin bag and bring to the boil, then lower the heat and simmer for 5 minutes. Turn off the heat and leave to cool and infuse for about an hour.

Squeeze the muslin bag back into the pan to extract as much flavor as possible, then discard it. Reheat the infused milk gently, then add the grated chocolate and stir until it has melted.

In a separate bowl, whisk the egg yolks with the sugar. Pour on the hot cream mixture and whisk gently to combine. Pour the mixture back into the rinsed-out pan and cook gently until it thickens to a custard consistency. You should be able to draw a distinct line through the custard on the back of a spoon. Remove from the heat immediately and cool in a sink of ice water. Stir from time to time as the mixture cools down.

Spoon the coffee cream into ramekins or little glasses and chill before serving.
MAKES 8

Dried fruit compote

Grapes, apricots and figs are all grown in abundance in Turkey, and after the harvest
a good supply is dried in the late-summer sun before being set aside for the winter.
Dried fruit compotes, known as *hoşaf*, are very popular throughout Turkey, where they
are sometimes served after the main part of the meal spooned over plain pilaf. *Hoşaf*
range from simple raisin compotes to brightly colored combinations of apricots, figs,
prunes and currants, sometimes with the addition of nuts.

You'll find the barberries and tiny wild Turkish dried figs in Middle Eastern food
stores, and some gourmet shops too.

9 ounces superfine sugar

1 cup water

½ stick cinnamon

2 cloves

4 cardamom pods

long piece of peel from 1 orange

long piece of peel from ½ lemon

3 ounces dried wild figs

3 ounces dried apricots

⅓ cup currants

¼ cup barberries

Combine the sugar and water in a heavy-based saucepan and heat gently, stirring
occasionally until the sugar dissolves. When the syrup is clear, add the spices and citrus
peels, then increase the heat and bring to the boil. Add the dried fruit and simmer for
5 minutes. Remove from the heat and leave the fruit to cool in the syrup.

Transfer to an airtight container and refrigerate until ready to use. The compote
will keep for up to a week.

SERVES 4–6

Sticky dried fig puddings

A variation on the universally popular sticky toffee pudding, this is a perfect winter warmer. The figs are less sweet and toffee-like than dates, and this particular recipe makes a surprisingly light sponge pudding.

As well as with the butterscotch sauce, you could also serve it with custard or lightly whipped cream.

½ pound dried figs, finely chopped

2 cups boiling water

1½ teaspoons baking soda

3 ounces unsalted butter (at room temperature)

9 ounces superfine sugar

3 free-range eggs

1 teaspoon ground ginger

9 ounces self-rising flour

BUTTERSCOTCH SAUCE

8 ounces unsalted butter

7 ounces heavy cream

12 ounces brown sugar

Preheat the oven to 350°F and butter twelve 5–7-ounce small metal molds, a 10-inch square cake tin or a 10 x 8 inch jelly roll pan.

Put the figs, boiling water and baking soda into a bowl, then stir well and leave to stand for 20 minutes.

Cream the butter and sugar in an electric mixer until light and fluffy. Add the eggs, one at a time, beating well after each addition. Mix the ginger into the flour, then sift onto the pudding mixture and fold in gently. Stir in the fig mixture and pour into the prepared molds, then bake for 15 minutes.

While the puddings are baking, make the butterscotch sauce. Combine all the ingredients in a heavy-based saucepan and bring to the boil, then lower the heat and simmer for 5 minutes. Stir occasionally, but don't overwhisk or the sauce will crystallize.

After 15 minutes baking, spoon a little sauce on top of each pudding, then return to the oven for a further 5 minutes, or until cooked when tested with a skewer.

To serve, unmold the puddings onto dessert plates, then invert them so the sticky surface is uppermost. Serve with extra sauce.

MAKES 12

Early morning in Gaziantep

[PICKLES AND PRESERVES]

Slightly perplexed to learn that we'd have to get up at 5 A.M. to enjoy this breakfast, we were even more alarmed to discover that it was going to be grilled liver kebabs—a challenge for anyone at that early hour, we felt.

he next morning saw us rising before the pigeons and the sunrise. We had arranged to meet a new friend, Filiz Hösukoğlu, for what we expected would be a rather challenging breakfast.

We'd met Filiz, a Gaziantep local, the previous day. She proved to be a font of knowledge about the city's culinary "must dos," turning up to lunch armed with a list of places to visit and people to meet. Her enthusiasm was infectious. "Tomorrow morning we will visit my friend Ali Bey and we will have *ciğer kebab*, a traditional Antep breakfast," she'd chirped. Slightly perplexed to learn that we'd have to get up at 5 A.M. to enjoy this breakfast, we were even more alarmed to discover that it was going to be grilled liver kebabs—a challenge for anyone at that early hour, we felt.

Our taxi edged its way down a narrow alleyway near the town market toward a crowd of men gathered outside a tiny hole-in-the-wall diner. We stumbled, bleary-eyed, over to Filiz, who was chatting cheerfully to Ali Bey, the liver chef. The air was blue with smoke rising from the grill and the place was bristling with purpose. Little clusters of tough-looking men crouched against the wall, or squatted on stools around low tables eating. Others were milling around in front of the grill, leaning in every now and then to help Ali Bey turn the skewers or to offer suggestions.

We stood around stomping our feet in the chilly morning air, admitting to Filiz, somewhat cautiously, that yes, it did indeed smell quite delicious. We sat down, squeezing in next to a balding man in an open-necked shirt and leather jacket, who glanced at us bemusedly. A few moments later Ali Bey came over to show what was on offer for breakfast. He proudly thrust a large tray of neatly arranged kebabs

Little clusters of tough-looking men crouched against the wall, or squatted on stools around low tables eating. Others were milling around in front of the grill, leaning in every now and then to help Ali Bey turn the skewers.

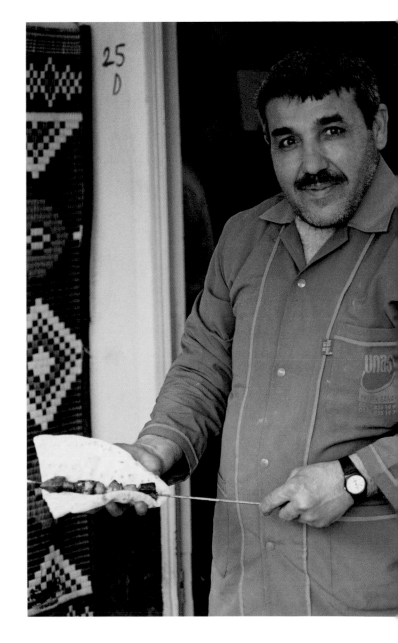

under our noses for us to choose. As well as calf's liver there were also kebabs of diced heart or kidney. In each case, the chunks of variety meats were alternated with lumps of lamb's tail fat to keep them moist over the fierce heat of the grill.

Greg's eyes lit up and he chose one of each; the rest of us were more restrained. Ali Bey whisked our selections off to the grill while his teenage son brought over the traditional kebab accompaniments. Onto the table went a battered tin plate of fresh parsley, mint and green onions; next came four little bowls of ground cumin, sumac, salt and chile flakes; and finally, bottles of cold *ayran*, the traditional yogurt-drink accompaniment for liver kebabs.

A little while later Ali Bey returned to our table brandishing our cooked kebabs. He deftly off-loaded them into soft floppy circles of flat bread and we sprinkled on our preferred garnishes. By now it was nearing 7 A.M. and most of his customers had taken themselves off to work. He sat down next to us, smiling, pleased to see how much we were enjoying breakfast. With Filiz translating, Ali Bey told us that he'd been working the liver grill for nearly forty years, having taken over the business from his father, Haydar. Every morning he got out of bed at 3 A.M. in order to select and prepare the best-quality variety meats for his customers. His *ciğerci* was open at 5 A.M. sharp and the last customers were served at 7 A.M.

He laughed when we asked him about this seemingly bizarre custom of eating kebabs for breakfast. "You know, Turks in this part of the country really love variety meats, but the liver kebab, it's a real Gaziantep thing," he explained. "In the winter it's cold and snowy here and liver kebabs make a good hot start to the day before you head off to work. And anyway, everyone knows liver is good for you; it builds up your strength and your blood."

We were ready for some exercise, so we said our good-byes and set off back to our hotel. The streets were coming to life. Bakeries and pastry shops were doing a

Stalls were festooned
with garlands of dried
eggplant, okra or
chiles, others were
piled high with hunks
of gently oozing
honeycomb or marbled
blocks of halvah.

brisk trade and, as we approached the covered markets, stall-holders were setting up their stands for the day. We wandered up and down the spice section, fascinated by the gleaming jars of pickles and the wide range of dried herbs and spices on offer. There were countless varieties of red pepper flakes to choose from as well as massive barrels of red pepper paste, each with a slightly different flavor.

Stalls were festooned with garlands of dried eggplant, okra or chiles, others were piled high with hunks of gently oozing honeycomb or marbled blocks of halvah. We drooled over the range of dried apricots and *pestil*—dried fruit leathers—and inspected bottles of myriad types of molasses from grape and carob, to mulberry and sumac. Metal buckets of all shapes and sizes contained yogurt and different kinds of brined cheese; *tulum*, a crumbly white goat's cheese, was especially fascinating as it is drained and matured in the goat's hairy hide. We were also curious to see displays of *tarhana* wafers. *Tarhana* is similar to Lebanese *kishk*, it's made from a fermented mixture of wheat and yogurt that is dried in the sun. In Turkey it's more commonly sold in powdered form, which is used to make a sort of instant soup.

On the outskirts of the noisy copper bazaar we passed a row of forlorn-looking Kurds, squatting on the pavement with their wares spread out on thin blankets in front of them. Among the thin nylon tracksuit pants and Day-Glo orange socks there were little mounds of vine leaves and plastic tubs of fresh green almonds. A trio of hollow-cheeked men in baggy suits tended a large samovar of bubbling tea and, all of a sudden, breakfast seemed a long time ago. It was time to head back to our hotel for a spot of refreshment and a bit of a sit down.

Pickles and preserves

While in Istanbul we found ourselves staying in the same neighbourhood as Asri Turşucu, one of the city's oldest and best-known pickle shops. Most days, as we set out on our daily adventures around the city, we would somehow find ourselves in front of this small corner shop, drawn by the stunning window display of pickles, gleaming like jewels in the morning sunlight. Inside, too, the shelves were stacked high with jars of all shapes and sizes.

One morning we did a quick tally of the produce on offer, identifying jars of cucumbers, red and green peppers, chiles, cabbage, beets, string beans, onions, okra, tomatoes, garlic and stuffed eggplant. And then there were more unusual items, such as medlars, pinecones and whole ears of corn, as well as a variety of pickle juices for drinking. Eventually we stopped counting, realizing that in Turkey just about every vegetable or fruit can and will be pickled!

The tradition of preserving summer's bounty is certainly alive and well in Turkey, and there are pickle shops in almost every town and village. In the cities, naturally enough, fewer people have the opportunity or time to indulge in home pickling, but in rural areas, come harvest time, it's still an annual tradition to lay down the season's surplus produce to brighten up mealtimes through the long cold winters.

All manner of vegetables are pickled in a simple vinegar-brine solution and fruits are preserved whole in sugar syrup or made into jams and jellies. The hot summer sunshine also makes it easy to dry fruit and vegetables. Tomatoes, peppers, apricots, figs and grapes are dried whole, or fruits are pounded into pastes and dried to form chewy fruit leathers known as *pestil*. Turkish markets stock an extraordinary range of *pestil*, sometimes jazzed up with nuts or coconut and rolled up to make a sweet called *kume*.

One of the most widely used Turkish preserves is *pekmez*, a sort of molasses made from boiled fruit pulp. *Pekmez* is traditionally used as an all-purpose sweetener, and in many rural areas villagers still prefer it to sugar. It's generally made from grapes, but we also found versions made from pomegranates and mulberries, quince, apple and date. *Pekmez* is poured over desserts and ice creams, or eaten as a sort of dip with bread. I use it with abandon, sloshing it into soups, stews and sauces, and even salad dressings, where it adds an indefinable sour-sweetness that I adore.

Spicy eggplant relish

If there is one ingredient that best sums up Turkey, it must undoubtedly be the humble eggplant. In the summer, the markets are overflowing with mounds of eggplants in myriad shapes and sizes; in the winter, strings of dried eggplants hang like exotic necklaces in the bazaars, waiting to be reconstituted in water, stuffed and braised in oil. In Turkey the eggplant is the king of the vegetables and lends itself to endless cooking styles, from grilling to baking, stuffing, pureeing, marinating, pickling and even being candied or turned into jam. It would be fair to say that I love eggplant as much as the Turks do!

2 large eggplants, peeled and
cut into ¾-inch cubes

sea salt

3 ounces olive oil

2 large onions, grated

8 cloves garlic, roughly crushed

1 tablespoon freshly ground black pepper

2 tablespoons sweet paprika

2 tablespoons ground cumin

2 large vine-ripened tomatoes, skinned,
seeded and diced

6 long red chiles, thickly sliced

2 tablespoons superfine sugar

juice of 2 lemons

Put the cubed eggplant into a colander and sprinkle liberally with salt, then leave for 30 minutes or so to drain. Briefly rinse, then pat dry and set aside.

Heat the oil in a large, heavy-based frying pan. Squeeze the grated onion well to extract as much juice as you can, then add to the pan with the garlic and spices and sauté over a high heat for 5 minutes. Add the tomatoes and chiles and cook for 2 minutes, then add the sugar and the eggplant cubes and season with salt.

Cook over a low–medium heat for about 30 minutes, stirring frequently to make sure nothing catches and burns. Toward the end of the cooking time add the lemon juice. Remove from the heat and allow to cool. The relish will keep in the refrigerator for up to a week.

MAKES 4 cups

Sweet pickled garlic

This recipe was inspired by an eighteenth-century Ottoman recipe. The strength of the garlic softens in the pickling liquor, and the cloves make a wonderful accompaniment to cold meats or salads.

2¼ pounds garlic
2 tablespoons coriander seeds
1 tablespoon white peppercorns
2 cups white-wine vinegar or apple vinegar
1 quart water
2 tablespoons honey
2 tablespoons currants

Separate the garlic cloves and remove any excess papery skin. Place in a large, non-reactive saucepan with the remaining ingredients except for the currants and bring to the boil. Lower the heat slightly and simmer for 10–15 minutes, until the garlic is tender. Remove from the heat and stir in the currants.

Divide the ingredients between the two sterilized 1-pint jars, then seal and turn them upside-down a few times to distribute the ingredients evenly. Leave in a cool, dry place for a month before using. The garlic will keep in the refrigerator for up to a month after opening.

MAKES 4 cups

Pickled onion rings in rose vinegar

These lightly pickled onion rings are delicious with cold and smoked meats and make a great addition to any salad—especially tomato salads. This is not a pickle to set aside and store—it needs to be eaten soon after it's made. My vegetable supplier calls the long red onions I use here "Tuscan onions." The main benefit of using them for this pickle is that when cut the rings are fairly even in size, and not too large.

3 ounces red-wine vinegar
½ teaspoon sea salt
1 teaspoon mild honey
2 long red onions, cut into thickish rings
splash of rose water
slivered pistachios to serve (optional)

In a bowl, stir the vinegar, salt and honey until the salt and honey have dissolved. Add the onion rings and toss thoroughly, then leave to macerate for an hour. Just before serving, add a splash of rose water and, if you like, a scattering of slivered pistachios.

SERVES 4

Pickled Onion Rings in Rose Vinegar
(opposite)

Partly dried tomatoes with pomegranate

Partly drying really ripe tomatoes in a very slow oven—or in the full sun of summer—concentrates the sugars. Sweet-sour pomegranate molasses complements the flavors beautifully. Use them as part of a meze selection— as you would sun-dried tomatoes—in salads, pilafs or sauces, or as an accompaniment to cold or cooked meats.

4½ pounds small vine-ripened roma tomatoes, cut in half lengthwise

3 ounces extra-virgin olive oil

2 tablespoons pomegranate molasses

sea salt

freshly ground black pepper

Preheat the oven to 120°F. Place the tomatoes, cut-side up, on metal racks fitted into baking trays (you'll probably need two). Whisk together the oil and pomegranate molasses and lightly brush each tomato with this. Sprinkle with salt and pepper and bake for 5 hours until the tomatoes have shrunk and shrivelled. Remove from the oven and leave to cool on the rack.

Arrange the cooled partly dried tomatoes in layers in a shallow container, separating each layer with greaseproof paper. They will keep in the refrigerator for up to 10 days.

MAKES 2¼ pounds

Pickled cucumbers with fennel

In her wonderful book *500 Years of Ottoman Cuisine*, Marianna Yerasimos writes that eighteenth-century Ottoman recipes combined fennel with cucumbers and garlic to make a wonderful crunchy appetizer. I love the mild aniseed flavor of young fennel and was inspired to create this pickle. It makes a wonderful addition to any meze table.

700 pickling cucumbers

6 baby fennel bulbs

4 small bullet chiles, pricked with the point of a small knife

8 cloves garlic

1 tablespoon fennel seeds

1 tablespoon coriander seeds

1 stick cinnamon, broken in half

4 cups water

⅔ cup white-wine vinegar

pinch of sea salt

2 tablespoons sugar

Wash the cucumbers, then prick them all over with a thin skewer or toothpick. Trim the stalks of the fennel bulbs evenly and cut the bulbs into quarters lengthwise.

Divide the cucumbers, fennel, chiles and garlic between two sterilized 16-ounce jars, layering them with the spices as you go and making sure that a piece of cinnamon stick goes into each jar.

Bring the water, vinegar, salt and sugar to a boil in a large, non-reactive saucepan. Pour the boiling liquid into the jars, ensuring there are no air pockets and that the vegetables are submerged. Seal the jars and turn them upside-down a few times to distribute the ingredients evenly. Leave in a cool, dry place for a week before using. The pickles will keep in the refrigerator for up to a month after opening.

MAKES 4 cups

[Clockwise from left] Pickled Cucumbers with Fennel (opposite), Partly Dried Tomatoes with Pomegranate (opposite), Spicy Eggplant Relish (page 311)

Long green pepper pickle

This pickle is made from long, mild green peppers—although it works equally well with hot peppers. Pickled peppers and chiles are often served at the start of a Turkish meal to stimulate the appetite.

2¼ pounds long green peppers

2 red serrano chiles

4 cloves garlic

1 tablespoon coriander seeds

1 quart water

1¾ cups white-wine vinegar

2 ounces sea salt

1 cup mint leaves, washed and dried

Wash the peppers and chiles, then prick them all over with a thin skewer or toothpick and set aside in a large ceramic bowl or dish.

In a large, heavy-based, nonreactive saucepan, combine the garlic, coriander seeds, water, vinegar and salt. Bring to the boil and pour over the peppers and chiles. Leave to macerate until cold.

Return everything to the saucepan and return to the boil. Divide the mint between two sterilized 1-pint jars, then divide the pepper mixture as well and pour in the liquid. Seal the jars and turn them upside-down a few times to distribute the ingredients evenly. Leave in a cool, dry place for a week before using. The pickles will keep in the refrigerator for up to a month after opening.

MAKES 4 cups

Snow almonds or walnuts

Soaking nuts in chilled water over several days causes them to swell up and become wonderfully crunchy. In Turkey these nuts are often served on a bed of ice, which keeps them moist and cold. Serve them with predinner drinks as a refreshing nibble—they seem to go especially well with rakı.

7 ounces raw almonds or walnuts

Put the nuts into a container and cover with cold water, then seal and refrigerate for 3–4 days.

Drain the nuts and rub away the skins. Rinse well, then return to the container and cover with fresh cold water. Leave until ready to serve—up to a week.

MAKES 9 ounces

Candied walnuts

This walnut praline makes a great garnish for all sorts of desserts, especially creamy mousses or ice creams, where they add a lovely sweet crunch. I also use them in the apricot ice cream for the Flower of Malatya (page 282).

⅓ pound superfine sugar
2 tablespoons water
7 ounces walnuts

Combine the sugar and water in a heavy-based saucepan over a gentle heat, stirring occasionally to dissolve the sugar. When the syrup is clear, increase the heat and bring to a rolling boil. Cook for about 5 minutes until the syrup reaches the thread stage at around 225°F (a drop of the syrup will fall from a wooden spoon in a long thread).

Add the walnuts to the pan—the sugar mixture will crystallize as the oils come out of the nuts. Lower the heat and stir gently until the crystallized sugar dissolves back to a caramel. This will take around 10–15 minutes. Carefully pour the hot caramel onto a cookie sheet lined with parchment paper or greased aluminium foil. Smooth with the back of a fork and allow to cool and harden. When cold, break into chunks with a rolling pin, then pound to crumbs in a mortar and pestle.
MAKES 9 ounces

Baharat

Baharat is a sort of all-purpose spice mix used widely around the Middle East and Turkey. The Arabic word literally means "spices"—and the spice recipe varies from region to region and family to family. Many spice shops will sell their own house blend. This is a fairly typical Turkish-style blend with just a touch of heat. It's infinitely versatile and I like to use it in braises and slow-cooked stews. Mixed with oil and crushed garlic it makes a terrific marinade for lamb chops and roasts and for barbecued game or poultry.

5 tablespoons sweet paprika
5 tablespoons freshly ground black pepper
¼ cup ground cumin
2 tablespoons ground coriander
2 tablespoons ground cinnamon
1 teaspoon hot paprika
1 teaspoon ground nutmeg

Mix the spices thoroughly and store in a jar for up to 3 months.
MAKES 7 ounces

Flavorings

Turkish cooking makes excellent use of a wide range of herbs, spices and other aromatics—although never allowing them to dominate the flavor of the core ingredient of a dish.

Herbs are used in large quantities, with mint, dill and parsley being the most popular. Herbs are generally used fresh—and they are certainly available in abundance—although occasionally dried herbs are preferred for specific dishes. For instance, some soups and dips, such as *cacık*, call on dried mint, often in addition to the fresh herb—the dried herb provides a mellow, subtle background flavor, while the fresh provides a top note that lifts the palate. There are also clear regional preferences, of course, with basil, oregano and thyme featuring especially prominently along the Mediterranean and Aegean coastlines. Interestingly, unlike Arab cooking, where the fresh herb dominates, coriander is rarely used in Turkish cooking.

In the ancient world, the very earliest spice routes from the Orient passed through Anatolia on their way west, so it's not surprising that allspice, cinnamon and cumin are popular in the rural Turkish kitchen, while Istanbul cooks have always had a rather lighter hand. With the discovery of the New World in the fifteenth century new ingredients such as tomatoes, peppers and chiles flooded into Anatolia and were taken up with alacrity.

It is perhaps the capsicum family that is now the most important ingredient in Turkish cooking as it is responsible not only for the fresh peppers and chiles enjoyed with nearly every course of every meal, but also for the dried, ground and flaked preparations used in myriad ways every day.

The best red peppers are said to grow in southeastern Turkey near Kahramanmaraş, Gaziantep and Şanlıurfa, with each variety having its own distinctive flavor. Urfa peppers are dark red or purple-black and lend a wonderful smoky depth to dishes. The dark-red peppers from Maraş are full-bodied and aromatic, while Antep's peppers are lighter red and a little milder. All these red peppers have a high oil content, and look moist and a little shiny, rather than dull and dry. Sometimes they will be roasted before use, which turns them a blackish color and makes them more potent.

Of the dried peppers, red pepper flakes—*kırmızı biber*—have a particularly special place in Turkish cuisine, and range from sweet and mild to fiercely hot depending on the region. As well as being used in all sorts of savory dishes, they are often stirred into sizzling butter (sometimes with dried mint) to make a wonderful final touch to soups.

Hot or mild Turkish red pepper flakes are available from specialty or Turkish food stores and are well worth hunting out for their distinctive flavor, which

is more warm and spicy than really hot. Once you've enjoyed their smoky aroma and rich, earthy flavor you'll be hooked.

Paprika is another pepper preparation that's used with abandon in the Turkish kitchen. Its flavor is sweeter and milder than that of the red pepper flakes, but this too varies in strength and style depending on the region. Turks tend to use sweet paprika and hot paprika; smoked paprika, often sold as Hungarian paprika, is used to a lesser degree.

As well as being used on their own, spices and dried herbs are often combined in Turkish cooking to make spice mixes. These differ depending on their use—some will be sweeter, some spicier, some more pungent. The following are some of my favorite combinations.

Poultry spice mix

This spice mix is a lovely balance of sweet, salty, sour and hot. I use it with all sorts of poultry dishes, as well as with other white meats such as rabbit, veal and pork. It also works very well with vegetable dishes—especially those featuring eggplant, zucchini or fennel.

⅓ cup ground allspice

2 tablespoons ground cinnamon

2 teaspoons hot paprika

2 teaspoons ground sumac

1 teaspoon freshly ground black pepper

Mix the spices thoroughly and store in a jar for up to 3 months.
MAKES 2 ounces

Köfte spice mix

A universally popular spice mix that works with all sorts of *köfte* and *şiş* kebabs. You can also use it in a marinade for grilled beef or lamb dishes. The dried mint makes it taste particularly Turkish.

⅓ cup ground cumin

⅓ cup dried mint

⅓ cup dried oregano

2 tablespoons sweet paprika

2 tablespoons freshly ground black pepper

2 teaspoons hot paprika

Mix the spices thoroughly and store in a jar for up to 3 months.
MAKES 6 ounces

Seafood spice mix

The addition of fennel seeds and lemony coriander makes this blend particularly well suited to fish dishes, especially those using crustaceans. Mix it with flour and use it to dust pieces of fish for pan-frying or grilling. Its slight curry flavor also lends itself to egg dishes, legumes and vegetables, even pilafs.

⅓ cup sweet paprika

2 tablespoons ground cumin

2 tablespoons ground coriander

1 tablespoon freshly ground black pepper

1 tablespoon ground fennel

Mix the spices thoroughly and store in a jar for up to 3 months.
MAKES 4 ounces

Lamb spice mix

The warmth of cumin combined with sweet and hot paprika bring out lamb's natural sweetness beautifully. Try mixing this with a little oil and rubbing it onto a leg of lamb before roasting, or sprinkle it onto tiny chops or lamb loins before grilling or frying.

2 tablespoons ground cumin

2 tablespoons sweet paprika

1 tablespoon hot paprika

1 tablespoon ground nutmeg

1 tablespoon freshly ground black pepper

Mix the spices thoroughly and store in a jar for up to 3 months.
MAKES 2 ounces

The essence of Turkey

[SWEET TREATS AND DRINKS]

The beauty and scale of Topkapı unfolds in a series of linked courtyards, and we passed through a succession of lush gardens, ornately vaulted stone chambers and exquisitely tiled pavilions …

O n our last day in Istanbul, we walked across the Galata Bridge from Beyoğlu to Sultanahmet. Things were exactly the same as they'd been a few weeks before, except then there had been a chill wind blowing off the Bosphorus and the March drizzle had smudged the spires and domes of the Old City skyline into a soft gray monochrome. Now the weather was warmer, tulips were blooming and the scent of spring was in the air.

Pushing our way through the jostling crowds around the Eminönü ferry terminal, we headed west to trudge up the hill toward the Topkapı Palace. We wandered along a street named Soğukçeşme Sokak, with its quaint old wooden houses built right up against the palace walls, until we found ourselves outside the Imperial Gate.

The residence of the Ottoman sultans for four centuries, the Topkapı Palace is perfectly situated on the top of a hilly wooded promontory at Seraglio Point. There were monasteries and public buildings on this site in Byzantium times, but the massive complex of pavilions and gardens that occupy the site today was built by Sultan Mehmet II after his dramatic conquest of Constantinople in 1453.

The beauty and scale of Topkapı unfolds in a series of linked courtyards, and as we passed through a succession of lush gardens, ornately vaulted stone chambers and exquisitely tiled pavilions it was easy to believe that at its peak this place was more a miniature city than a royal residence.

The administrative heart of the entire Ottoman Empire was gathered here at the palace; government and cabinet ministers, foreign ambassadors and the elite military corps known as the Janissaries all lived here, side by side with the sultan

and his harem. When the Ottoman Empire was at the height of its power, the kitchens fed an average of 5,000 people every day. On feast days and other special occasions this number could easily double—you can only wonder what the food bills would have been like.

It was a lot of mouths to feed and, from the very beginning, food was of prime importance to palace life. When he built the Topkapı, Mehmet II included a huge four-domed kitchen, and over successive centuries this was gradually extended to form the complex that remains today. As we discovered, beneath the distinctive twin rows of domes and chimneys was a whole little world in its own right: the kitchen complex was not just where cooking was done, but it also housed pantries and storerooms, administrative offices, sleeping quarters for kitchen staff, a mosque and a bathhouse.

The palace kitchens were manned by a brigade of highly specialized staff. At its largest, there was a team of almost 1,400 cooks and assistants, including pilaf chefs, baklava chefs, *köfte* makers and kebab chefs, bakers, confectioners and pickle makers, to name but a few. And in the way that chefs in today's finest restaurants devote a lot of their time to reading magazines and cookbooks from countries all around the world, the chefs of Topkapı Palace did the same in their day, borrowing ideas from far-flung lands and adapting and reinventing them for the sultan's pleasure.

Of course, the palace cooks were lucky. As the Ottoman Empire expanded, so did their repertoire. Not only was Constantinople itself a vast food market, with new and exotic foodstuffs coming in every day from all corners of the empire and beyond, but the growth of the empire led to a continuous exchange and cross-fertilization of culinary ideas and recipes across its lands and peoples, providing plenty of inspiration for the chefs.

By the time of Suleiman the Magnificent—the Empire's golden age—cooking had been elevated to an art, and food was celebrated in song, poetry and exquisitely painted miniatures. Chefs competed to create ever-greater culinary masterpieces and foreign visitors to the court returned home to tell tales of lavish banquets,

where 300 or more dishes were eaten on floors spread with richly embroidered cloths against a backdrop of tinkling fountains and music in the air.

Relics of this devotion to the pleasures of the table are still on display. In the kitchens we inspected pots and pans, kettles and cauldrons and all sorts of other cooking paraphernalia, as well as a vast collection of Chinese porcelain. Other rooms housed displays of the more delicate trappings of this elite lifestyle; we gazed, awestruck, at dishes from İznik painted with tulips, carnations and pomegranates, delicately engraved pudding spoons and jewelled carafes.

We wandered happily around the buildings and gardens, making our way toward the far end of the palace grounds to a broad terrace overlooking the water. We stood for a while in the warm sunshine gazing out to where the Golden Horn, the Bosphorus and the Sea of Marmara meet, and then over to the Asian shore in the distance.

We had one more mission before our Turkish journey came to an end. Clambering off a busy streetcar back at the Eminönü waterfront, we headed for the Spice Bazaar. We cut through the imposing Yeni Mosque, emerging on the other side to the ablution fountain where we looked across to the rooftops of the Spice Bazaar, domed like some strange metal egg carton. In the chambers above the imposing gatehouse entry were the windows of the famous Pandeli restaurant, one of the oldest and most prestigious in the city. But, for now, we walked inside the bazaar to see where the palace cooks did their shopping.

Little has changed in Mısır Çarşısı—the "Egyptian" Spice Bazaar—since it was built in the early seventeenth century. Now, as then, along its cavernous, dimly lit walkways you could find spices from the Orient, caviar and tea from the Black Sea, olives from Greece and exotic fragrant oils from Arabia. We squeezed our way up and down the crowded walkways and it was as if we were reliving our entire Turkish journey of the last five weeks. At one stall we found olive oil from Ayvalık, at another there was *tulum* cheese in a traditional goatskin sack and bright red smelly *pastırma* from Kayseri, while around the corner, we spotted Aleppo pepper flakes, pistachio coffee and *tarhana* from Gaziantep.

Produce from all around the country was available—dried apricots from Malatya, golden raisins from İzmir, wild greens from the Aegean coast, fish from the Bosphorus and the Mediterranean. There were great dark oozing blocks of honeycomb, buckets of creamy yogurt, sackfuls of bulgur wheat, necklaces of tiny dried okra, and mounded displays of nuts, fruits and sweets as far as the eye could see. All this great Anatolian abundance was on display right here in the heart of Istanbul.

Emerging into the sunshine, we found that the narrow streets outside the Spice Bazaar were chaotic. It was just an ordinary weekday, but it seemed as if the entire population of the city was here doing business or its daily shopping. We pushed our way through the heaving crowds of shoppers—past the *simit* sellers with their trolleys of bread, past stalls offering pomegranate juice or a glass of hot *sahlep*, past eager young Turks keen to sell us plastic dolma-rollers and gypsy women offering bunches of luridly tinted carnations—and ducked into a small teahouse to catch our breath.

The noise of the crowd faded away and we sat for a moment in silence, our conversation stilled by a sudden sense of melancholy. Although unvoiced, I was sure that we shared the same thought: "It's too soon to leave this place." I pulled out my notebook and flicked back through the pages; five weeks' worth of scribblings rose up from the pages in a tangle of disjointed words, phrases and expressions. Every meal we'd eaten had its own story—in the names of the new friends we'd made, the restaurants visited, the ingredients discovered, the dishes tasted. It is true that the purpose of our journey had been about the small, simple things of daily life … about food and eating and cooking. But the real joy had been in the way these small things revealed this country's history and the lives of its people.

Every meal we'd eaten had its own story—in the names of the new friends we'd made, the restaurants visited, the ingredients discovered, the dishes tasted.

I glanced down at my notebook again, at the jottings of quotes and notes of conversations we'd had, and memories and faces came flooding back. In my mind's eye I could see Talat Çağdaş ladling hot sugar syrup over a tray of golden baklava; Musa Dağdeviren talking animatedly of his passion for Anatolian peasant food; Filiz and The Fish Doctor, and Hüsna Baba with his sea urchins; Emine with her enchanting smile and Sedat pouring us yet another glass of rakı. All these people, and many more, had shared their passions, had helped and taught us, had fed and hugged us and had shown us their Turkey. Our journey had certainly been a celebration of food, but what would the food be without the people?

A moment later, a waiter appeared, setting down on the table in front of us pretty little tulip-shaped glasses of strong, sweet tea. As we thanked him, he smiled and asked the same question that we'd been asked so many times over the last few weeks: "Where you from? You spik Ingleez? You like Turkey?" We smiled back and assured him that, yes, we did like Turkey very much indeed.

Sticky apricots stuffed with clotted cream

Deep amber and ivory in tone, these popular Turkish sweet treats are exquisitely pretty—and they taste sensational. Make sure you use good-quality, large dried apricots; in Turkey the best apricots come from Malatya and these are exported all around the world. It can be difficult sometimes to find whole dried apricots, in which case you'll have to use apricot halves and sandwich them together. The cream used in Turkey is *kaymak*, a thick clotted cream made from buffalo milk. Lightly sweetened mascarpone, crème fraîche and strained yogurt are the best alternatives if you can't find *kaymak*.

Pekmez, or grape molasses, is available from Turkish food stores.

1½ cups water

2 tablespoons superfine sugar

½ stick cinnamon

6 cardamom pods, lightly crushed

2 tablespoons *pekmez*

1 tablespoon lemon juice

9 ounces dried apricots (preferably whole)

9 ounces clotted cream, mascarpone or Strained Yogurt (page 54)

additional superfine sugar

2 tablespoons finely ground or slivered unsalted shelled pistachios

Combine the water and sugar in a heavy-based saucepan and heat gently, stirring occasionally, until the sugar dissolves. When the syrup is clear, add the cinnamon, cardamom, *pekmez* and lemon juice, then increase the heat and bring to the boil. Add the apricots, then lower the heat a little and simmer for 20 minutes. Remove the pan from the heat and leave the apricots to cool in the syrup.

Remove the apricots from the syrup and let them drain for a moment in a sieve. Reserve the syrup. Sweeten the cream with a little sugar to taste. If you are using whole apricots, slit them carefully along one side and fill them generously with cream. If using apricot halves, sandwich them together with a spoonful of cream. Arrange the stuffed apricots on a serving plate and chill. When ready to serve, sprinkle each apricot with pistachios and drizzle with a little syrup.

SERVES 4–6

Nightingale nests

⅔ cup walnuts
½ cup unsalted shelled pistachios
2 heaped tablespoons superfine sugar
½ teaspoon ground cinnamon
6 sheets phyllo pastry
melted unsalted butter

SUGAR SYRUP
7 ounces superfine sugar
7 ounces water
1 stick cinnamon
long piece of peel and juice from
½ lemon

Preheat the oven to 350°F. Grease a baking tray.

To make the syrup, combine the sugar, water, cinnamon stick and lemon peel in a heavy-based saucepan and heat gently, stirring to dissolve the sugar. Bring to the boil, then lower the heat and simmer gently for 5 minutes. Remove from the heat, then add the lemon juice and set aside to cool.

Pulse the nuts, sugar and cinnamon to fine crumbs in a food processor.

To make the nightingale nests, work with one sheet of phyllo at a time and keep the rest covered with a damp tea towel. Place a sheet of pastry on your work surface and brush with a little melted butter. Fold the phyllo sheet in half, bringing the short sides together. Swivel the pastry rectangle so a short side is facing you. Brush with a little more butter and scatter on a generous amount of the nut mixture.

Lay a long metal skewer or a chopstick across the end of the phyllo rectangle facing you and roll the pastry around it and away from you to create a tight log. Brush the pastry log with melted butter. With the skewer still in place, gently push both ends of the pastry log inward, wrinkling up the pastry, until the log is around 5 inches long. Gently pull out the skewer and coil the wrinkled log into a "nest" shape. Use a spatula to lift it onto the prepared baking sheet. Continue working with the remaining phyllo sheets and nut mixture until you have six neat bird's nests—you should still have some nut mixture left.

Brush the nests with butter and bake for 20 minutes, or until golden brown.

Shortly before the end of the cooking time, bring the syrup to a boil. Remove the pastry nests from the oven and set the jelly-roll pan on a high heat on your stove top. Cook for a minute, turning continuously (this helps make the bottoms of the pastry good and crisp). After a minute pour on the boiling syrup, then immediately remove the pan from the heat. Leave the pastries in the pan to soak up the syrup as they cool.

When ready to eat, fill the middle of the nests with more of the nut mixture and serve.
MAKES 6

Turkish coffee

Making coffee is something of an art form in Turkey. It is prepared and served as a way of signalling respect and affection for one's guests. You will usually be asked to specify whether you wish to drink it *az şekerli* (with a little sugar), *orta şekerli* (with a moderate amount), *çok şekerli* (with a lot of sugar) or *şekersiz* (without sugar). To enjoy Turkish coffee, you need to get your head around the fact that the coffee is not strained before serving, and that the sugar is added to the coffee as it brews, not afterward. The grounds that remain at the bottom of the cup are used for fortune-telling.

It's best to make Turkish coffee in a *cevze*, a small, long-handled pot, but a small saucepan will suffice.

2 tablespoons finely ground, medium-roast Turkish coffee
¾ cup water
sugar to taste

Combine all the ingredients in a *cevze* and stir well. Bring to the boil slowly over a low heat. Watch the pot carefully: remove the *cevze* from the heat as soon as a thick foam forms on the surface and begins to rise. Carefully divide the foam (not the liquid) between two small coffee cups, being careful not to disturb or disperse it.

Return the *cevze* to the heat and boil briefly. Pour the coffee into the cups carefully and slowly, again being careful not to disperse the foam. Serve right away.
SERVES 2

Coffee and coffee houses

Europeans have the Ottomans to thank for introducing them to coffee. Originating in Ethiopia, the wild coffee arabica bush is believed to have been cultivated by African tribesmen from the sixth century AD, who enjoyed it for its stimulating properties, rather in the same way that we enjoy it today. From Ethiopia, the use of coffee spread over the Red Sea to Yemen, and then its popularity swept rapidly through Arabia.

By the sixteenth century, the consumption of coffee had become fashionable in Mecca, Damascus and Constantinople, where the first true coffee house was established in 1554. Despite efforts by the pious to ban it because of concerns about its mind-altering properties, coffee drinking spread like wildfire. Within a few decades Constantinople was full of coffee houses and by the end of the sixteenth century there were reputedly more than 600 coffee houses in the city alone.

The pleasure of coffee was embraced by the Ottoman Empire. By 1700 there were coffee houses as far afield as Venice and Marseilles. In 1669, Sultan Mehmet IV sent an emissary to the courts of Louis XIV to woo the palace with various Ottoman delights: coffee was served from delicate long-spouted ewers, ladies' hands were sprinkled with rose water and all manner of sweets were served. Subsequently, coffee was peddled around the country by wandering coffee vendors sporting traditional Turkish costume as a mark of their trade.

Vienna's love affair with coffee dates from the Ottoman siege of the city in 1683, when retreating Turkish armies reputedly left behind sacks of coffee beans that they'd brought with them. An enterprising Pole, Franz Kolschitsky, who was familiar with coffee having once served as an interpreter in the Ottoman army, prepared the beans in the traditional manner and thus introduced the Viennese to the delights of drinking coffee.

It's not hard to see why coffee was such an instant hit, especially in Muslim countries where alcohol was prohibited. In fact, the English word *coffee* comes from the Turkish *kahveh*, which comes from the old Arabic word for wine—*kawhah*.

Coffee houses have largely always been men's domain. The earliest coffee houses were often constructed as pavilions, and, as is the case with fancy restaurants today, the most favored were the ones with a good view of the city, the Golden Horn or the Bosphorus. Customers reclined upon low benches and smoked fragrant tobacco—sometimes opium—through slender water pipes. Entertainment was provided and they generally operated as a kind of gentleman's club, where men would while away the hours chatting or reading the daily newspapers. Over time, coffee houses became inextricably linked with prayer. Often sited next to mosques, these two institutions were generally the main places for social gathering in a village or town.

Today coffee houses—*kahve*—tend to be rather down-at-the-heels, dingy places, and they continue to be more often frequented by men than by women or family groups. Inside you'll find little groups of men playing cards or backgammon and smoking endlessly. And despite the name and the long history, the drink of choice in coffee houses these days tends to be tea!

Ayran

This chilled yogurt drink is popular all over Turkey, especially in the summer months. It's sold in bottles and little cartons, and in some villages it's sold churned from large wooden barrels to make it light and fluffy. *Ayran* is the drink to serve with kebabs and *köfte*. When we ate our liver kebab breakfast in Gaziantep, chef Ali told us that he couldn't conceive of eating any meal without *ayran* and that, when he was growing up, if there was no *ayran* on the table his grandmother would refuse to eat the meal.

2 cups chilled Greek-style yogurt
1 cup chilled water
½ cup crushed ice
sea salt
dried mint to serve (optional)

Blend all the ingredients, except the dried mint, in a blender until light and frothy. Serve immediately in tall chilled glasses, sprinkled with a little dried mint, if you like.
SERVES 4

Tamarind *sherbet*

Tamarind—or "Indian date" as it translates from the Turkish—has a wonderfully tart flavor and is used to make this lovely thirst-quencher. Restaurants and wandering drink vendors often sell this chilled drink in the summer months.

9 ounces tamarind
1 quart water
9 ounces superfine sugar

Soak the tamarind in the water overnight.

The next day, bring the soaking tamarind to the boil slowly, then remove the pan from the heat and leave to cool. Strain through muslin into a clean jug, then stir in the sugar until dissolved. Decant into a sterilized bottles and refrigerate.

This *sherbet* will keep in the refrigerator for up to five days. After opening, drink within two days. Serve chilled, with extra sugar if you like.
MAKES 1 quart

Turkish delight martini

This exquisitely pretty martini combines the classic Turkish delight flavors of chocolate and rose water. You can buy rose-flavored syrup, which tints this cocktail the palest of pink hues.

½ lemon or lime

drinking chocolate

1½ ounces vodka

3 teaspoons white crème de cacao

3 teaspoons good-quality rose syrup

2–3 drops rose water

rose petals to garnish (optional)

Rub the rim of an elegant chilled martini glass with the lemon or lime, then dip into a saucer of drinking chocolate.

Combine the vodka, crème de cacao and rose syrup in a cocktail shaker with a handful of ice. Stir well, then strain into the martini glass. Add a few drops of rose water and garnish with rose petals, if you like.

SERVES 1

Hazelnut martini

The spiciness of chiles and vodka and the tang of lime combine beautifully with warm, sweet cinnamon and Frangelico to make a wonderful cocktail for winter evenings.

Adding a stick of cinnamon to one part sugar and two parts water makes for a heady sugar syrup to use here. Reserve a few tablespoons of the cinnamon syrup and candy a few chiles to use as a garnish—it'll take this martini to another height altogether!

1 ounce pepper vodka or chile-infused vodka

1 ounce Frangelico

3 teaspoons lime juice

1 teaspoon cinnamon sugar syrup

candied chiles or chile flakes to garnish

Combine the vodka, Frangelico, lime juice and sugar syrup in a cocktail shaker with a handful of ice.

Stir and strain into a chilled martini glass. Garnish with candied chiles or sprinkle with chile flakes.

SERVES 1

[From left] Turkish Delight Martini
(opposite), Pomegranate *Caprioska*
(page 347)